The Theory of Morality

Alan Donagan

The Theory of Morality

The University of Chicago Press
Chicago and London

The University of Chicago Press, Chicago 60637
The University of Chicago Press, Ltd., London

00 99 98 97 96 95 94   8 9 10 11 12

Library of Congress Cataloging in Publication Data

Donagan, Alan.
  The theory of morality.

  Bibliography: p.
  Includes index.
  1. Ethics.   I. Title.
BJ1012.D57   170   76-25634
ISBN 0-226-15567-6

For Bruce Benjamin
21 October 1924 – 22 March 1963
In Gratitude and Affection

וְנִשְׁמוֹת הַצַּדִּיקִים בְּיַד אֱלֹהִים
The Wisdom of Solomon, 3:1

"One should never direct people toward happiness, because happiness too is an idol of the market place. One should direct them toward mutual affection. A beast gnawing at its prey can be happy too, but only human beings can feel affection for each other, and this is the highest achievement they can aspire to."

"Oh no, I want happiness, you'd better leave me with happiness," Oleg insisted vigorously, "Just give me happiness for the few months I have before I die. Otherwise to hell with the whole...."

" ... Happiness is a mirage." Shulubin was emphatic, straining his strength to the utmost. He had turned quite pale. "I was happy bringing up my children, but they spat on my soul. To preserve this happiness I took books that were full of truth and burned them in the stove. As for the so-called 'happiness of future generations,' it's even more of a mirage. Who knows anything about it? Who has spoken with these future generations? Who knows what idols they will worship? Ideas of what happiness is have changed too much through the ages. No one should have the effrontery to try to plan it in advance. When we have enough loaves of white bread to crush them under our heels, when we have enough milk to choke us, we still won't be in the least happy. But if we share things we don't have enough of, we can be happy today! If we care only about 'happiness' and about reproducing our species, we shall merely crowd the earth senselessly, and create a terrifying society."

Alexander Solzhenitsyn,
Cancer Ward

Contents

Preface

When most people I encounter discuss a moral question, the considerations they advance conform to a set of related patterns, even though those patterns are sometimes at odds with the philosophical doctrines they profess. Neither phenomenon is surprising. Both in Europe, and in the societies whose cultures descend from Europe, moral traditions are still being transmitted in association with religious ones; and the major religions of those societies, Judaism and the various branches of Christianity, agree in the main about morality. Moreover, much of the literature of those societies has been occupied with predicaments that are intelligible only in terms of their common moral tradition. And yet, on the other hand, philosophy and the social sciences in those societies have for the past century been dominated by movements which repudiate that moral tradition.

Undergraduates soon discover that most of the systems of philosophical ethics they study are hard to reconcile with the grounds on which they have been brought up to make moral judgements. In my own undergraduate days, only one system was advanced as being a theoretical account of received morality: namely, the new intuitionism of Broad and Ross. But it seemed unacceptable. Under the influence of logical positivism, I found it epistemologically hard to swallow. A little later, W. D. Falk led me to doubt whether it did not exclude every intelligible motive for acting morally. And, at the same time, Marxism was undermining my confidence in traditional morality itself. Was it anything more than an ideological defence of a social order doomed by its inner contradictions?

The writings of George Orwell, which I first read in the late forties, placed all these matters in a new light and determined the form in which I have conceived the problems of moral philosophy ever since. To begin with they persuaded me that any acceptable form of social order, whether socialist or not, must rest on moral foundations, which are in principle ascertainable at any period, and permanently valid. Marxist humanists now acknowledge this. In addition, by setting forth the traditional duties of honesty and veracity as more than the merely *prima facie* duties recognized by Broad and Ross, Orwell showed that the new intuitionism could provide no foundation for them. It had become clearer what morality was, but more obscure how it could be philosophically justified.

A possible answer to the latter question was suggested by Stephen Toulmin's *Examination of the Place of Reason in Ethics*, and by various papers which appeared in the philosophical journals at the same time. If, as Aristotle and Kant both held, reason is practical as well as theoretical, can Orwellian morality not be justified by showing it to be required by practical reason? Although I was ultimately to conclude that this suggestion was correct, I should have been unable at that time to put it to good use, because the only conceptions of nontechnical practical reason of which I could then make anything drew either upon Hume's theory of sympathy or upon Hobbes's theory of a rational social contract. Fortunately, I was soon afterwards attracted to other investigations.

In the decade that followed, in which I wrote on moral theory only incidentally, two things occurred that have left marks on the present study. The first was that Benjamin Nelson, then a colleague at Minnesota, introduced me to moral theology and to the history of casuistry in Christianity. He recommended me to look into the references in Kirk's *Conscience and Its Problems*, and so, as I later discovered, to traverse with a guide a path Whewell had found for himself. The second was the appearance in 1958 of G. E. M. Anscombe's paper, "Modern Moral Philosophy." At last, somebody writing in a philosophical journal had affirmed the traditional moral position I had found in Orwell, and with a like clarity and force. At the same time, however, she had expressed a disturbing doubt whether an adequate philosophical justification of the morality she described is possible, as distinct from a religious one.

Her reason was that the conception of moral law implicit in that morality is religious not only in origin but essentially. Exploration of the concept of practical reason may yield a theory of moral virtue like Aristotle's, but not a theory of moral law. In so concluding, she dismissed Kant's contributions to the theory of practical reason as tendentious and muddled. Had I not become persuaded that she was mistaken, as a result of reading Kant's ethical writings with a succession of advanced classes at the University of Illinois, I could not have embarked on the present study. What Aquinas wrote about natural law, read in the light of Germain Grisez's important paper on the Thomist first principle of practical reason, confirmed me in this.

The moral tradition associated with the Jewish and Christian religions is incompatible in various respects with other venerable moral traditions, for example that of Hinduism. Hence a theory according to which that tradition was simply derivable from a theory of practical reason would imply that those who follow others, for example Hindus, are either deficient in practical reason or inept at exercising it. By forcibly pointing this out, in discussing a paper of mine read in Melbourne in 1968, Professor James Mackie, of Monash University, led me to conclude that a moral system must have a double foundation: a theory of practical reason, and a theory of the nature of moral agents. In what follows, I have been at pains to set out what the moral system I present presupposes about the nature of moral agents; but the establishment of those presuppositions is destined for separate investigation.

By the time I began the first draft of the present study, in the spring of 1970, the custom of beginning books on what is now called "normative ethics" by attempting to establish fundamental principles had come to seem wrongheaded. As I saw the matter, the middle part of moral theory, like the middle part of mathematics, is far better understood than either its application to highly specific cases or the establishment of its fundamental principles. Setting aside the principle of duties to God, I did not think that there was much doubt about what the fundamental principle of traditional morality is, in view of the similar formulations of it by Aquinas and Kant. But, since either of those formulations seemed to me far more persuasive in itself than any attempt to explain why it is persuasive, I resolved to reserve my attempt to justify my preferred formulation until the final chapter.

At every stage of my research I have benefited from discussion with colleagues and students, to whom I offer my gratitude, regretting that the magnitude and continuousness of my appropriations have made particular acknowledgment impossible. Some particular debts, however, can be identified: to the colloquia of the University of Texas at Austin, and the University of Chicago, at which portions of drafts were critically discussed; to Aquinas College, Grand Rapids, which invited me to present my views on Aquinas's theory of natural law before a distinguished and critical Aquinas memorial colloquium; to J. B. Schneewind, who transformed my view of Sidgwick, partly by severe criticism in correspondence, and partly by allowing me to read portions of his forthcoming definitive study, and who later kindly read the typescript of the present work; and finally, to the first of the readers who reported to the Chicago University Press on my draft: while gratifying my vanity by recommending its prompt publication, he or she beneficently delayed its appearance and improved its contents by five dense pages of acute criticism.

Two friends, B. J. Diggs and Henry B. Veatch, despite their different disagreements with much I have to say, tactfully encouraged me throughout the long process of research and writing; nor did they complain when I molested them with copies of my drafts. Their support, and that of my wife, who spared time from demanding researches of her own to help me to set in order my more tangled pages, have been beyond any possible return.

The first partial draft of this study was made possible by grants of study-leave by the University of Chicago in the spring terms of 1970 and 1971. The award of a fellowship by the American Council of Learned Societies, together with financial support from the University of Chicago, afforded me leisure to write second and third drafts between spring 1972 and autumn 1973. The present text is a revision of the latter. I am deeply grateful both to the council and to the university; and, within the university, to the family of the late Joseph Regenstein, whose munificent benefaction enabled me to work in the most agreeable of libraries.

Finally, for converting my scribble into elegant typescript, I offer my thanks to Kay Wertz.

Note on the Second Impression

Elizabeth Anscombe, Jesse de Boer, Wayne Booth, Antony Flew, Newton Garver, Marjorie Grene and J. J. C. Smart have kindly drawn my attention to a number of misprints and mistakes, most of which it has been possible to correct. Corrections of substance are on pp. 16, 106, 137, 173, 205, 206, and 252.

1

The Concept of a Theory of Morality

1.1 What a Theory of Morality Is a Theory of

Moral philosophers often find themselves at cross-purposes, because they have made up their minds neither about what a theory of morality is a theory of, nor about what a philosophical theory of it would be.

Morality, in the sense in which it will be investigated here, has to do with *mores*: that is, with generally accepted norms of individual conduct. There is a usage, advocated by Nietzsche and now standard in sociology, according to which any system of mores is a morality. Nietzsche believed that moralities, so understood, are "symptoms and sign languages which betray the processes of physiological prosperity or failure," towards which an inquirer who had not fallen under the spell of one of them would take the attitude of a psychological diagnostician. At least one of his own diagnostic efforts is well known, namely, his identification of two ideal types of morality: the master moralities, "with which the healthy instinct defends itself against incipient decadence"; and the slave moralities, "with which this very decadence defines and justifies itself."[1]

Unless impartiality too is to be treated diagnostically, it demands that, before following Nietzsche down this all-too-human path, we make some inquiry into what 'morality' meant to moralists. The most superficial investigation shows that it did not mean "system of mores." Rather, it stood for a standard by which systems of mores, actual and possible, were to be judged and by which everybody ought to live, no matter what the mores of his neighbors might be.

Whether or not this standard is a chimaera, as Nietzsche persuaded himself that it is, can only be settled by examining it.

In the Western intellectual tradition, the first reasonably clear conception of morality as a standard for judging systems of mores seems to have been formed by the Stoics. The Stoic ideal, as described by Diogenes Laertius, was

> to be in accordance with Nature, that is, in accordance with the nature of man and that of the universe, doing nothing which the universal law is wont to forbid, that is, the right reason which pervades all things and is coextensive with Zeus. [2]

Cicero's doctrine that, whether or not there was a written law against rape when Tarquin was king, Tarquin's rape of Lucretia was illegal, as violating eternal law, was thoroughly Stoic. His argument for it even echoes Diogenes Laertius:

> [Before there was a written law] reason [*ratio*] existed, having sprung from the nature of things, impelling [men] to right action, and summoning [them] from wrongdoing. This reason began to be law, not when it was written down, but when it originated; and it originated simultaneously with the divine mind. Hence the true and supreme law having to do with commanding and forbidding is the right reason of Jupiter the highest [Cicero, *de Legibus*, II, 4, 10].

In Stoic theory, the relation between Nature and reason is hard to disentangle, and Nature is extraordinarily elusive. Hence Nature, as a principle distinct from reason, became less and less important to the later Stoics, and to philosophers influenced by Stoicism. What mattered was that the "true and supreme law" was held to be both willed by the highest of the gods and enjoined by reason. These two characteristics are inseparable, because the divine law expresses the divine mind, which is necessarily rational. Yet, although insepa-rable, they are distinct; and, from the point of view of moral philosophy, the one that is fundamental is rationality.

This was more evident to the Stoics, who respected popular poly-theism, than it is to strict monotheists, like Jews and Christians, who take all divine commands, whether or not they form part of the supreme divine law, to express divine providence and wisdom. The Stoics, in treating as poetically true such pious tradition as that, after his death, Romulus revealed himself as a god to Proculus Julius and commanded that a temple be dedicated to him, could hold such commands to express no more than a god's arbitrary pleasure. Nor would it have made any difference if the god had issued a command that was universal: say, that everybody who passed down the street in which his temple was to be erected should perform an act of worship. It is true that it is a genuine divine law that all men should obey the gods; but it no more follows that everything the gods command is divine law than it follows, because it is martial law that every soldier should obey the lawful commands of his superiors, that those commands themselves are martial law.

A divine command expresses divine law if and only if it expresses divine reason. And if it be assumed, as it was by the Stoics, that human reason is in principle adequate for the direction of human life, it follows that, so far as it has to do with the regulation of human life, the content of the divine law can be ascertained by natural human reason, and its force appreciated, without any direct reference to the gods at all. By contrast, divine commands that do not express divine law can only be known by revelation, whether from the mouth of the god himself, or through intermediaries.

Hence it was a mistake for Professor Anscombe to contend that morality can intelligibly be treated as a system of law only by presupposing a divine lawgiver. Her inference was also mistaken that, if those who deny the existence of a divine lawgiver choose to discuss ethical topics, they should follow Aristotle's example, and do it by way of a theory of the virtues. [3]

The conception of morality as virtue is not an alternative to a conception of it as law. Taking virtue, in the usual Aristotelian way, to be a disposition having to do with choice, consisting in a mean determined by a rational principle, namely, the principle by which a man of practical wisdom would determine it, the conception of morality as virtue presupposes that, in situations calling for moral choice, practical wisdom can determine whether or not a given choice accords with a rationally determined mean. With respect to the virtue of justice, Anscombe herself declares that, "in normal circumstances," it is unjust "to deprive people of their ostensible property without legal procedure, not to pay debts, not to keep contracts, and a host of other things of the kind." [4] The inference is irresistible that to each precept of moral virtue of the form, "In normal circumstances, to act in such-and-such a way would be unjust (or contrary to some other specific virtue, such as courage or temperance)," there is a precept of moral law that is its counterpart:

namely, "In normal circumstances, to act in such-and-such a way would be morally wrong." And if the former can be arrived at by natural human reason, the latter can too.[5]

The Stoics, rather than Aristotle or Plato, are to be credited with forming the first reasonably clear conception of morality: not because they had a theory of divine law, but because they conceived the divine law as valid for all men in virtue of their common rationality. Had Aristotle thought of 'ethical virtue' as something which all men could share, he would have essentially anticipated the Stoic conception, even though he made little of the connection between virtue and a law of reason. But he did not. Although he acknowledged that artisans, women, children, and slaves each had their appropriate virtues—the dispositions by which each might be good of their kind—he thought of ethical virtue proper as the virtue of a free citizen. The practical wisdom (*phronesis*) which determines the mean in which ethical virtue consists is directed to the good of the respective cities of which its possessors are citizens. Obviously there is a strong moral element in Aristotle's theory of ethical virtue; but he did not succeed in distinguishing moral virtue as such, the virtue of a man as a man, from political virtue, the virtue of a citizen of a good city. Aristotle did indeed distinguish between a good citizen and a good man; for a good citizen of an oppressive or predatory city will be a bad man. But it did not occur to him that the good to which a man's virtue as a rational being is directed may not be that of his city.[6]

Although it is less obvious in them, both Judaism and Christianity also distinguish between a divine law that is binding upon all men by virtue of their rationality and special divine commandments addressed to particular individuals and groups.

Judaism may be defined as acceptance of the Torah, or teaching of Moses, as declared in the Pentateuch, developed in later scriptures, and interpreted by generations of rabbis. It consists partly of Halachah, or precepts of conduct, and partly of Haggadah, or edifying teachings other than precepts. Although the Torah is held by Jews to contain nothing that is not implicit in the Pentateuch, the task of making implicit Halachah explicit is never complete since new situations continually call for new applications.

While the whole Torah does not purport to be binding upon all mankind, part of it does. Even in biblical times, the Jews had come to distinguish from mere heathens those gentiles who recognized that part of the Mosaic Halachah which applies to gentiles and Jews alike. As interpreted by Maimonides, rabbinic teaching about this universal law is that it consists of seven 'Noachite' precepts. Six of them were given to Adam: the prohibitions of idolatry, of blasphemy, of murder, of adultery, and of robbery, and the command to establish courts of justice. The seventh was given to Noah: the prohibition of eating a limb from a living animal.[7]

That all the righteous men of the nations of the world have a share in the world to come is received Jewish doctrine; and the balance of authority takes the righteous men of the nations to be all who observe the Noachite precepts, whether as divinely revealed or as inherently reasonable. It is true that Maimonides, apparently because of his philosophical doctrine that natural human reason does not suffice to establish the Noachite precepts, maintained that those who observe them upon any ground other than that they are laid down in the Torah as holding for all Noah's progeny, must do so for mistaken or inadequate reasons, and so cannot be truly righteous. But because such a position would exclude from a share in the world to come most of Noah's descendants, who have never heard of the Torah, and because it lacks either scriptural or Talmudic authority, the preponderant Jewish opinion has rejected not only it, but also the philosophical premise upon which Maimonides advanced it, that natural human reason does not suffice to establish the Noachite precepts.[8]

Christian authority agrees with Jewish. St. Paul taught that, although only Jews can break the law of Moses, because only they know it, gentiles nevertheless find "in their own natures a rule to guide them, in default of any other rule"—a law "written in their hearts"—and they break that.[9] The dismal counterpart of universal knowledge of divine law is universal guilt.

Christian moralists have been divided about the sense in which the universal part of the Mosaic law is written in the hearts of all men. The stricter opinion was that the bulk of the Ten Commandments are written in every heart, in the sense that nobody can be ignorant of them except through some wilful misuse of his mind, and that, consequently, ignorance of the law is always culpable. Anthropological knowledge of the varieties of human mores has made such a view incredible; but it has not touched the less strict opinion that certain common conceptions underlying the Torah are accessible to everybody, although, since even these may be obscured and distorted by the bad mores of the society in which he is brought up, a man's education will limit how much of the universal part of the

Mosaic law he can discover for himself. On this view, a normal adult in a reasonably decent society may be ignorant of parts of morality that are relatively obvious, but he cannot be utterly ignorant of the conceptions that underlie it; and these conceptions provide him with a rule, however rudimentary, by which he can guide his conduct.

Stoic, Jewish, and Christian thought are therefore substantially agreed in this: that there is a set of rules or precepts of conduct, constituting a divine law, which is binding upon all rational creatures as such, and which in principle can be ascertained by human reason. This universal or common code is what Jews and Christians came to refer to as "morality" or "the moral law" (*lex moralis*). They also called it "the law of nature" (*lex naturae*) and "natural law" (*lex naturalis*), because they believed that the moral law applies to man by virtue of his nature as a rational being, and is known to him primarily by the exercise of natural human reason.

Aquinas described the natural law as a certain "participation in the eternal law by rational creatures" (*participatio legis aeternae in rationali creatura*), and observed, a propos the Mosaic law or *Lex Vetus*, that "since moral precepts have to do with what pertains to good mores, which is what conforms with reason, and since every judgement of human reason derives in some way from natural reason, it is necessary that all moral precepts belong to the law of nature."[10] This conception of the moral law is not sectarian. If it was held by Aquinas, it was also held by the Reformer John Calvin, who, although he made more than Aquinas did of a point on which they were agreed, that because of his "dullness and obstinacy" a man needs a written law "to declare with greater certainty what in the law of nature is too obscure," nevertheless did not question that the moral law is the law of nature.[11]

The conception of morality as a law common to all rational creatures by virtue of their rationality, although endorsed by the Stoic, Jewish, and Christian religious traditions, is not itself religious. Except with regard to divine worship, neither Stoics, Jews, nor Christians found it necessary to resort to premises about the existence and nature of God in stating the reasons for the various provisions of the moral law. All three, it is true, believed that what is grounded on those reasons is part of the universal divine law, because they believed that finite human reason participates in the infinite divine reason. In consequence, they thought that common morality is upheld by God, and so has a religious sanction as well as the purely moral one that violating it violates human rationality.

In revealed religions like Judaism and Christianity, which teach ways of life that include but go beyond common morality, the boundaries in those ways of life between what is common morality and what is not are easily lost sight of. To Jews endeavoring to live a full Jewish life, and to Christians endeavoring to live a full Christian life, it is of little moment whether or not something required of them as Jews or Christians is also required of them merely as rational creatures. Anybody who thinks of a religious way of life as a seamless whole, in which common morality is comprehended and sanctified, will come to find it as natural to fulfil the obligations peculiar to his religious faith as to fulfil those that are not. Such a person will be constantly tempted to mistake commandments binding upon him by virtue of what he takes to be religious truth for moral laws binding upon human beings as rational, even though his own religious doctrine condemns his error.

How else can the Jewish conviction be accounted for that the seventh Noachite commandment is part of common morality? It does not appear to be contrary to our nature as rational creatures to eat a part cut from a living animal, for example, to eat a live oyster, unless it involves cruelty. And how else can the Christian conviction be accounted for that Jesus' severer pronouncements on divorce are morally definitive? It is not absurd to maintain that the Christian conception of marriage as monogamous and indissoluble is a higher and better one than any other; but that is not to declare it binding upon all human beings as rational.

Judaism and Christianity have nevertheless bequeathed us a definite general conception of what the theory of morality is a theory of: it is a theory of a system of laws or precepts, binding upon rational creatures as such, the content of which is ascertainable by human reason. Jews and Christians not only affirm the existence of such a system, they also identify it with part of the code of conduct they take to be binding on themselves by virtue of religious truth. These doctrines raise two philosophical questions, which a theory of morality must answer. First, is there such a system of laws or precepts, or is it a chimaera? And second, if there is such a system, is it the one with which Judaism and Christianity identify it, or some other?

The first of these questions cannot be affirmatively answered independently of answering the second; for it must remain in doubt whether any system of specific precepts is binding on rational creatures as such until such a system is produced and shown to be binding on them. However, in the great ages of religious philosophy, even those who did not question the philosophical demonstrability of the moral system contained in the Mosaic Torah, nevertheless considered that system to have been far more solidly established by divine revelation than it could ever be by philosophical reasoning. And so not only Maimonides, in *Mishneh Torah,* but even Aquinas, in *Summa Theologiae,* preferred to treat the moral law theologically. In both works, the investigation of philosophical problems is ancillary to that of theological ones. It is only a slight exaggeration to say that the ages of faith brought forth the idea of a pure moral philosophy but not the thing.

Why Kant was the first major philosopher to work out a complete philosophical theory of morality may partly be explained on similar lines. In France and Britain, the centers of philosophical research in the seventeenth century, incomplete theories of morality abounded, as philosophers who stood by traditional Christianity, confronted with the radical unorthodoxies of Hobbes and Spinoza, upheld the rationality of the principles of Christian morals. But, although these defenders of orthodoxy saw that they must demonstrate Christian moral principles philosophically, without the help of revealed theology, most of them judged it superfluous to derive from those principles a system of definite precepts, or to apply that system to difficult cases of conscience (*casus conscientiae*)—a study known as "casuistry." Such tasks were left to moral theologians; and in the eighteenth century they continued to be, throughout most of Europe.

In the German universities, however, under the influence of Christian Wolff, moral philosophy was taught in a systematic way, independently of revealed theology. The structure of the courses that were given is exhibited in the two textbooks of Alexander Gottlieb Baumgarten: *Initia Philosophiae Practicae Primae,* having to do with fundamental principles, and *Ethica Philosophica,* in which a system of specific precepts was derived from those principles.[12] Hence, when Kant's study of Rousseau's *Emile* and *Du Contrat Social* had led him to think of common morality as grounded in autonomous reason, the Wolffian tradition provided him with materials which he could transform into a serious moral philosophy.[13] How he went about this task may be followed in his *Lectures on Ethics,* for which he used Baumgarten's textbooks;[14] and in two published works: *Grundlegung zur Metaphysik der Sitten* (1785), written in his full maturity, in which he laid the foundations; and

Die Metaphysik der Sitten (1797), written in his old age, in which he erected a moral system upon them. That the greatest thinker of the German enlightenment, by way of Shaftesbury, Hutcheson, and Hume, of the Wolffians, and finally by way of Rousseau, should in the end have arrived at the position that the common morality he learned from his pietist parents was after all not a matter of revelation or of feeling, but of ordinary human reason (*gemeine Menschenvernunft*), and that the business of philosophy was to explore common moral knowledge, not to deny or supersede it, testifies to the power of the traditional conception of what morality is.[15] While, as a whole, the Critical Philosophy was revolutionary, Kant repeatedly protested that it reaffirmed not only the traditional moral code but also the traditional philosophical conception of that code as purely rational.

From the point of view of the present inquiry, however, the chief importance of Kant's *Grundlegung* and *Metaphysik der Sitten* is exemplary. I have tried to describe in general terms, with historical allusions, what a philosophical theory of morality would be. These great works, whatever their defects, are classical specimens of the thing.

1.2 Morality as a Disposition of Affection and Conduct

Although they were received from the first as classics, Kant's ethical writings were widely regarded as definitive of a dead tradition, not as models for future research. This may in large part be put down to Hegel's objection that Kant's "exclusively moral position" cannot make sense of concrete ethical life. Morality (*die Moralität*), conceived as a law binding upon all rational creatures by virtue of their rationality, was identified both by Kant and Hegel with "the pure unconditional self-determination" of a rational will. But Hegel argued that although such self-determination accounts for the "infinite autonomy" of ethical life, it must ultimately reduce it to "an empty formalism." It provides moral duty with identity, but not with content, and so cannot rise above preaching an empty duty for duty's sake.[16]

If the pure self-determination of a rational will is abstract and empty, where is a specific content for ethical life to be sought? Hegel's answer was: in the mores of an actual ethical community (*sittliches*

Gemeinwesen). In such a community, he declared, "it is easy to say what man must do, what are the duties he has to fulfil in order to be virtuous: he has simply to follow the well-known and explicit rules of his own situation. Rectitude is the general character which may be demanded of him by law or custom."[17]

Outside the ethical life (*Sittlichkeit*) of willing conformity to the mores of an actual ethical community, morality is an empty form: a devotion to duty for duty's sake, which lacks a rational ground by which anybody's specific duties may be determined. "As one of the commoner features of history," Hegel remarked, "for example, in Socrates, the Stoics, and others, the tendency to look deeper into oneself, and to know and determine from within oneself what is right and good, appears in ages when what is recognized as right and good in contemporary mores [*in der Wirklichkeit und Sitte*] cannot satisfy the will of better men."[18] But although better men may divine that something is wrong with contemporary mores, Hegel contended that they can provide no specific alternative that is rationally grounded. Their withdrawal into an inner life is therefore an "evaporation" of actual life into abstract "subjectivity"—into virtu-ousness without grounded virtues.[19]

"The moral point of view . . . is defective because it is purely abstract": that is the core of Hegel's case against morality.[20] It is *Sittlichkeit* evaporated into subjectivity; and although, as a stage in philosophical inquiry, "it is right enough to evaporate right and duty into subjectivity, it is wrong if this abstract groundwork is not condensed out again."[21] It follows that the proper subject of philosophical ethics is not morality but *Sittlichkeit*; and that a well-constructed ethical system will be, not a theory of morality, but a theory of what fills the empty form of morality with content. However they differ from him and from one another, philosophers who have accepted Hegel's doctrine of the emptiness of the moral point of view have, like him, inevitably become critics of morality. They are not immoralists; that is, they do not acknowledge any precepts as precepts of morality, and flout them. Rather, they assert that the a priori principles of morality, being abstract, cannot generate any specific precepts at all.

Hegel's observations on morality contain much that is true. A moral life cannot be solely the conscious following of explicit moral precepts. Since good morals are characteristically displayed in emergencies, which deny opportunity for reflection, they must in some measure consist in what Michael Oakeshott has called "a habit of affection and conduct."[22] Such a habit or disposition is revealed as much in what a man does not do as in what he does: it is a sort of fastidiousness or taste. And the tradition of such a disposition, although variable, will be stable. The kind of change which belongs to it, as Oakeshott has remarked, "is analogous to the change to which a living language is subject: nothing is more habitual or customary than our ways of speech, and nothing is more continuously invaded by change."[23]

That morality is characteristically found embodied in such dispositions of affection and conduct is part of what Hegel meant when he contended that morality receives content only in the *Sittlichkeit* of an ethical community. But he seems also to have meant that the content of the *Sittlichkeit* which embodies morality must be more than moral. Oakeshott's analogy of language is useful here. The grammar of a language is ascertained from the usage of those who speak and write that language well. Its authority is that of the speech and writing which exemplifies it. But speaking or writing well is more than doing so grammatically: being grammatical is a necessary condition of it, but not a sufficient one. And so it is with the relation of morality to acting well: nobody can act well unless he acts morally; but, for the most part, to act well it is not enough to act morally. A life the sole object of which was to obey the moral law would be aimless and empty.

A morality largely confined to restrictions on how one may pursue legitimate ends, which lays down only the most general conditions on what ends may be legitimately chosen, has sometimes been thought to be incomplete, if not mutilated. Alasdair MacIntyre, for example, has depreciated the virtues characteristic of such a morality as "secondary," on the ground that "their existence in a moral scheme of things as virtues is secondary to . . . the notion of another primary set of virtues which are directly related to the goals which men pursue as the ends of their life."[24] And, writing in 1964, he went on to compare unfavorably British society from the middle of the nineteenth century, in which, because of the depth of class divisions, the only moral virtues all its members have been able to agree upon are secondary, with American society in the same period, in which the same goals have been pursued by members of all classes. The American class structure, he contended, "allows for there being a national community of values"; the British one "only allows that national community of values to exist at the level of. . . the secondary virtues."[25]

Even if class divisions in Britain are deeper than in the United States, the sociological contrast MacIntyre depicted is dubious. Because Americans of all classes mostly agree on the rationality of a fundamentally capitalist economic system, he credited them with sharing the same goal in life—success in terms of that system. Yet capitalism is attractive as an economic system in part because it is consistent with any number of different life plans, and imposes none; that may even be why many Americans are attached to it. Very few of those whose chief object in life is business success imagine that object to be morally mandatory, or regard those who reject it as immoral. And no way of life which permits a variety of specific goals—no free way of life—can treat traditional moral virtues like fairness as secondary to any virtue which is merely requisite for the attainment of some specific goal. On the contrary, it will refuse to treat as either primary or moral any virtue the sole ground of which is that it is requisite for the attainment of this or that specific goal. The moral virtues are those without which you cannot, conformably to your rationality, pursue any goal whatever.

Neither of the two truths we have identified in Hegel's criticism of morality need be denied by traditional moralists. In religious traditions such as Judaism and Christianity, moral education, as the transmission of dispositions of conduct, is a matter of initiation into the life of a religious community; and in civilized pagan cultures it is a matter of initiation into the life of those cultures. Morality is characteristically learned as one learns to speak one's mother tongue grammatically: not by formal instruction, in times set aside for it, but by conversation and by participation in a common life. And one learns it incidentally to learning how to act well.

Nor did Kant deny that characteristically the capability of acting morally consists in dispositions of action and affection, and not of deliberation, or that such dispositions are usually found only in members of ethical communities. His reverence for the nontheoretical morality of ordinary folk should have placed this beyond question. Moreover, by teaching that every man has a natural end, happiness; that different persons and cultures have found happiness in different ways of life; and that morality is the common condition of every rational way of seeking happiness, he made it equally plain that a life that was merely moral would have been unimaginable to him. And, even more strongly than Oakeshott, he maintained that common morality is disclosed in what a man will not do: it consists in the limitations he observes in his pursuit of happiness.

In drawing attention to the limits both of the place of morality in human life, and of theory and deliberation in morality, Hegel asserted nothing that traditional moralists could not have approved. But they vehemently disapproved his more ambitious doctrine that morality has no content except that which the *Sittlichkeit* of ethical communities can supply. For they insisted that the restrictions ordained by practical reason on how one may pursue one's ends are specific. They conceived the conditions imposed by morality upon conduct to be analogous to those imposed by the grammar of a particular language upon speech in that language. By taking it to be a mere empty form which any coherent way of life whatever would have, Hegel reduced morality to something analogous to grammaticality in general.

Yet his reasons for so degrading morality are obscure. In his *Philosophie des Rechts* he sometimes wrote as though he were merely developing the implications of Kant's position.[26] Now it is true that Kant described his fundamental principle of morality as being purely formal, like all principles of reason. And his first formula for that principle, *Act only according to that maxim by which you can at the same time will that it should become a universal law,*[27] helped to create an impression that he took it to be empty. But that impression cannot be sustained. In Kant's terminology, "formal" principles are contrasted with "material" ones, that is, with principles grounded in experience and interest.[28] There is no implication that they are compatible with any content whatever. Moreover, he went on to maintain that his fundamental principle presupposes that action has an end prescribed by reason and not by interest or whim, to wit, rational nature itself; and that, accordingly, it has a second formula, equivalent to the first, namely, *Act so that you treat humanity, whether in your own person or in that of another, always as an end and never as a means only.*[29] It is therefore evident that he did not think of the formal first principle of morality as devoid of content.[30]

Today, however, the doctrine that reason can generate none but purely logical and hence empty a priori principles is so widely received that Hegel's defenders may think to claim for him the credit of anticipating it. And unquestionably, the *onus probandi* lies upon those who assert that pure reason furnishes substantive moral principles, not upon those who deny it. Anybody who offers to construct a theory of morality on the model of Kant's thereby undertakes to demonstrate how its principles are required by pure reason. Yet even though this undertaking must be reserved for what follows, it can be shown at once that Hegel himself conceded too much to the point of view of morality to have been able consistently to deny all content to its principles.

Although he was not much interested in the problem of how a man is to conduct himself when his will cannot "find itself" in the mores of his society, Hegel nevertheless recognized the problem and discussed it. It was the problem of Socrates, and of the Stoics. What, for example, must a deeply thoughtful man do if he finds himself a member of a society in which the institution of slavery is recognized? Presumably having in mind such things as the Stoics' denial of the validity of the master-slave relation, even as they were compelled to observe the laws regarding it, Hegel agreed that in such a situation one has no choice but "to try to find in the ideal world of the inner life alone the harmony which actuality has lost"—or has never had.[31] It was in this spirit that Epictetus imagined a slave as thus addressing his master: "Zeus has set me free; do you think that he intended his own son to be enslaved? But you are master of my carcass; take it."[32] Yet, even though the Stoics could not draw content for the empty self-determination of their wills from the *Sittlichkeit* of their ethical community, Hegel himself confessed that they were "better men than their fellows" and that their repudiation of slavery was right. How can this be rendered consistent? There is indeed the expedient of declaring that it was according to the *Sittlichkeit* of his ethical community, and not of their own, that Hegel judged the Stoics better men than their contemporaries; but, since such accidental and external superiority could have no philosophical significance, his own principles forbade him to adopt it. And there appears to be no other way of justifying his verdict than to concede that the ideal world of the Stoics' inner life had content as well as abstract form.

Hegel did not perceive that a pure morality of affection and conduct—a morality the content of which is wholly a matter of sharing the unselfconscious mores of an actual community—is weak both internally and externally. Its internal movement, Oakeshott has observed, which "does not spring from reflection on moral principles, . . . does not amount to moral self-criticism." Hence it has little power of recovery if, as is probable, "it degenerates into superstition, or if a crisis supervenes."[33]

The process of degeneration may be studied in moral traditions with a history of reflection on principles but in which the practice of self-criticism has fallen into disuse. According to received Catholic doctrine, it is morally wrong to serve in an unjust war: that is, a war not undertaken for a just and grave reason and with a right intention, or one that is not waged in a just way, or one in which there is no reasonable chance of accomplishing what is intended.[34] Although this definition contains moral terms requiring interpretation, there is large agreement among Catholic moralists that various specific reasons for undertaking a war are unjust or inadequate, that various specific intentions are wrong, and that various specific ways of waging it are barbarous. Nor is it seriously doubted that, by one or more of these criteria, many of the wars fought by Catholic states have been unjust. However, it is also held that some wars are just and necessary; and that, if such a war is in prospect and can be effectively waged only by a conscript army, then it will be a citizen's moral duty to obey a law of universal military conscription.

What, in this system, is the moral duty of a man conscripted for military service in what he is persuaded is an unjust war? If he is convinced, there is no question: he must refuse to serve. But only if he is convinced. If he is in doubt he has no such duty. He must, of course, try to resolve his doubt; but if he cannot, he may consent to serve. For it is his duty to obey the morally lawful commands of the state; and he cannot know that the call to serve is morally unlawful, unless he knows that the war in which he is called to serve is unjust. He may therefore assume that a war his own country is waging is just, unless he has good reason to believe that it is not.

Interpreted straightforwardly, this is mere common sense. Everybody has a general duty of loyalty to his country. Hence, if there is evidence that a war his country is waging is just, a man cannot be blamed for accepting that evidence in good faith, even though he knows that, governments being what they are, it may well be fraudulent. But what if there is plain evidence that the war is unjust?

Consider one of the rare cases which, by good fortune, have been documented. By 1943 it must have been difficult for any intelligent Catholic in Germany who read the newspapers to have been in any doubt at all that, by Catholic criteria, his country was waging an unjust war. A pious Austrian farmer, Franz Jägerstätter, saw what was obvious.

> [W]henever rulers have declared war against other countries [he wrote in a memorandum], they usually have not broken into their

lands in order to improve them or perhaps give them something. Thus, if one is fighting against the Russian people, he will also take as much out of that country as can be put to use here. If we were merely fighting Bolshevism, would other things like iron, oil wells, or good grainlands have become such important considerations?[35]

Given that the war was unjust, as it plainly was, was it not his duty to refuse induction into the German army? Jägerstätter consulted his parish priest, and ultimately his bishop.

Since the punishment for refusal to serve in the German army was death, the Catholic clergy cannot be blamed for not advocating it. But there was no question of open advocacy. What Jägerstätter sought was private counsel about the legitimacy of a conclusion he had reached wholly by himself, on evidence available to anybody. Neither of the clergy he consulted questioned the truth or the relevance of that evidence. Yet they told him that neither they nor he, a relatively uneducated man, were in a position to make an informed judgement about the justice of the war; and that therefore the conclusion he had reached about it was doubtful.

In a private statement subsequently written in prison Jägerstätter demolished this sophistry.

> For what purpose . . . [he asked] did God endow all men with reason and free will if, despite this, we have to render blind obedience; or if, as so many also say, the individual is not qualified to judge whether this war started by Germany is just or unjust? What purpose is served by the ability to distinguish between good and evil?[36]

Neither his sagacity nor his constancy were shaken. He was condemned to death, and beheaded.

After the war, the bishop who had tried to turn him from his course made it clear that his example was on no account to be followed. He was a martyr to his conscience, yes: but to "an inculpably erroneous conscience." It was not Jägerstätter but the "heroes" of the *Wehrmacht* who "conducted themselves . . . in the light of a clear and correct conscience."[37]

Is it possible to find in this anything but the depravation of the *Sittlichkeit* of an ethical community whose members had lost the habit of moral self-criticism? What was done under Nazi rule matters less than what was thought and said afterwards. In his profound charity, Jägerstätter himself excused the compliance of the clergy with Nazism as intended to "spare the faithful many agonies and martyrs."[38] While few would dare cast a stone had it been affirmed after the war that the members of the *Wehrmacht* who had believed it their duty to serve had been inculpable, although in error, the denial that Jägerstätter's conscience had been "clear and correct" was an open scandal.

Hegel disparaged the point of view of morality on the ground that, being abstractly rational, it could find content for its judgements only in the mores of some actual community. The case of Jägerstätter reveals an opposite process. The moral theory of Catholic Christianity furnished specific precepts on the subject of legitimate war service, which applied to the case in question on the basis of stated facts which were not questioned. But, by recourse to the mores of their actual community, Jägerstätter's spiritual advisers were able to evaporate the precepts whose applicability to his case they could not dispute. For, according to those mores, apart from such fanciful possibilities as a war with the declared intention of destroying the Church as an institution, no individual citizen was deemed capable of assuring himself that any war his country proposed to wage was unjust. Here, what is exposed as empty, as lacking specific content, as allowing any filling whatever, is not *Moralität*, but *Sittlichkeit*.

1.3   Intuitionism: Old and New

In English-speaking countries the moral theory known as intuitionism has been widely advanced as connecting the conception of morality as a system of specific precepts binding upon rational creatures as such with the conception of it as an unselfconscious disposition of affection and conduct.

The position taken by most intuitionist moralists from the mid-seventeenth century to the early nineteenth may be summed up as follows. In uncivilized societies, moral thinking is, from various causes, defective and discordant, and so unsuitable as a point of departure for moral theory. In civilized societies, by contrast, whatever may be their cultural differences, the fundamental principles according to which moral thinking is carried on are the same. For the most part, such thinking is unselfconscious, and the thinker is quite unaware of the premises upon which he proceeds. However, it is susceptible of theoretical analysis; and, when analysed, is revealed as presupposing specific precepts, which may be precisely formulated and systematically ordered. Such systematization will inevitably rectify moral deliberation in various ways, just as grammatical analysis rectifies speech, but only by bringing to light rules and precepts implicit in how people actually think and speak.

The moral system thus elicited, according to the intuitionists, is deductive. With the help of factual premises, some of the precepts it contains are derivable from others, by way of ordinary syllogistic reasoning. But the moral precepts which are ultimate, that is, which are not thus derivable from others, are per se binding upon rational creatures as such, exactly as Descartes declared the ultimate principles of any pure science are. They are, in Cartesian terminology, "intuitions": that is, "undoubting conception[s] of a pure and attentive mind, . . . generated solely by the light of reason, and . . . more certain than deduction itself, because simpler."[39] An intuition thus has two characteristics: it cannot be doubted by anybody who has it, while he has it; and, springing as it does from the light of reason, it cannot be false. There is disagreement among intuitionists about how many ultimate moral intuitions there are: whether one or two, or a much larger number. But there is no disagreement that moral thinking in all civilized societies has a common systematic structure, which can be elicited by analysis, or that the underived precepts in that system are intuitions in the full Cartesian sense.

The implicitly systematic character of moral thinking was virtually unquestioned by intuitionist moralists from Ralph Cudworth and Henry More in the seventeenth century to William Whewell in the nineteenth. John Locke and Samuel Clarke went further than most, and pressed the comparison of moral science to mathematical, as in Locke's notorious profession of confidence "that if Men would in the same method, and with the same indifferency, search after moral, as they do mathematical Truths, they would find them to have a stronger Connection one with another, and a more necessary Consequence from our clear and distinct *Ideas*, and to come nearer perfect Demonstration, than is commonly imagined."[40] Without going so far, the great majority nevertheless agreed that it was the ultimate precepts or principles, the *noemata moralia* as More called them, which were intuitively known, and that the others were known only by deduction. There were some differences of opinion about how difficult the process of derivation was, and how certain its results. Bishop Butler, indeed, ventured to deny that it was ever difficult at all. "[L]et any plain honest man," he wrote, "before he engages in any course of action, ask himself, Is this I am

going about right, or is it wrong? Is it good, or is it evil? I do not in
the least doubt but that this question would be answered agreeably
to truth and virtue, by almost any fair man in almost any circumstance."[41] But not many followed Butler in this, even though in the
eighteenth century casuistry was neglected.

The last major work in this older British intuitionist tradition was
William Whewell's *Elements of Morality*, the first edition of which
appeared in 1846. Intuitionism had been under attack from the
point of view now generally known as utilitarian both by latitudi-
narian Christians such as William Paley, in his *Principles of Moral
and Political Philosophy* (1785), and by infidels such as Bentham
and his followers. Against this "low" view of morality, Whewell
proposed to defend the "high" nonutilitarian view, returning to the
tradition of Clarke and Butler but modifying it by admitting that
intuitive knowledge is progressive. He maintained that intuitive
understanding of first principles, in morals as in the natural sciences,
improves from generation to generation. However, it is doubtful
whether Whewell's theory of progress in intuition is consistent with
intuitionist doctrine. The Cartesian conception of pure science
demanded that the intuitive principles on which it is erected be
certain and indubitable; and intuitions capable of progressive
change would be neither. For this reason Whewell's system may also
be classified as a transitional one, in which British intuitionism
began to transform itself into something more like Kantian rationalism. Another element in Whewell's system which may be considered transitional was his view that some intuitive principles, such
as the principle of justice, *that each man is to have his own*,
presuppose the existence of social institutions, such as some form of
property; and that the specific duties arising from those principles
will vary according to whatever forms of those institutions are in
force.[42]

A principal cause of the demise of the older intuitionism, and of
the very different shape of its revivals in the twentieth century, was
the criticism of Sidgwick. Sidgwick's view of intuitionism is enig-
matic. He did not deny merit to it: indeed, he protested that the
intuitional morality was his as much as it was any man's.[43] And he
expounded it, in general terms, both accurately and fairly.[44] In
particular, he drew attention to its doctrine that the intuitions
presupposed in ordinary moral thinking are not known to ordinary
moral thinkers; that only trained theorists are capable of identifying
them; that their exact formulation is difficult and disputable; and

that apparent intuitions may have to be rectified to make them compatible with one another.[45] Yet, notwithstanding these admissions, he laid it down that for a precept to be intuitively known it must satisfy the following four conditions: (1) that it be clearly and precisely formulated; (2) that its self-evidence be ascertained by careful reflection; (3) that it be consistent with other propositions received as intuitively evident; and (4) that experts in the subject do not dissent from it.[46] Armed with these conditions, he made havoc of intuitionism through ten remorseless chapters. For even in those departments of morality most thoroughly explored by intuitionists, such as those of veracity and contract, he could argue, and did, that the precepts which really are commonly accepted fail to satisfy condition (1), that they be clearly and precisely formulated; and, on the other hand, that those enunciated by intuitionist moralists, although they may satisfy conditions (1) and (3), of clarity, precision, and consistency with one another, are too controversial to satisfy condition (4).[47]

It is perplexing that Sidgwick should have forgotten that, according to his own exposition, intuitionists must reject his fourth condition. Their doctrine that the fundamental principles of the system implicit in ordinary moral thinking, once accurately formulated, will be indubitable to any pure and attentive mind that considers them, does not entail that they will be self-evident at once to any theorist to whom they are presented. Moral theorists going about their difficult work, even intuitionist theorists, can seldom bring a pure and attentive mind to bear upon results that traverse their own. And although individual intuitionists hoped that their own results were final, the intuitionist school made no such claim. Intuitionism was a method to be followed, but no more than any other could it assure those who followed it of success. Yet intuitionists could claim, and did, that since their results did not diverge haphazardly and unsystematically, they could be interpreted as approximating, in different degrees, to the true system that was sought.

The strategy of Sidgwick's attack on intuitionism was not only misdirected, it diverted him from bringing a pure and attentive mind to intuitionism's successes. Thus he complained that "Common Sense seems doubtful" about how to resolve numerous casuistical problems about contracts and veracity.[48] Now it is undeniable that ordinary folk are puzzled by such problems and that the solutions proposed by individual intuitionists vary; but it by no means follows that they have not been solved by intuitionist methods, and even less that they cannot be.

One example must suffice. Sidgwick represented the intuitional method as baffled by the problem of whether a promise is binding if it has been obtained by a material concealment. He hazarded the opinion that whether the concealment was "wilfully produced," or whether the error was "shared by the promisee or produced in some way unintentionally," might be circumstances affecting a decision. But he simply did not notice that Whewell professed to have solved this very class of cases by recourse to his Principle of Truth. "[T]he false supposition releases the promiser," Whewell wrote, "so far as it was included in the Common Understanding [of what the Promiser is to do for the Promisee]." And he sensibly added: "Yet it must be very difficult for the Promiser to know how far his Promise is hypothetically understood. And therefore, to avoid the moral trouble which such doubts produce, it is wise in such cases to express the condition on which the Promise is given."[49] This resolution is almost a commonplace among Roman Catholic moral theologians. Michael Cronin, for example, has laid it down that

> It is only in so far as error excludes consent that it vitiates contract. . . . there is always a core or subtance which a man stipulates for and concerning which there should be no mistake. . . . Mistake . . . vitiates contract only in so far as it affects this central core.[50]

Of course neither Whewell nor Cronin would have denied that common sense is doubtful about this solution, in the sense that most nontheoretical persons would flounder when the question was first put to them. But Sidgwick's question was whether the intuitional method is capable of solving it; and the answer seems to be that it is.

Such was Sidgwick's authority among philosophers inclined towards intuitionism that they received his criticism of the older intuitionist position as decisive. And so, instead of trying to vindicate a view they thought exploded, they set out to construct a new intuitionism that would satisfy Sidgwick's conditions. Yet the task appeared to be impossible. For, according to Sidgwick's first three conditions, only clear and precise precepts, which are self-evident upon reflection, will do as intuitions; and according to his fourth, these precepts must be accepted by all qualified persons. There are indeed vague generalities which satisfy the fourth; but they, being what they are, cannot satisfy the first three.

The difficulty was nevertheless overcome by C. D. Broad and W. D. Ross, working independently of one another. Their solution was to reinterpret as statements of pertinent moral considerations the vague generalities almost nobody will deny. When such a maxim as "In general, you should not break your word!" is reinterpreted as equivalent to "For a proposed course of action to involve breaking your word is always a consideration against doing it," it looks precise as well as uncontroversial. Under this treatment, popular maxims yield a store of moral intuitions.

Unfortunately, the new intuitions did not suffice for moral guidance, as the precepts of the older intuitionism had done. When a man finds himself in a situation in which it would suit him to do something by which he would break his word, it is not enough for him to know that there is a consideration against doing that thing; what he wants to know is whether, in that situation, that consideration is decisive.

Broad and Ross recognized this problem and hoped to solve it by discovering a procedure for arriving at moral judgements about what to do in particular situations. The one they settled on has two stages. The first is to review the various courses of action that are possible, taking note of all characteristics that count for or against choosing them. To carry out this first stage, it is not enough to possess the supposedly universal power intuitively to perceive, of a characteristic brought to one's attention, whether an action's having that characteristic counts in favor of doing it, or against doing it, or neither. A moral agent must also be familiar with all the more significant characteristics that count for or against doing the actions that have them. He must, in short, be morally well brought up. Supposing that he is, and that he succeeds in reviewing all the morally significant characteristics of the various courses of action open to him, he may then proceed to the second stage: that of weighing the various considerations against one another, in order to judge what course of action is indicated by the greatest balance of favorable considerations over unfavorable ones.

Broad compared the second stage to perceptual judgement.

> When it comes to estimating resultant fittingness from component fittingnesses and unfittingnesses . . . we are soon reduced to something analogous to those perceptual judgments on very complex situations which we have constantly to make in playing games of skill.[51]

And Ross was emphatic that judgements at the second stage are not intuitive. Thus, of one important intuitive consideration, that a proposed action would be the keeping of a promise, he declared that intuitionism implies no more than that it is "independent and *sui generis*"; it certainly "implies no particular view about the relative weight of this [consideration] as compared with others."[52] Hence,

[when] there is more than one claim upon our action, [and] those claims . . . conflict, . . . while we can see with certainty that the claims exist, it becomes a matter of individual and fallible judgement to say which claim is in the circumstances the overriding one. In many such situations, equally good men would form different judgements as to what their duty is.[53]

The most familiar objection to the newer intuitionism is moral: that it allows ordinarily respectable persons to do anything they are likely to choose, and to have a good conscience in doing it. While "speciously strict," as Peter Geach has remarked, it "leads in fact to quite laxist consequences."[54] For in any situation calling for a choice between socially possible alternatives, each alternative will, *ex hypothesi*, be supported by some consideration; and, since the new intuitionist theory confers no definite weight on any consideration, every agent may assign to each of them whatever weight seems good to him.

Philosophically, the chief objection must be that it is fraudulent to describe what the new intuitionists take to be the process of moral deliberation as one of "weighing" or "balancing" considerations. For that metaphor to be appropriate, there must be a procedure for ascertaining the weight of each consideration, either comparatively or absolutely, a procedure analogous to that of putting objects on a balance or scale. It is an appropriate description, even a happy one, for deliberation in terms of a moral system in which different considerations are ordered serially; for in such deliberation, which consideration has priority over the others is determined by reflecting on their respective places in the series—a process unquestionably analogous to weighing different objects in order to find the heaviest. But by repudiating anything that might order the various considerations it acknowledges, and accepting as "weighing" or "balancing" any process whatever in which a man, hesitating before alternatives supported by different considerations, without conscious insincerity overcomes his hesitation, the new intuitionism deprives that description of any definite sense. Hence its laxist consequences.

Although Sidgwick's objections to the older intuitionism were unsound, and although, even had they not been, exchanging it for the newer one would have been a poor bargain, intuitionism in ethics, whatever its form, is vitiated by the same fundamental error that has caused its decay in science and metaphysics: the Cartesian doctrine that a deductive science must derive from principles which, solely by the light of reason, are indubitably evident to a pure and attentive mind.

Descartes' implicit argument for his erroneous doctrine was one of success: that, by following the method laid down in his *Discours*, he himself had found fundamental principles that qualify as intuitions, not only in "first philosophy," but also in mathematics, physics, and the scientific study of the soul. In the late nineteenth and early twentieth centuries, when empiricists, idealists, and pragmatists united in denying intuitive status to any alleged principle in any branch of inquiry, the impugned claim of success was supplemented by a negative argument to the effect that, if there were no intuitions, then no deductive science would be possible. It was rightly agreed on all sides both that the principles of a fundamental deductive science, if they really are principles, cannot themselves be deductively derived from any propositions yet more ultimate, and that if the principles of a fundamental science are to ensure the truth of the propositions derived from them, they must possess a title to truth prior to that of any deduction. And it was reasonably assumed that a perfectly rational being contemplating such principles would find them self-evident; for such a being would be in possession of all considerations pertinent to their truth, and would weigh them accurately. It was then inferred that no rational being whose mind was less than perfectly rational could perceive the necessary truth of such principles unless its grasp of them was the same as that of a perfectly rational being: that is, unless it rightly perceived them as indubitably self-evident when it contemplated them with a pure and attentive mind.

While the decay of Cartesian intuitionism in philosophy of mathematics and philosophy of science has damaged the argument from success for intuitionism in ethics, it has not destroyed it. And the negative argument for intuitionism continues to find adherents, although it is now sometimes turned against the view that morality can be presented as a deductive system. In its anti-deductivist form

it runs: there can be no deductive system of morality unless its
principles are intuitions; no moral principles are genuine intuitions;
therefore, there can be no deductive system of morality.
For the present it must suffice to dispose of the negative argument
for intuitionism, although in the sequel (see 2.4 and 7.3–4) the
implicit argument from success will be met by presenting common
morality as a deductive system, the fundamental principle of which,
although there is reason to think it true, is not a Cartesian intuition.

The flaw in the intuitionist negative argument is its step from the
reasonable assumption that a perfectly rational being, contemplating the principles of a fundamental deductive science, would
find them self-evident to the conclusion that an imperfectly rational
being could not grasp the necessary truth of those principles unless
it did so in the same way. In general, propositions are received as
principles of deductive sciences because attempts to think in terms
of their contradictories break down. Sometimes, as with reflection
on a fundamental logical principle like the law of contradiction, in
which it becomes evident that to deny the principle would make
nonsense of the acts of assent and dissent out of which reasoning
itself arises, the result may be admitted to qualify as a Cartesian
intuition. More often, however, as with the principle that the
relation of temporal priority is logically transitive, it may not. There
are various considerations upon which human beings, recognizing
their imperfect rationality, may reasonably accept a proposition as a
fundamental necessary truth; but what those considerations may be,
in a given investigation, cannot be laid down in advance.

Just as an imperfectly rational being, in reasonably accepting a
proposition as a fundamental necessary truth, need not directly
perceive it to be so when he contemplates it with a pure and attentive
mind, so he need not imagine it to be indubitable. Intuitionists
themselves, confronted with alleged intuitionist systems that are
mutually incompatible, have always conceded that a conviction of
the indubitability of an alleged truth is not necessarily accompanied
by knowledge. But, if knowledge be conceived as the acceptance of a
proposition, upon adequate grounds, as true, it is even more
important to recognize that knowledge of a necessary truth is not
necessarily accompanied by a sense of its indubitability. An imperfectly rational being may accept a proposition as necessarily true on
grounds which a perfectly rational one would recognize at once to be
adequate, and yet be disquieted by doubt as to whether those
grounds are adequate.

1.4   The Philosophical Interest of the Hebrew-Christian Moral Tradition

Few philosophers would have been ready to believe that the fundamental principles of morality are intuitively known unless they had felt themselves to be members of an ethical community and to share in its dispositions of affection and conduct. From Cudworth to Sidgwick, and from Sidgwick to Broad, the British intuitionists, old and new, did feel this. Their intuitive convictions drew sap from roots in a common life. Yet, notwithstanding that they tended to represent the traditional morality of their society as a datum to be investigated, in itself unselfconscious and unreflective, that morality originated, as we have seen, in rules laid down on theoretical grounds by Stoic philosophers and Christian theologians. And while it has gone some way towards reconversion into a habit of behavior and affection, it has "never," as Oakeshott observed, "been able to divest itself of the form in which it first emerged."[55] In consequence, even as partly reconverted into a morality of habit, the traditional morality of the Western world must remain largely unintelligible to anybody unwilling to investigate its philosophical and religious foundations.

Ever since the middle of the nineteenth century, most academic philosophers in the English-speaking world have been unwilling to do so, with results to which, in a celebrated passage, John Rawls has drawn attention.[56] Traditional morality has been able to find a place in secular academic philosophy only in the form of intuitionism, which is, to use Rawls's word, "unconstructive." The principal constructive alternative has been utilitarianism, all the varieties of which derive from Bentham's greatest happiness principle, the principle that acts are right in proportion as they promote the happiness of sentient beings. The academic position of utilitarianism has been secure ever since Sidgwick defended it both as providing a foundation for the morality of common sense and as remedying its deficiencies. Yet, although the extent of their divergence is disputed, utilitarianism is evidently incompatible with traditional morality. And even among academic philosophers traditional morality has remained too strong, as a disposition, for many of them to have been able to embrace utilitarianism with a tranquil mind. Unfortunately, the only other constructive doctrine to have gained academic recognition has been perfectionism, which is representatively expressed by Nietzsche's answer to his own question: "[H]ow can your life, the individual life, retain the highest value, the deepest significance? ... Only by your living for the good of the rarest and most valuable specimens."[57] Few academics have been able to endure that. By contrast, utilitarianism has enough in common with traditional morality to be considered a rival to it on something like its own terms. And so academic moral philosophy has become dominated by a theory alien to the habitual morality that has survived, not only in society at large, but in academic philosophers themselves.

A number of moral philosophers, among whom Frankena, Gert, Gewirth, Nagel, and Rawls are conspicuous, have recently developed nonintuitionist theories designed to correspond more closely than utilitarianism with our actual moral tradition. It is significant that none of them endorses what MacIntyre has referred to as the "undergraduate-essay commonplace that Kantian ethics is riddled with incoherences."[58] Yet, although each has drawn attention to misunderstood or neglected sides of the work of this or that classical moral philosopher (as Frankena has to Butler and Hume, and Gert to Hobbes), with the exception of Frankena all conclude that, down to the present century, essential parts of the structure of an adequate moral theory have remained to be completed.

However, another approach is possible, an approach which, if I am not mistaken, was followed by Kant himself. In this approach one provisionally accepts as sound and complete the work of the moral theorists (some of them theologians) who shaped the habitual morality that survives in our society, and one tries to isolate the philosophical core of what they had to say about that morality. Nor must it be forgotten that, in doing so, one is taking them at their own word. For not only did both Jewish and Christian thinkers reach substantially the same conclusions about what, in their respective ways of life, was the moral law common to all mankind, they also agreed that their results were accessible to all men by virtue of their common reason. It will be convenient to call this intellectual tradition the "Hebrew-Christian" tradition.[59]

There is, it must be confessed, an obvious objection to approaching moral theory by way of this tradition. Quite apart from particular beliefs about God and his relation to the world that they ascribed to divine revelation, both Jews and Christians shared a number of philosophical beliefs about the existence and nature of God, and about the nature of the world, of man, and of human action, which are presupposed by their teachings about morality but which are by no means shared by all intelligent human beings in all civilizations. How then can morality as the Hebrew-Christian tradition conceives it be truly common?

Fortunately, as the inquiry that follows will show, the part of Hebrew-Christian morality that depends on beliefs about the nature of God (for example, the prohibition of idolatry) is separable from the part that has to do with the duties of human beings to themselves and to one another. (There are some minor exceptions, such as the prohibition of suicide, which is justified both on nontheistic and on theistic grounds.) By restricting our inquiry to the latter part, which is much the greater, and which covers all the topics with which secular moral theory has to do, this objection, to the extent that it turns on the theistic character of the Hebrew-Christian moral tradition, is avoided.

The remainder of the objection, however, must be faced. Every part of common morality, as the Hebrew-Christian moral tradition conceives it, rests on presuppositions about the nature of the world, of man, and of human action, which are rejected both in some venerable cultures, such as Hinduism and Buddhism, and in some post-Christian theories of man, such as B. F. Skinner's radical behaviorism. Although these presuppositions are shared by most people in our society, perhaps not always consistently, and are in my opinion philosophically defensible, it is of course necessary that they be defended. Yet their defence must be destined for a separate investigation. In constructing a moral theory no more is necessary than to identify and state any controversial metaphysical presuppositions that distinguish it from its rivals.

That the Hebrew-Christian tradition, as a matter of historical fact, has determined the substance of the received morality of the Western world, is sufficient reason for studying it philosophically. And if what is presupposed in that tradition about man and his world should also be true, there would be an even stronger reason. For it is unthinkable that a traditional consensus about the substance of morality, maintained for over two millennia through great social and cultural changes, should be accidental. Such a consensus may be in error; but if so, its error must lie deep: not in its conscious calculations, which have been repeatedly scrutinized and probed, but in what is unreflectively presupposed in it. On the other hand, if its fundamental presuppositions are true, there is a strong ante-

cedent probability that the traditional consensus as to the substance
of morality is also true.

1.5   The Investigation Proposed

The shape of the investigation now proposed is dictated by the
various considerations that have been presented.
It will fall into two parts. In the first, I shall try to develop, as a
philosophical system, that part of common morality according to the
Hebrew-Christian tradition which does not depend on any theistic
belief. In the second, I shall investigate the truth of that system,
partly by examining the external objections that have been made to
it, chiefly from a consequentialist point of view, and partly by
exploring the considerations on which its first principle has been put
forward.

The mode in which the first part will be presented shall be as
impersonal as I can make it. For, since the system I shall try to
develop is not my invention, it will be open to any reader to question
whether I have presented it correctly. Aquinas long ago pointed out
that any statement of the content of common morality in the
Hebrew-Christian tradition must become more controversial as it
becomes more specific. [60] And, although my presentation of it will be
comparatively general and unspecific, I cannot escape taking sides
on a number of disputed questions, about my answers to which I am
less confident the less they have been approved by others. What I am
interested in, and presume that my readers will be interested in, is
what really belongs to common morality as traditionally understood,
and not my own views as such or, indeed, anybody else's.

Do I accept the system I proceed to work out? In the end, I shall
argue that it is sound in principle. But in the process of deriving it,
the sole question with which I shall occupy myself is internal:
namely, given that its metaphysical presuppositions are those I
identify, and given that its first principles are what I find them to be,
what specific conclusions follow? In each case, the answers I shall
give will be my own. But it was mere prudence to inquire into those
that were given by theologians and philosophers whose work has won
acceptance as authoritative; and I found, as I had expected, that
even on matters of vehement dispute, my task would seldom be more
than to choose among answers already given.

The order in which the system will be developed is logical. I shall begin by identifying the presuppositions about nature, man, and human action that underlie the whole of it. Certain additional presuppositions made only in part of it will be reserved for discussion in connection with that part. The two kinds of question the system professes to answer will then be distinguished: those about the rightness or wrongness of actions in themselves; and those about the culpability or inculpability of doers in doing them. Since answers to questions of the second kind presuppose answers to questions about the first, I describe them as "first-order" and "second-order" questions respectively. Finally, I shall attempt to ascertain what ultimate principles are recognized in the Hebrew-Christian tradition and, having done so, to determine the way in which specific precepts are to be derived from them.

The body of the system can then be derived: first of all, the precepts having to do with first-order questions; and then, after laying down certain further presuppositions about the "interior" of action, in particular about intention and will, those having to do with second-order questions. One feature of how first-order questions will be treated should be mentioned. Many of them have to do with relations in which an agent stands to an institution. Although it is sometimes held that part of a moralist's task is to design institutions, the weight of the Hebrew-Christian tradition, I shall argue, is against this. Some institutions (slavery, for example) are immoral, and voluntary participation in them is wrong. But most institutions, and a fortiori most of their forms, are neither ordained nor forbidden by common morality, but permitted. In some cases, for example the institution of the family, Judaism and Christianity both teach that there is a certain form of it which is divinely ordained; but it does not follow that either Jews or Christians must hold it morally obligatory for societies which do not share their religion to adopt their form of the family. Problems about what moral obligations are generated by institutions in process of change will be seen to be particularly difficult.

Having exhibited common morality as a system, and ascertained its principal specific precepts, I shall conclude the first part of the investigation by considering whether this system is consistent. Since it will have been shown to derive from a single first principle, by way of a large number of specificatory premises in which a nonmoral concept in that principle is unfolded, it is undoubtedly consistent if its first principle is self-consistent and if its specificatory premises are consistent with it, themselves, and one another. But the nonmoral concept contained in the first principle and unfolded in the specificatory premises is so rich that none of these conditions can be assumed to obtain. The consistency of the system can therefore be established only indirectly, by examining the kinds of contradiction that are alleged to arise within it. This will lead to an examination of the ordering principles that have been held to be intrinsic to its specific precepts; and in particular of the Pauline principle that evil is not to be done that good may come of it, and of various forms of the principle of the double effect.

After common morality, as traditionally conceived, has been presented as a philosophical system—or, as Kant might have expressed it, after we have made the transition from common rational knowledge of morality to philosophical—the second part of the investigation may begin. This will in turn fall into two parts. In the first, external objections to the system developed will be considered. These arise from cases, often described as "cases of necessity," in which it is maintained that to observe the precepts of common morality would be calamitous. It will be argued that, although on some occasions that may indeed be so, the precepts of common morality are such that, given its presuppositions, predictions that calamity can only be averted by violating them must always be doubtful. It will also be argued that it is very doubtful whether any consequentialist alternative to common morality can be justified on consequentialist grounds.

Finally, the grounds on which the first principle of common morality has been held to be binding on all rational creatures as such will be considered. They will be shown to involve a kind of teleology that is very widely misunderstood and hence neglected: namely, a teleology in which the end for the sake of which an action is done is not something to be produced by doing it but something already in existence to be respected in doing it. It will be contended that acceptance of such a teleology is a condition upon conceiving one's actions as rationally autonomous; and the nature of the necessity of that condition will be explored.

A theory of morality will thereby have been constructed. For, if what has been done is sound, a system of specific precepts will have been derived from a first principle the observance of which will have been shown to be a condition upon rational action. For a rational creature to violate the precepts of such a system would be to violate his own rationality.

2 Presuppositions and Principles

2.1 Human Beings and Their World

Morality, as conceived in the Hebrew-Christian tradition, applies to rational creatures as such. In the Hebrew scriptures, the first wrongdoer, the Father of Lies, was not a human being but one of the mysterious creatures popularly called angels, who according to Aquinas are not even corporeal. Yet, since the only rational creatures with whom human beings are historically known to have had personal or social relations are other human beings in this world, the only part of morality to have been embodied in traditional habits of conduct has had to do solely with human beings inhabiting worlds of the kinds they have believed themselves to inhabit. In attempting to expound the content of morality in specific detail, traditional moralists have had no choice but to confine themselves to that part of it about which moral traditions have been specific; and it would be affectation not to take example by them.

It would also be philosophically unrewarding. Exotic problems about what precepts apply to rational creatures who can at will read one another's minds, or who are protected by metallic exoskeletons,[1] and how they differ from the precepts applicable to human beings in worlds like our own, call for ingenuity rather than for philosophical insight.

By contrast, working out what are the specific requirements of morality for human beings, living in the kind of world they do, is not at all straightforward. For not only do human cultures differ from one another principally in the different conceptions they have of what human beings are, and of what kind of world they inhabit, but it is peculiarly difficult to determine within any culture what its conceptions of man and of his world are. Nobody ordinarily has occasion to put into words what is presupposed about something in virtually everything he or those with whom he speaks have to say about it. Just because our conceptions of the fundamental nature of man and of our world are presupposed in nearly everything we say about them, they are seldom expressed in anything we say. Characteristically, we become aware of what we presuppose when we encounter human beings whose intellectual traditions are not ours, and, finding that what they say on various specific subjects having to do with man in the world diverges radically from what we say, we proceed to trace the divergence to their rejection of presuppositions we were not aware of making.

What is distinctive in the presuppositions of the Hebrew-Christian moral tradition about the nature of human beings and their world can therefore be most economically ascertained by way of the clues afforded by the differences between its prescriptions for human conduct and those of some comparably rich alien tradition: Hinduism, for example. Nearly all Hindu prescriptions about human conduct are a matter of caste—the caste into which the agent is born. Each Hindu follows the way of life laid down for his or her caste, which is different from that laid down for any other, and regards himself or herself as forbidden to become intimate with the members of any other; not merely may Hindus not marry outside their castes, they may not even eat outside them. "[A]part from avoidance prohibitions," Arthur Danto has remarked, "nothing in India ever was worked out that would serve as a general ethic overarching the differences between castes, treating men, as it were, as equals in some ways."[2]

While Hindus consider it meritorious to pursue, in approved ways, both wealth (*artha*) and physical, especially sexual, pleasure (*kama*), morality in the main consists of doing one's duty (*dharma*) as a member of a caste. Except for that duty, which will require him to do various things for others—for members of his family, for his associates in common enterprises, for the poor, and so forth—a man owes nothing to others. "Each of us," Danto sums up the teaching, "must find his way, and though it is a plight we have in common, essentially there is nothing we can do for one another."[3]

Although Hinduism usually horrifies Westerners when they first encounter it, as a system, it is difficult to object to on its own presuppositions about the fundamental character of human beings and of their world. It takes every human being to be, at bottom, a soul (*atman*). Before its incarnation in its present body, every soul has a long history of previous incarnations, not all of them necessarily human; and the series will continue after death, until, by purification, the soul attains liberation (*moksha*). The series of incarnations takes place according to the law of Karma, which ordains that a soul's every evil act of will necessarily brings about a situation, perhaps in a subsequent incarnation, in which either that evil is expiated or another evil act of will is committed. No soul endures any suffering or degradation except as part of this necessary process. Since acts of will are free, the law of Karma does not necessitate any individual evil act by which anybody suffers. Yet no suffering caused to one soul by another's evil action is unnecessary. Hence, if the evil action which caused that suffering had not been performed, as it might not have been, equivalent suffering would nevertheless have been produced from some other source. [4]

Hindus simply reject such Jewish and Christian doctrines as that a man may not stand idly by while another is a victim of violence, although they endorse intervention against violence when the *dharma* of one's caste requires it. On their own principles, they are right. Most justifications of such intervention make two assumptions: that there can be undeserved suffering; and that, in many cases, the sum of evil in the world will be less if violence is resisted than if it is not. But if the world is as Hindus believe, both these assumptions are false. There only appears to be undeserved suffering, because it is not perceived that the sufferer is a soul with many lives before the present one: the law of Karma assures us that no soul suffers except as is necessary to purify itself of past wrongs. And the sum of evil consists of two kinds of items: bad acts of will and the bad Karma they produce. Bad acts of will cannot be prevented by violence, although some of their physical manifestations may be; rather, they are provoked by it. Hence resistance to evil cannot reduce the sum of evil in the world. No soul can avoid suffering and evil except by religious purification; and each soul must purify itself. The only way, in the end, in which any soul can help another is indirect: by advice and example.

Comparison with Hinduism at once forces into the open two fundamental presuppositions of the Hebrew-Christian tradition. The first may be formulated as follows:

(1) *Man, considered as a moral agent, is a rational animal.*

Against the Hindu doctrine that, as moral agents, human beings are souls transmigrating through a series of bodies, the Hebrew-Christian presupposition is that they are rational animals. According to Hinduism, a human agent is not strictly an animal at all: he is a soul undergoing the illusion of being in a human body. His animality is a temporary state he is in; it is not part of his essence. According to the Hebrew-Christian tradition, a human agent is essentially an animal. He came into existence when his animal life began; and he will not exist as an agent after death until his soul regains his animal body at the resurrection. True, his soul survives his bodily death; but as a disembodied soul, he is not a full human agent. On the other hand, as a rational animal, man is quite unlike any other animal now known to him. He is autonomous, in the sense that he acts in the light of conceptions he has formed of himself, of others, and of his world, according to principles of action he has chosen, and for which, allowing for the limits of his knowledge, he is responsible.

The second Hebrew-Christian presupposition that is brought to attention by comparison with Hinduism is:

(2) *The world man inhabits is a system of nature, in which events occur according to morally neutral laws.*

A "morally neutral" law is one that is formulable without mentioning, explicitly or implicitly, the moral properties of actions: that is, whether actions of certain kinds violate, are consistent with, or are required by the moral law. For example, there are laws of nature by which it can be deduced that if you shoot a man through the brain, then his other vital functions will shortly cease. But whether your shooting of him was right or wrong can make no difference to what will follow in the course of nature. There can be no law, such as the Hindu law of Karma, according to which, besides its consequences according to neutral laws of nature, such an act will have additional natural consequences by virtue of its moral properties.

Recent moralists have often ignored the limitations imposed by this presupposition on the scope of traditional morality. While it does not excuse them from examining cases that may arise in systems of nature the laws of which differ from those we believe to obtain as a matter of fact, it does require that any case to be considered could occur in a possible system of nature in which human life could subsist.

Moralists sometimes perplex themselves with such cases as this.

Somebody dear to you is dying of a painful disease; by writing the words, "Let him die!" on a piece of paper given to you by a Mephistophelian stranger, you can work an instant cure but thereby will untraceably cause the death of somebody utterly unknown to you in a foreign country. Should you write the words? Before an answer is attempted, it should be asked whether any set of laws of nature is possible, according to which writing certain words on a piece of paper could have such consequences. For unless one is, traditional morality implies nothing whatever about the case. It is not confined to what can actually happen; but neither does it take account of fairy tales.

The second presupposition also excludes from consideration the notorious problem put by Ivan Karamazov to his brother Alyosha in Dostoevsky's novel:

> " . . . imagine that it is you yourself who is erecting the edifice of human destiny with the aim of making men happy in the end, of giving them peace and contentment at last, but that to do that it is absolutely necessary, and indeed quite inevitable, to torture to death only one tiny creature, the little girl who beat her breast with her little fist, and to found the edifice on her unavenged tears—would you consent to be the architect on those conditions? Tell me and do not lie!"
> "No, I wouldn't," Alyosha said softly.[5]

The problem Dostoevsky propounds is not like that depicted in the gospel stories of the temptation of Christ, in which the diabolic ruler of this world promises to give what he can give—riches and power—as a reward for a crime. On the contrary, in Dostoevsky's story you discover that it is in your power to bring about genuine peace and happiness for all mankind, but that the nature of things is such that, in order to ensure it, you must torture a child to death. Here again, it is necessary to demand, in what possible system of nature could a deed of that kind be a necessary element in causing that outcome? Whoever may maintain that there is such a possible system owes us some account of it.

Common morality as traditionally conceived absolutely forbids, as we shall see, either torturing or murdering the innocent, no matter what may be gained thereby in any possible system of nature. But no reason has been given to fear that, by accepting those absolute prohibitions, we may be abandoning the hope of making mankind happy in the end.

2.2   Actions, Circumstances, and Consequences

Besides the presuppositions it makes about human agents and their world, the Hebrew-Christian tradition also makes certain special presuppositions about human action. But since these additional presuppositions distinguish its conception of human action from others in which its more fundamental notions about man and the world are also taken for granted, they cannot be elicited by comparisons with traditions such as Hinduism, which reject those fundamentals. There appears to be no alternative to the laborious method of a systematic survey.

Common morality, as the Hebrew-Christian tradition understands it, has to do with human actions both objectively, as deeds or things done, and subjectively, as the doings of agents. Objectively, they are either permissible or impermissible; subjectively, either culpable or inculpable. For the purposes of this and the subsequent chapter, however, it will suffice to consider them objectively.

Expressions referring to actions are sometimes ambiguous. Thus, phrases of the form "*A*'s action in *F*-ing" may refer either to an individual action or to a kind of action. Taken as an individual action, Brutus's action in murdering Caesar was a single, unrepeatable event; but it may also be taken as any one of several kinds of action, for example, as tyrannicide, or murder, or treachery. Taken as the action-kind, tyrannicide, Brutus's action is repeated every time anybody kills a tyrant. On most occasions, of course, the context of what is said makes plain whether an action referred to is an individual or a kind; when it does not, I shall resort to the cumbrous expressions "individual action" and "action-kind."

Individual actions are events, namely, events consisting in the doing of something by an agent. The ontological status of events is disputed—understanding by "ontology" that branch of philosophy in which an attempt is made to determine what fundamental kinds of entities must be acknowledged in order to account for the truth of true propositions, and what need not. If a sentence expressing a true proposition contains a referring expression, then the kind of entity for which that expression stands must be acknowledged by ontology, unless a paraphrase of that sentence can be given, expressing the same proposition, which contains neither referring expressions for that kind of entity nor expressions whose reference is obscure. A familiar example of this procedure is the demonstration that the odd entities apparently referred to by expressions of the form "the average X" (whether the average Englishman, the average Tibetan yak, or what you will) may be eliminated from ontology, by providing paraphrases in which the apparent referring expression, "the average X," is replaced by words with comparatively non-problematical reference, like the common nouns for which "X" is a place-holder.[6]

Unlike the existence of substances, the occurrence of events can be reported without using any expression apparently referring to an event. In order to report that wombats exist, I must employ an expression that apparently refers to wombats; but in order to report the occurrence of Brutus's murder of Caesar, I need only say "Brutus murdered Caesar," which contains expressions referring to Brutus, to Caesar, and, if predicables are referring expressions, to a dyadic relation referred to by the two-place predicable " ... murdered...."[7] P.T. Geach has argued that no expression that apparently refers to an event does so in fact, in the sense required by ontology: that for every true sentence in which such expressions occur, a paraphrase can be found "in which persons and things are mentioned but in which events do not even appear to be mentioned."[8]

Yet it is far from certain that paraphrases can be found, containing no expression whose reference is obscure, for sentences in which causal relations are ascribed to events; for example, "The catching of the ball by the fieldsman caused the bruising of his fingers." It is true that the proposition expressed by this sentence would be expressed more idiomatically by, "The fieldsman bruised his fingers because he caught the ball," which contains no expression that apparently refers to events. Unfortunately, it also contains a connective, "because," whose sense in such contexts has not to my knowledge been plausibly analysed except as signifying a causal relation between events.[9]

It is true that the concept of causation has not become much clearer than it was when Bertrand Russell proposed the extrusion of the word "cause" from the philosophical vocabulary, on the ground that it was too "bound up with misleading associations."[10] However, the standard view of a kind of causation I shall call "event-causation,"[11] namely, that in which one event, say E_1, causes another, say E_n, is that in such a case E_1 must be a member of a set of events, $E_1 \ldots E_m$, none of them redundant and all occurring at the same time, such that, under some set of descriptions, the occurrence of E_n is deducible from the occurrence of $E_1 \ldots E_m$, according to the laws of nature. That is, E_1 is one of a set of nonredundant conditions jointly sufficient for E_n.[12] As Davidson has pointed out, no causal proposition such as that E_1 caused E_n implies or presupposes any specific law of nature, or any proposition about the occurrence of any other specific event. Nor, in order to have good reason to believe that E_1 caused E_n, is it necessary to know what other events, together with E_1, are jointly sufficient for E_n, or under what descriptions or by what laws of nature the occurrence of E_n is deducible from the occurrence of E_1 and of its fellows.[13]   *Event causation*

This is but the beginning of an analysis of event-causation, which nobody, to my knowledge, has satisfactorily completed. Various studies strongly suggest that some reference to a context of inquiry is implicit in all assertions about event-causes. J. S. Mill pointed out that, in different contexts, different events in the set of conditions jointly sufficient for another event are selected as its cause;[14] and recent studies have made progress in classifying contexts of inquiry and matching different contexts with appropriate kinds of event-causes. Although all this falls far short of an analysis of event-causation, it is nevertheless enough to go on with.

I shall assume, accordingly, that actions are events of a certain kind, and that events are a special category of individuals. Like individual substances, they admit of different true definite descriptions, that is, different descriptions purporting to apply to one individual only. "The tyrannicide committed by Brutus," for example, is one true definite description of Brutus's murder of Caesar; "the murder Brutus committed as a result of conspiring with Cassius" is another.[15]   *Action Description*

Actions may be described either as actions or merely as events. The description "the funny thing that happened on the way to the Forum," may describe an action, but it does not describe it as an action. Descriptions of actions as actions, which I shall call "action-descriptions," necessarily describe them as doings or as deeds. And any such description—their characteristic form is that of the formula "the doing of X by A at t"—may be supplemented in either of two ways while remaining an action-description.

The first such way is by adding a description of the circumstances in which the deed described was done. Since a circumstance of something metaphorically "stands around" or surrounds it, a circumstance of a deed is conceived as obtaining at the same time as

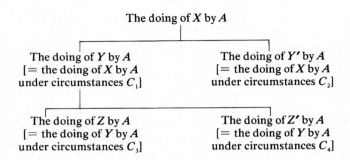

**Fig. 1   A descent tree for an
action-description**

the deed is done. However, circumstances include such things as the existence of evidence, the tendering of advice, and the presence of natural signs, all of which may refer to the past or to the future. A juryman may render a verdict of guilty despite the circumstance that the evidence of guilt is weak; an investor may buy certain shares in view of the circumstance that his broker predicts that they will appreciate; and a prospector may drill a well on instinct, disregarding the circumstance that geological signs are wanting that oil was formed where he drills. It is also convenient, and not theoretically objectionable, to classify as circumstances of an action any mental states of the agent that are neither explicitly nor implicitly described in the action-description itself. And so, when a thief steals in hope of a large gain or in fear of punishment, I shall treat that hope and that fear as circumstances in which he steals.

When an action-description of the form "the doing of X by A" is supplemented by a description of circumstances, as in "the doing of X by A under the circumstances C," the supplemented description will sometimes be a sufficient ground for a new action-description, in which the circumstances C are not mentioned. The supplemented description, "the surreptitious taking of M by A, under the circumstances that M did not belong to A, and M's owner had not given A leave to take it," is a sufficient ground for a new description of A's action, namely, "the theft of M by A."

The set of those action-descriptions of the same action, which are either sufficiently grounded upon other action-descriptions of it supplemented by descriptions of its circumstances, or are action-descriptions of it upon which, so supplemented, others are sufficiently grounded, may be arranged in trees of descent.[16] Figure 1 is the schema of such a tree.

The taking of a chalice (X) by A may be larceny (Y) and promise-breaking (Y'); it may also be burglary (Z) and sacrilege (Z'), given the circumstances: that the chalice did not belong to A and he had not been given leave to take it (C_1), that he had given a promise not to take the chalice (C_2), that he took it by night after breaking into the building where it was kept (C_3), and that the building where it was kept was a church (C_4).

Of two action-descriptions, D_1 and D_2, D_2 may be said to be "less primitive" than D_1, if D_1, supplemented by a description of circumstances, is a sufficient ground for it. In any tree of action-descriptions, the description from which the others descend is the most primitive or "basic" description in that tree. However, it does not follow, with respect to action-descriptions of the same action belonging to such trees, that there is one tree of descent to which they all belong, and therefore one description which, in terms of circumstances, is most primitive or basic.

A second way in which an action-description may be supplemented is by adding a description of the causal consequences of the action it describes. By a "causal consequence of an action" I mean an event that follows, according to laws of nature, from a set of nonredundant events, occurring at the same time, of which that action is a member and from which, in the relevant context of inquiry, that action is singled out as event-cause. As we shall see, not everything that is colloquially describable as a "consequence" of an action is a causal consequence in this sense.

Action-descriptions supplemented by descriptions of the causal consequences of the actions they describe may be sufficient grounds of new action-descriptions, in which those causal consequences are not mentioned. And sets of such action-descriptions, the members of which are either, when supplemented by descriptions of causal consequences of the actions they describe, sufficient grounds of others, or are sufficiently grounded by others so supplemented, may also be arranged in trees of descent. The following action-descriptions, for example, may be so arranged: (i) "Brutus's stabbing of Caesar," (ii) "Brutus's killing of Caesar," (iii) Brutus's enraging of Antony," and (iv) "Brutus's felling of Caesar." Of the descriptions in this series, (i), supplemented by "with the causal consequence that Caesar died," sufficiently grounds (ii), and supplemented by "with the causal consequence that rage arose in Antony" sufficiently grounds (iii); and then (ii), supplemented by, "with the causal consequence that Caesar's body collapsed," sufficiently grounds (iv). It may be remarked that each of the new action-descriptions in this sequence, namely (ii), (iii), and (iv), is analysable as a description of the form "*A*'s causing of *X*." Thus "Brutus's killing of Caesar" is analysable as "Brutus's causing of Caesar's death," and "Brutus's enraging of Antony" is analysable as "Brutus's causing of rage to arise in Antony."[17]

Since the expression "*A*'s causing of *X*" is inescapably an action-description, there appears to be no limitation upon the possibility of grounding new action-descriptions on descriptions of the causal consequences of actions. This is borne out by the parlance of common lawyers, according to which the causality of an agent's deed is sometimes said to "reach through" events subsequent to it to other and more remote events.[18] However, neither in law nor in common morality is it held that the causal "reach" of an action can extend to any and every subsequent event that would not have occurred had it not occurred.

In this connection, two cases in Hart and Honoré's *Causation in the Law* have become standard.

(i) A forest fire breaks out, and later investigation shows that shortly before the outbreak A had flung away a lighted cigarette into the bracken at the edge of the forest, the bracken caught fire, a light breeze got up, and fanned the flames in the direction of the forest.[19]

(ii) A throws a lighted cigarette into the bracken which catches fire. B, just as the flames are about to flicker out, deliberately pours petrol on them. The fire spreads and burns down the forest.[20]

In both these cases, the event describable as "the throwing by A of a lighted cigarette into the bracken," is one of a set of conditions jointly sufficient for the fire, and it is not redundant: if it had not occurred, the other conditions specified would not have been sufficient. Yet only in case (i) can A's action in throwing the cigarette be correctly described as the causing of the fire. Let us see why.

An action, as conceived by common law, is a deed done in a particular situation or set of circumstances; and that situation consists partly of matters external to the agent, such as the weather and the nature of the landscape, and partly of his own bodily and mental states, such as that he is standing by bracken at the edge of a forest. Should he be deprived of all power of action, the situation, including his bodily and mental states, would change according to the laws of nature. His deeds as an agent are either interventions in that natural process or abstentions from intervention. When he intervenes, he can be described as causing whatever would not have occurred had he abstained; and when he abstains, as allowing to happen whatever would not have happened had he intervened. Hence, from the point of view of action, the situation is conceived as passive, and the agent, *qua* agent, as external to it. He is like a deus ex machina, whose interventions make a difference to what otherwise would naturally come about without them.

On this conception of action, an agent's state of mind with respect to his deed makes not the slightest difference to how that deed may correctly be described. Whether he is aware or unaware of what its consequences are, whether he would or would not have done it had he been aware of them, whether he is pleased or displeased with them, have no bearing on whether or not those consequences would have followed in the course of nature had he not done what he did. And so, on this conception, it does not matter, in case (i), whether or not he believed, intended, or hoped that a breeze would get up, and fan the flames kindled by his cigarette, or that a forest fire would follow: what determines whether his throwing away his cigarette was the causing of the fire is simply whether, his situation being what it was, the outbreak of fire followed from his deed in the course of nature.

Hart and Honoré observed that in common law, as in prescientific common sense, a further distinction is drawn, according as the consequence does or does not follow in the *normal* course of nature. Abnormal occurrences within the course of nature are either intrusions into causal systems that are usually closed, as when a meteor strikes the earth's surface, or coincidences. Although both intrusions, in this sense, and coincidences occur in the course of nature, it is usual in common law to regard some of them as "extraneous" or "intervening" factors which "break" the chain of causation from action to consequence. Hart and Honoré cite a dictum of Lord McDermott, that if a workman injured in the course of his employment gets burned because the hospital he has entered catches fire, or if he is maimed because the ambulance taking him from the hospital to a convalescent home is involved in a street accident, his being burned or maimed would not be a result of the original injury.[21]

One source of the tendency to treat abnormal events as breaking the chain of causation is that it is easy to conceive them as interventions. This is explicit in the description of certain extraordinary abnormalities as "acts of God." Yet if, as is now commonly believed, abnormal events are as much a part of the course of nature as normal ones, there can be no ontological ground for distinguishing them, as links in causal chains, from normal ones.

Further light is thrown by considering case (ii), in which the causal chain linking A's throwing away of his cigarette to the outbreak of the forest fire does not contain any abnormal events but does contain a second action, B's pouring of petrol on the dying flames in the bracken. Now it is a general principle of the traditional legal doctrine of tort, that

> the free, deliberate and informed act or omission of a human being, intended to produce the consequence that is produced, negatives causal connexion.[22]

Such an action is held to be a *novus actus interveniens* through which the causal influence of a previous action cannot reach.

There is an obvious philosophical objection to this. Are not human beings themselves parts of nature, and are not their actions natural events? If they are, then if an action affects other human beings, and elicits responses from them, those effects and those responses also occur in the course of nature. Hence, according to what was said in connection with abnormal events, there can be no ontological ground for distinguishing a *novus actus interveniens*, considered as a link in a causal chain, from any other natural event.

This objection might be met in either of two ways. The first would be to concede that human actions are natural events, occurring in the course of nature, and to distinguish certain causal sequences from others on moral grounds, even though causally—or ontologically—they do not differ at all. In many moral traditions, nobody but a deed's agent or agents may be held responsible either for it or for the consequences that flow from it. And consequences that would not have occurred but for an *actus interveniens* flow from it, rather than from any action prior to it. Therefore the doer of a prior action may not be held morally responsible for those consequences. In the moral traditions in question, it is natural to describe a *novus actus interveniens* as, morally speaking, cutting short the consequences of prior actions, even though, ontologically speaking, it does not.

On this way of looking at the matter, in a sequence of causal consequences of an action, any kind of event whatever that cuts off moral responsibility for whatever comes after it, may be said, morally speaking, to cut short the chain of causal consequences before it. Hence if abnormal events are held to cut off moral responsibility, they too may be held, morally speaking, to cut short the causal consequences that flow from a preceding action.

The second way of meeting the objection that a *novus actus interveniens*, being a natural event, cannot, as a link in a causal chain, differ from any other natural event, would be to distinguish the causation of human actions from that of other natural events. Not only uninstructed common opinion, but a venerable philosophical tradition, holds that human actions are not mere links in chains of event-causation. According to the position in question, human actions are not, strictly speaking, caused by other events at all, although they may be reactions or responses to them. Rather, they are caused by agents. Aristotle drew the distinction between event-causation and what may be called "agent-causation"[23] by an example: "The stick moves the stone and is moved by the hand, which again is moved by the man; in the man, however, we have reached a mover that is not so in virtue of being moved by something else."[24] Whereas the three events—the movement of the hand, the movement of the stick, and the movement of the stone—form a chain of event-causes and effects, the cause of the movement of the hand is not another event but a substance—a man. Although the relation of a man to his own actions is an ancient paradigm of causation (it underlies the scholastic conception of the divine creator as first cause), many philosophers nowadays profess to find it unintelligible. The only possible reply is that, in any respect in which agent-causation is unintelligible, event-causation is unintelligible too: it will be time to attempt to elucidate the nature of the power by which an agent acts when the nature of the necessity by which one event gives rise to another has been analysed.[25]

If the theory be accepted that actions are caused by agents, and not by other events, a limitation on the causal reach of actions follows at once. Suppose that an event C, which would not have occurred unless an action A_1 had occurred, is traced back to A_1 through another action A_2. A_1 cannot have been a member of a set of conditions jointly sufficient for A_2; for, *ex hypothesi*, A_2 is not caused by other events. But, in that case, A_1 cannot have been a member of a set of conditions jointly sufficient for C; for C would not have occurred unless A_2 had occurred. Accordingly, any secondary action through which a putative causal consequence is traced back to a primary action alleged to be its cause, must be held to break the putative causal chain. If, an action A_1 having been performed, the event C subsequently comes about in the course of nature, then C must come about without the help of any further action.

The difference between these two ways of upholding the doctrine that a *novus actus interveniens* cuts short the consequences of an action goes down to the foundations of legal and moral theory. Those who prefer the first way take principles of legal or moral responsibility as ultimate and use them to distinguish the causal consequences of actions, legally and morally speaking, from their causal consequences, ontologically speaking. Neither in law nor in morality, they hold, do judgements of responsibility for the alleged consequences of actions turn on whether those allegations can be independently established. On the contrary, verdicts of responsibility should be reached on appropriate legal or moral grounds, and whatever agents are held responsible for should, by virtue of that, be classified as consequences of their actions. Although this approach has captivated legal theorists, inspiring them with the hope of avoiding the quagmire of the theory of causation, it has not found much favor in the courts. "[A]n impartial consideration of the way in which courts have decided [the relevant cases]," according to Hart and Honoré, "does not confirm the modern view that in using the language of causation they have merely given effect to their conceptions of justice, expediency, or chosen policy."[26] On this point, moral theory sides with the practice of common law. Primarily, an agent can be held morally responsible only for his actions. Derivatively, he may be held responsible for an occurrence that is not one of his actions if certain of his actions constituted the causing of that occurrence. But to judge him responsible for an occurrence he did not cause, and to give that judgement a semblance of justice by couching it in the language of causation, would be corrupt—and not only linguistically.

The Hebrew-Christian tradition, as I understand it, conceives human actions as interventions by human agents in the ordinary course of nature, thereby presupposing a distinction between event-causation and agent-causation. In my opinion, both this conception of action and the presupposition about causation on which it rests are philosophically defensible, independently of moral theory. But to defend them would require a complete independent inquiry into the nature of human action: an undertaking almost as large as that of working out a theory of morality. And so, in action theory as in metaphysics, it is possible to do no more than state what the Hebrew-Christian tradition presupposes. The justification of its presuppositions must be reserved for separate investigations.

Although it is clear enough in principle, the doctrine that a *novus actus interveniens* cuts short a chain of causal consequences must be explored a little further before it can be safely applied.

Consider the following case. A poisoner orders that a chocolate cake be made. While it is being made, he distracts his cook's attention and adds powdered arsenic to the sugar the cook is about to use. He then engages a parcel service to box and deliver the cake to his victim: whereupon one person takes the order, another collects the cake, another boxes it, and yet another delivers it. After it has been delivered, the victim's servant, believing his master to have ordered it, serves it at supper. Pleased, the victim cuts a slice, eats it, and dies of arsenic poisoning. Obviously it would be absurd for the poisoner to disclaim causing his victim's death by poison; and yet there can be no doubt that his own action in adding arsenic to his cook's sugar only led to his victim's death by way of a long series of intervening actions: by his cook, by the various employees of the parcel service, by his victim's servant, and finally, by his victim himself. How, then, consistently with the doctrine that a *novus actus interveniens* cuts short the chain of causal consequences flowing from an action, can the poisoner be said to have caused his victim's death at all?

The solution is that, although the adding of powdered arsenic to the cook's sugar cannot by itself be described as the causing of the victim's death, it was not the poisoner's only action. A man may act either in his own person, or by his agents, or partly in his own person and partly by his agents. And his agents may be voluntary and witting, or unwitting. When one man acts as the agent of another, witting or unwitting, he does not cease to be the agent or doer of what he does; but because he acts as the agent of the other, that other is also held to be an agent in his action, and the principal agent. What is done by a secondary agent for a principal is imputed to that principal as his own deed. A man becomes the voluntary and witting agent of another, either by agreeing to do something at his request or at the request of his accredited representative, or by acting as a functionary in an institution whose services the other engages. In our example, the poisoner's cook was his voluntary agent in the first of these ways, and the various employees of the parcel service were his voluntary agents in the second. On the other hand, a man acts as the unwitting agent of another when that other takes advantage of someting he does by anticipating that he may do it and surreptitiously intervening in such a way that his doing it will subserve some purpose of the other's.[27] In our example, the victim's butler and the victim himself were taken advantage of in this way, so that they acted as unwitting agents of the poisoner, subserving his purpose.

On this analysis, the action which caused the victim's death was a complex one, composed of a number of constituent actions, only one of which the poisoner did in his own person, and the remainder of which were done by his witting or unwitting agents. In the sequence of events between that complex action and the victim's death, there was no intervening action. Hence the poisoner did indeed cause his victim's death, but not solely by what he did in his own person.

When a man entices, induces, or persuades others to do something, and they do it, common law rightly imputes agency to him as well. But it is a mistake, and an unnecessary although not uncommon one, to explain this causally, by regarding the enticing, inducing, or persuading as an action whose causality reaches through whatever is done under that enticement, inducement, or persuasion, to its consequences. Actions done under enticement, inducement, or persuasion remain actions: that their agents were enticed, induced, or persuaded may reduce their responsibility, but it cannot annul their agency.

A similar mistake is found in some legal treatments of acts of omission or commission by which wrongdoers are given an opportunity which it is the agent's duty to deny them. A man whose duty it is to guard a certain entrance to a bank, but who, by leaving his post, gives robbers an opportunity to enter, is sometimes said to cause the loss of whatever the robbers take. This seems to me to be as absurd as to say that he causes the robbers to rob. What is correct is that he culpably *allowed* the robbers to rob and so made possible the loss of whatever they took. And for that, he may well be held responsible. But to describe the causality of the guard's dereliction as reaching, through the robbers' intervening action, to the loss to the bank that was its consequence, would corrupt a judgement of causality by groundlessly accommodating it to a judgement of moral responsibility.

Joel Feinberg has strenuously contested the doctrine that a *novus actus interveniens* cuts short the chain of a prior action's causal consequences. His method is to present a number of cases, in each of which, although the consequences of a prior action are traced through the intervening action of a second agent, he contends that the second agent can be likened to a pistol loaded and cocked, whose action is triggered by the original agent.[28] Here is one of them.

> Jones, a depositor in . . . [a] bank, was standing in line before the depositor's window when a bank robber entered, drew his gun, and warned "If anyone moves I'll shoot." The teller immediately grabbed something and dived to the floor. The bandit shot at him, and the ricocheting bullet struck Jones, still waiting in line, causing him severe injury.[29]

Feinberg comments that "The bank robber was all wound up to shoot, so to speak, at the slightest provocation; and the teller, perhaps inadvertently but effectively, provided that slight stimulus."[30]

Since Feinberg's discussion of this example appears to presuppose that actions have event-causes, his rejection of Hart and Honoré's doctrine that voluntary intervention negatives causal connection is not unexpected. However, he agrees with Hart and Honoré that not every causal consequence countenanced by his causal theory can ground new action-descriptions. Hence he proposes a variation of their restrictive doctrine: namely, that the less expectable an intervening action is, the more likely it is to negative causal connection.[31] How, on his own causal theory, low expectability could annul a causal link, he does not explain. Jonathan Bennett, however, seems to have captured his idea, without doing violence to the theory of causation, by simply restricting the incorporation of descriptions of causal consequences into action-descriptions. A consequence of a bodily movement made by an agent is more likely, he declares, to be "covered by the description of what [that agent] did," (i) the more confident the agent was that that consequence would ensue, (ii) the more "certain or inevitable it was" that that consequence would ensue, and (iii) the higher the degree of immediacy there was between that movement and its consequence.[32]

Although there is something persuasive in Feinberg's and Bennett's position, it has an implication which is hard to swallow. Suppose that one of Nero's praetorian guards, acting on orders, were to offer a Christian the choice of professing belief in the divinity of Augustus or having his throat cut. The unfortunate Christian would have reason to be completely confident that, were he to refuse the profession demanded, his death would follow. Furthermore, his death would, barring a miracle, ensue upon his refusal inevitably and immediately. By Feinberg's and Bennett's criteria, it would therefore follow that, by his refusal, the Christian would not only cause his own death but would also cause a confessor to be murdered: that is, he would be both a suicide and a persecutor.[33]

Such intolerable conclusions may be avoided, while allowing for what is persuasive in Feinberg's and Bennett's position, by distinguishing causing or allowing a wrong action by another from doing what will foreseeably be met with a wrong reaction.

A human being causes an event, as we have seen, either by directly making it happen or by directly making something else happen, which, as an intervention in the course of nature, is among a set of nonredundant conditions jointly sufficient for the event's occurrence. He allows an event to happen when he abstains from intervening in some way open to him, while being aware that, apart from interventions by others, the event both will happen if he does not intervene in that way and will not happen if he does.

As has been observed in connection with Feinberg's example of the undutiful bank guard, a man may be morally responsible for what he allows to happen, as well as for what he causes. But it does not follow that the distinction between causing something to happen and allowing it to happen makes no moral difference. In some cases, traditional morality forbids both causing X to happen and letting it happen; in others, it forbids causing X to happen, but permits letting it happen. Thus it is wrong both to cause harm to an innocent person and to let harm be done to him by others. On the other hand, it may be permissible to let something happen which it would be wrong to cause, if the only way of preventing it is forbidden. Thus, it would be wrong for a physician to prolong his patient's suffering; but it is permissible to let it be prolonged, if the only way in which he can promptly relieve it is by promptly bringing a certain medication, which he can do only if he drives dangerously, a forbidden action.

There is, however, a distinction between causing or allowing something to happen and acting when you foresee that something will happen only if you so act.[34] What an agent causes or allows to happen follows in the course of nature from his intervention or abstention. But what he can foresee is not confined to what follows in the course of nature. A man can often foresee (not infallibly) how others will react to what he does. And his foresight does not affect the causal status of their reactions. What they do, even though he foresees it, is neither caused nor allowed to happen by him.

It is true that, according to traditional morality, doing what will foreseeably be met with a wrong reaction is sometimes wrong. If, in pursuing his legitimate ends, a man finds that several effective courses of action are open to him, each legitimate in itself, but one of which will foreseeably be met with a wrongful reaction by somebody else, then it would be wrong for him to choose that course. And much of what Feinberg and Bennett say holds of such choices. They are more culpable the more confident the agent is that the course chosen will be met with a wrongful reaction; and if the agent fails to foresee what is foreseeable, he is the more culpable the more obviously it is foreseeable and the more immediate is the connection between action and reaction.

Yet the distinction between causing or allowing something to happen, and doing what will foreseeably be met with a wrongful reaction is morally important. In traditional morality it is unconditionally forbidden (omitting certain minor and contested exceptions) to cause the death of a materially innocent person; and it is likewise unconditionally forbidden to commit such a crime as treason, even though refusal to commit it will, according to a credible threat, foreseeably be followed by the murder of an innocent hostage. In terms of the distinctions we have drawn, that an event is foreseen or foreseeable as resulting from a reaction to a certain action is one of the *circumstances* of that action; and that an action is done under such a circumstance does not make the occurrence of what was foreseen or foreseeable its causal consequence.

Colloquially, the word "consequence" is sometimes used as a synonym for "causal consequence"; but it is also used in a far wider sense, now common in academic philosophy, according to which the distinction between a causal consequence and a foreseeable outcome is obliterated. One event is the consequence of another, in this wider sense, if it happens after it but would not have happened had certain alternatives to that other event happened. More technically: an event E_2 is a consequence of an event E_1, if and only if E_2 happens after E_1, and an alternative event E_3 is possible, such that if E_3 were to have happened instead of E_1, then E_2 would not have happened. The conception of E_3 as a possible alternative to an actual event E_1 may be informally elucidated for noncomplex events as follows: let D_a be a true state description of the universe during the interval from t_1 to t_{1+n}, the period of the occurrence of E_1; then E_3 is an alternative to E_1 just in case D_p is compatible with the laws of nature, D_p being a state description of the universe during an interval of the same duration as that from t_1 to t_{1+n}, which is identical with D_a in all respects except that according to it E_3 occurs and E_1 does not.

Specimens of this wider use of "consequence" are found both in the consequentialist affirmation, "The rightness or wrongness of an action is determined solely by whether or not its consequences are better than those of any of its alternatives," and in the anti-consequentalist one, "The principles of morality are to be observed whatever the consequences."

It has been objected that, according to the theory of action outlined earlier in this section, sentences such as those expressing these affirmations are unintelligible, because nothing is, in itself, either a consequence of an action or not: depending on which is chosen from the many true descriptions of an action, the same event may be either a consequence of it or a part of it.

This is a complete misunderstanding. That an action can be truly described by reference to its consequences in the wider sense, as by reference to its causal consequences and circumstances, in no way entails that its consequences are part of it. However, it is legitimate to distinguish the consequences of an action per se from its consequences relative to some description. The consequences of an action per se are those events which would not have happened had the agent taken certain alternatives to it open to him, and which are not directly referred to in any basic or minimal description of it. The consequences of an action relative to a certain description are that subset of its consequences per se which are also consequences of events to which direct reference is made in that description. Thus, the moving of Brutus's dagger through the air was a consequence of the action described as "Brutus's assassination of Caesar" per se but not relative to that description, as his subsequent death at Philippi probably was.[35]

2.3   First-Order and Second-Order Moral Questions

Common morality is first of all a system of laws or precepts about human actions considered objectively, as deeds. The most familiar form in which its laws are expressed is prohibitory: that actions of certain kinds are unconditionally contrary to reason, and hence cannot be performed by a human being inasmuch as he is rational. That actions of certain kinds are unconditionally contrary to reason of course implies that reason is practical as well as theoretical. *How* reason can be practical is a topic that will be investigated in the final chapter, on the foundation of common morality. For the present, it is enough that common morality presupposes that it *is*.

The most elementary acts of practical reason are not propositional but prescriptive, and are expressible by sentences of the form "Actions of kind K may (may not) be done." By contrast, the most elementary deliverances of common morality about human actions, considered objectively, are strictly speaking about prescriptions about them. Thus a moral law or precept of the form "Actions of kind K are (are not) contrary to reason," may be analysed as "Practical reason itself—that is, anybody's practical reason, provided that no error is made—prescribes that actions of kind K may not (may) be done." That an action is contrary to reason, or not, is therefore a fact about it, by way of being about what practical reason prescribes with regard to it.

The elementary deliverances of common morality are therefore true or false according to the realist, or correspondence, theory of truth. They are true if and only if practical reason, functioning without error, would make certain prescriptions. Thus elementary moral prohibitions of the form "Actions of kind K are unconditionally contrary to reason" are true just in case practical reason, functioning without error, would prescribe that actions of kind K unconditionally may not be done: or, in a more recent idiom, just in case anybody in any possible world, who thinks about the matter to a practical conclusion and makes no error, prescribes that actions of kind K unconditionally may not be done.

Any proposition of the form "Actions of kind K are unconditionally contrary to reason," may be more conveniently expressed as "No action of kind K is (morally) permissible." Here the word "permissible" is used figuratively. Agents are figuratively thought of as permitting themselves to do what they do, and as refusing themselves permission to do what they abstain from doing. Then, by a simple extension, actions which are contrary to reason are thought of as those which, as rational creatures, agents are not able to permit themselves to do. Thus an action is morally impermissible— an agent, as rational, is figuratively not able to permit himself to do it—if it is contrary to reason; and it is morally permissible if it is not.

In what follows, I shall call a "precept" any universal proposition of common morality with respect to the permissiblity of any kind of human action considered objectively. In using the word "precept" in this way, I follow earlier moralists. Since the word is not now in frequent use, it is suitable for revival as a technical term; and it has fewer misleading associations than the word "rule." I shall also follow earlier moralists in referring to some of the more general and frequently cited precepts as "principles."

Every precept of common morality can be expressed in one or another of the following three forms:

(1) It is always (morally) permissible to do an action of the kind *K*, as such.
(2) It is never (morally) permissible to do an action of the kind *K*.
(3) It is never (morally) permissible not to do an action of the kind *K*, if an occasion occurs on which one can be done.

Precepts of the first kind state what morally may be done: what is morally legitimate or licit. Those of the second kind (the most familiar) are prohibitions. They state what ought not to be done: what is morally wrong or illicit. Those of the third are positive injunctions or statements of duty. They state what ought to be done: what is morally right or obligatory. Formulating all three in terms of a single concept confers obvious advantages in logical economy. And there is a gain in clarity. For example, the expression "right," which is commonly used to signify a positive injunction, is also used merely to indicate that something is licit. "You were quite right" may mean, "You did what it was not permissible not to do," and usually does; but it may also mean, "You did what it was permissible to do."

A moral system which confines itself to laying down what kinds of action, considered objectively, are permissible or not is considered in the Hebrew-Christian tradition to be incomplete. For both Judaism and Christianity, as religions, pay far more attention to the spirit in which a man acts than to whether objectively considered he does as he ought. A man who acts in a wrong spirit is held to blame, even though, objectively considered, he does everything he ought: and one who acts in the right spirit is not held to blame, even though he does what objectively he ought not. The act of blaming, like that of prescribing that something may or may not be done, is nonpropositional. I shall speak of it as "judicative." And, as with acts of prescribing, common morality makes higher-level assertions about whether or not judicative acts of blaming or abstaining from blaming are required by practical reason. Such assertions are expressible by sentences of the form "Practical reason, functioning without error, would (would not) blame anybody who did an action of kind K in a state of mind of the kind M." Sentences of that form are conveniently abbreviated to, "Doing an action of kind K in a state of mind of kind M is (is not) culpable."

Universal propositions to the effect that acting in a state of mind of a certain kind is or is not culpable are also precepts. For they are equivalent to universal propositions about the permissibility or impermissibility of certain kinds of human action, namely, certain kinds of judicative act. It may be observed that judicative acts themselves are not only, objectively considered, permissible or impermissible, but are also, subjectively considered, culpable or inculpable. Thus a man's absolving himself of blame for some wrong action may be a judicative act which, objectively considered, it is impermissible not to perform; and yet, subjectively considered, he may be culpable for performing it, because he does so without honestly considering the facts.

Precepts about the culpability or inculpability of agents in doing what they do would make no sense whatever unless their actions were in themselves, objectively considered, permissible or impermissible. Hence I shall refer to questions about the permissibility or impermissibility of actions as "first-order" moral questions, and to questions about the culpability or inculpability of agents in acting as "second-order" moral questions.

The distinction between first-order and second-order moral questions is related to a distinction drawn in Christian moral theology between actions considered materially and actions considered formally. Considered materially, an action is a deed, and no reference is made to the doer's state of mind in doing it. Thus an action is material stealing, or materially considered is stealing, if it is the forcible or surreptitious taking of what belongs to somebody else. Considered formally, an action is what its doer wills to do in doing it. Hence an action which materially is stealing may not be so formally, because the stealer may honestly believe that what he is taking is his own property.

In drawing this distinction, "material" and "formal" are used in Aristotelian senses. According to Aristotle, the final cause of a thing determines its form; and the final cause of an action is what the doer wills and intends in doing it. The material action, about the nature of which the doer may be mistaken, is that by which, successfully or unsuccessfully, he tries to do his will.[36]

In the Hebrew-Christian tradition, as I understand it, all questions of common morality are either first-order ones about the permissibility or impermissibility of actions or intentions, or second-order ones about the culpability or inculpability of agents. Of course, the tradition sanctions evaluative questions about actions which are not reducible to these. But we must remember that it does not reduce all questions about the evaluation of actions to moral ones.

Yet some philosophers have questioned whether a morality confined to questions of these two kinds is not impoverished. R. M. Chisholm, for example, has inquired whether an adequate morality would not find room for questions of at least two more kinds.[37]

Questions of the first of the two additional kinds are about whether actions of certain kinds are or are not supererogatory: over and above the call of duty. Here a distinction must be drawn. As traditionally conceived, a supererogatory action is one which promotes an end which it is morally obligatory to promote but in a way which is not obligatory because it demands too much of the agent. Traditional morality, of course, acknowledges that there are such actions, and its conceptual resources are adequate to describing them. There are also actions which are extraordinary, in that the agent meets extraordinary demands, but in which the end, while recognized as a good either by individuals or by societies, is one it is permissible but not obligatory to pursue. Such ends are: business success, scholarly achievement, athletic prowess. Extraordinary actions in pursuit of such ends are quite properly praised, especially by those who think the ends pursued to be worth pursuing; but only confusion could result from treating questions about praiseworthiness of this kind as moral.

Questions of the second of Chisholm's two additional kinds are about whether actions of certain kinds are not demeritorious or objectionable, even though they are not impermissible. (Chisholm's term for them is "offensive.") However, it is not clear that there are actions which are morally offensive but permissible. Thus offences such as self-righteousness, sloth, and want of consideration are morally impermissible; and, provided that there is no want of consideration, ill-breeding, affectation, and coarseness, while demeritorious, do not seem to be morally offensive. Here again, confusion would result from treating questions about offensiveness of the latter kind as moral.

2.4   The Fundamental Principle

Both Jewish and Christian thinkers have always held that the numerous specific precepts of morality are all derivable from a few substantive general principles, even though the conception of those precepts as binding upon rational creatures as such is compatible with the new intuitionist doctrine that the fundamental principles from which they derive are many. No Jewish or Christian moralist would dispute that the part of morality having to do with duties to God, which lies outside the scope of this investigation, derives from the principle in the Mosaic Shema: that God is one, and is to be loved with one's whole mind and heart (Deut. 6:5). And most of them have held that the part having to do with rational creatures, in their relations with themselves and with one another, also derives from a single first principle. Here, however, tradition has diverged, and two different principles have each won some recognition as fundamental. Some traditional moralists have maintained that the two, despite their obvious differences, coincide at a deeper level. Of these, the most distinguished was Kant, whose first and second formulas of the fundamental principle of morality philosophically restate the two apparently different traditional principles, and who declared that those formulas "are at bottom merely . . . formulations of the very same law."[38]

The more familiar of the two traditional candidates for recognition as the fundamental principle of morality, with respect to the relations of rational creatures to themselves and to one another, is also the more recent. In Judaism, its authority is talmudic. According to the Babylonian Talmud, a gentile once demanded of Hillel that he be taught the whole Law while he stood on one foot. "Do not do to your fellow what you hate to have done to you," Hillel told him. "This is the whole Law entire; the rest is explanation."[39] A similar saying of Jesus is preserved by Matthew: "All things whatsoever ye would that men should do to you, do ye even so to them."[40] Although one of these formulations is negative and the other positive, they are in fact equivalent; for to forbid an action of a certain kind, and to command one of its contradictory kind, are equivalent. The precept formulated in these two ways has become known as "The Golden Rule."

Two objections are commonly made to receiving the Golden Rule as the fundamental principle of morality. First, it excludes the possibility that it may be right to do anything to another which you would hate to have done to you. Yet, as Kant pointed out, the Hebrew-Christian code calls upon parents, teachers, and judges to do many things to others, for their good or for the common good, which most plain men would hate to have done to them. How many judges would not hate to be sentenced, if they were guilty?[41] Second, the Golden Rule *prima facie* fails to condemn any action which affects the agent alone (as suicide may), or any action between consenting persons, to which there is no other party.[42] Yet common morality as traditionally conceived certainly recognizes the existence of duties to oneself, and hence must forbid actions contributing to violations of those duties when done at the behest of somebody else.

Such objections can be forestalled by appropriate interpretations. For example, with respect to Hillel's formulation, a moralist might distinguish natural hating from unnatural; then, having laid it down that, in the Rule, hating is to be interpreted as natural hating, urge that it is unnatural either to hate getting one's just deserts or not to hate such wrongs to oneself as suicide. By such an interpretation, certain substantive principles of duty are in effect absorbed into the Rule. Other substantive principles can be introduced into it by other interpretations.

That the common objections to it can be forestalled by such interpretations, which are neither dishonest nor arbitrary, points to a characteristic of the Golden Rule which not only exposes its inadequacy as a first principle but also explains its ubiquity. For it is ubiquitous. The earliest known version of it, one very like Hillel's, is credited to Confucius; and others appear in all the major religions. It is a proverb in many languages. Nor does the evidence suggest that it was diffused from a single source.[43] The explanation is simple. What a man would or would not have another do to him is in part a function of the mores he has made his own. Hence in cultures whose mores differ radically, what the Golden Rule is taken to require or forbid will differ radically too. And so any system of conduct that can be put forward as rational can include it.

The variability of what, in different cultures, the Golden Rule is taken to require or forbid shows that it is accepted because of its form. It expresses the universality of the precepts of whatever system incorporates it. Its force is therefore, as Sidgwick pointed out, that of a principle of impartiality: in no system that incorporates it can it be permissible for A to treat B in a manner in which it would be impermissible for B to treat A, "merely on the ground that they are two different individuals, and without there being any difference between the natures or the circumstances of the two which can be stated as a reasonable ground for difference of treatment."[44] In its original form, Kant's first formula, "Act only according to that maxim by which you can at the same time will that it should become a universal law,"[45] has the same force. It is a rubric for an act of self-examination by which anybody may verify whether his judgement of how he may treat another has a place in the system of conduct he accepts, or whether it is an exception made in his own interest. But, obviously, no principle of impartiality that is common to different systems of mores can serve as the substantive first principle that distinguishes any one of them from the others.

Although the Golden Rule has always enjoyed popular esteem and has recently been recognized as an adequate substantive principle by so eminent a moralist as R. M. Hare,[46] most traditional moral theologians and philosophers have attached more weight to the second of the two traditional candidates for recognition as the first principle of morality. It is presented in a well-known passage that precedes the parable of the Good Samaritan in Luke's gospel.

> And behold, a certain lawyer stood up, and tempted [Jesus], saying, Master, what shall I do to inherit eternal life? He said unto him, What is written in the Law? how readest thou? And he answering said, Thou shalt love the Lord thy God with all thy heart, and with all thy soul, and with all thy strength, and with all thy mind; and thy neighbor as thyself. And he said unto him, Thou hast answered right; this do, and thou shalt live (10:25–28).

With the approval of Jesus, the "lawyer" (that is, student of Torah) here offers, as the fundamental principle governing the relations of human beings to themselves and to one another, an injunction from Leviticus, 19:18, *Love your neighbor as yourself.*

Although Jesus went on to interpret "neighbor" as standing for any human being whatever, in the passage from Leviticus the term strictly refers only to one's countrymen, so that a Jew's neighbors in a Jewish state would be his fellow Jews. However, rabbinical teaching as codified in Maimonides' *Mishneh Torah* joined the

passage in Leviticus to another in Deuteronomy, the two together
being equivalent to the principle in Leviticus as Jesus interpreted it:

> 206. To love all human beings, who are of the covenant, as it is
> said, 'Thou shalt love thy neighbor as thyself' (*Lev.* 19:18).
> 207. To love the stranger, as it is said, 'Ye shall love the stranger'
> (*Deut.* 10:19).[47]

In his most revealing philosophical remarks about common
morality, which are to be found in the treatise *de lege veteri* in his
Summa Theologiae, Aquinas recognized the two precepts in the
passage quoted from Luke as the first common principles of that
morality (*prima et communia praecepta legis naturae*).[48] To these
two precepts, all the precepts of the Mosaic decalogue, in which the
whole of common morality is in some sense contained, are related as
conclusions to common principles (*sicut conclusiones ad principia
communia*).[49] The first common principles are self-evident (*per se
nota*) to human reason, and the precepts of the decalogue can be
known from them straight off with a little thought (*statim . . .
modica consideratione*). As for the more specific precepts of
morality, although they can be inferred from the precepts of the
decalogue by diligent inquiry (*per diligentem inquisitionem*), only
the wise are capable of carrying out such inquiries. Ordinary folk
will therefore receive the more specific precepts by instruction
(*mediante disciplina sapientium*).

In the system of morality thus sketched, confining attention to the
part of it that is independent of any theological presupposition,
there is a single fundamental principle, held by Aquinas to be *per se
notum*, that human beings are to love one another as they love
themselves. From this primary and common principle (which
Aquinas also referred to as a *principium communissimum*)[50] all the
precepts of the Mosaic decalogue that do not rest on a theistic
premise, that is, all but the first four, can be derived with a little
thought. And from the precepts of the decalogue, in turn, skilled
moralists can derive the more specific precepts needed for resolving
problems of casuistry.

A problem, however, remains. In his preliminary discussion of
natural law in the treatise *de lege* (*Summa Theologiae*, I-II, 90–97,
esp. 94, 2) Aquinas did not even mention what in *de lege veteri* he
went on to recognize as its first and common precepts. Instead he
described the natural law as deriving from a "first precept" which
he also called "the first principle in practical reason (*primum*

principium in ratione practica): namely, that "good is to be done and pursued, and evil shunned" (*bonum est faciendum et prosequendum, et malum vitandum*).[51] What was the relation, in Aquinas's mind, between this first principle and the nontheistic *principium communissimum* that one is to love one's fellow human beings as oneself?

Germain Grisez has offered the only answer known to me that is consistent with what Aquinas wrote about both principles. The principle that good is to be done and sought, and evil avoided, is not primarily moral. It defines the fundamental condition that any movement or abstention from movement must satisfy if it is to be accounted an action at all. For no bodily movement can intelligibly be called an action unless it is presented as seeking or attempting some good, or shunning some evil. Even actions contrary to practical reason require "at least a remote basis" in it.[52] Wrong actions, so far as they are actions at all, are done in pursuit of something that seems good to the agent. However, any human being who thinks clearly must recognize that there are certain goods fundamental to human flourishing—to a full human life as a rational being: they include life itself, communicable knowledge, and friendship. With regard to human beings, whether oneself or another, the principle that good is to be pursued and evil shunned first of all forbids any action whatever directed against those fundamental goods; secondarily, it commands every human being, as far as he reasonably can, to promote human good generally, both directly (by actions good in themselves, such as acquiring knowledge) and indirectly (by producing the means for human flourishing, such as growing food). But the disposition to act and abstain from action in accordance with these commands and prohibitions is what loving yourself and others consists in. Hence the primary and common principle of the natural law may also be formulated as: *Act so that the fundamental human goods, whether in your own person or in that of another, are promoted as may be possible, and under no circumstances violated.* It is a principle of what Kant thought of as respect (*Achtung*), but of respect for certain fundamental goods. And, so interpreted, it plainly follows immediately from the first principle of practical reason.

Aquinas implicitly distinguished the love (*dilectio, amor*) of our own and others' humanity demanded by natural reason from the theological virtue he called *caritas* ("charity"; in Greek, *agape*). For he declared that all natural virtues—all dispositions to act as the natural law requires—"are in us by nature as an undeveloped aptitude, and not as fully perfected" (*secundum aptitudinem et inchoationem, non ... secundum perfectionem*), whereas the theological virtues, the greatest of which is charity, are infused by divine grace, "wholly from the outside."[53] Aquinas's doctrine of charity, which is fundamental to his moral theology, falls outside the scope of this inquiry. Roughly, he maintained that the virtues which are exhibited in actions done according to common morality, and are directed to natural human goods, must be "perfected" by directing them to man's ultimate supernatural end as divinely revealed, for which the infused theological virtue of charity in needed.[54] Charity comprehends every action demanded by the common morality required by natural reason, but directs them all to a further end, and an even more demanding one. Hence grace perfects nature. By affirming that the ends of theological virtues are not the same as those of the natural ones as such, but are more remote and comprehend more acts, Aquinas implied that his theory of the natural virtues—of common morality—does not logically presuppose his moral theology, and can be studied in its own right.

Although distinctions of this sort were once common property of orthodox Christianity in all its branches, there have recently been movements in Protestant moral theology to repudiate the doctrine that natural human reason can generate any moral laws at all: to proclaim *agape* (as theologians like to call it) as the sole valid guide for action; and, as the sole and sufficient rule of conduct, "Love, and do what you will!"

How this Augustinian injunction is supposed to guide conduct is far from clear, as W. K. Frankena has remarked; for the verb "to love" is desperately ambiguous.[55] In the mouths of orthodox theologians like St. Augustine or St. Thomas Aquinas, for whom traditional morality as embodied in the Mosaic decalogue is an expression of charity, one of the things enjoined is that the traditional moral law be obeyed. This position has been called "pure rule-agapism" by Paul Ramsey.[56] Others, taking what Frankena has judged "the clearest and most plausible view," have interpreted the law of love as a combination of a principle of benevolence, that we must produce good as such and prevent evil, with a principle of distributive justice.[57] Agapism of this sort would be a modified form of utilitarianism. Yet others have identified it with one or another of the pure forms of utilitarianism and have grappled with the familiar difficulties incurred (see below, 6.4–5). And finally, there are those who, confounding *agape* with diffuse affectionate sentiment, have reduced "Love, and do what you will!" to "Having ascertained the facts of your situation, allow nothing—and especially not the precepts of traditional morality—to deter you from what your affectionate sentiments may prompt!" It should surprise nobody that the results of this vulgar "situation ethics" are sloppy and incoherent. [58]

Except for the first, all these positions are incompatible with the traditional doctrine that the system of common morality embodied in the Mosaic decalogue is strictly derivable from the primary and common principle that humanity is to be loved as such. And the first position, "pure rule-agapism," has to do, not with the rational character of common morality but with its relation to the theological virtue of charity. Our task is to inquire into the meaning of the primary and common principle, understood as knowable by ordinary human reason. And, as regards that inquiry, the only alternative to the interpretation of Aquinas proposed by Grisez, correctly, as I shall hereafter assume, is Kant's second formula of the fundamental principle of morality, *Act so that you treat humanity, whether in your own person or in that of another, always as an end, and never as a means only.* [59] Although, like Aquinas's, according to the interpretation by Grisez which I accept, this formula is teleological, it takes the ends of actions to be human beings themselves, not the human goods that may be realized in them.

In recent generations, many British moralists have objected that humanity, or rational nature, is not the sort of thing that can be an end in itself. "[B]y an end," Sidgwick complained, "we commonly mean something to be realized, whereas 'humanity' is, as Kant says, a self-subsistent end." [60] Ross dilated upon this, arguing that "ends . . . in the ordinary sense of the word men are not. For an end is an object of desire, and an object of desire is something that does not yet exist." And on no better ground, he complacently pronounced "the notion of self-subsistent ends" to be "nothing but an embarrassment to Kant." [61]

Far from embarrassing Kant, it is more probable that such cavils would have astonished him. Nor do I think he would easily have been persuaded that, among Sidgwick's and Ross's countrymen, the belief that the ultimate end of an action is the existing being for whose sake it is done was any less common that it was among his own.

For this familiar conception he might, indeed, have invoked

theological authority. "[T]he ultimate end of any maker, as a maker, is himself," Aquinas wrote; "we use things made by us for our own sakes, and if sometimes a man makes a thing for some other purpose, this is referred to his own good, as either useful, or delectable, or fitting [*honestum*]."[62] Obviously, a man who makes things for his own use or pleasure does so ultimately for his own sake; but even when he does something as "fitting," for example, when he observes the terms of his contract with his employer, Aquinas held that he does so as due to himself as well as to his employer. Nor should it be forgotten that not all actions are primarily directed to the use or pleasure of the being who is their ultimate end. This is most evident in actions whose ultimate end is God; for, since God is perfect, nothing anybody does can benefit him in any way at all. "God is the end of things," Aquinas explained, "not in the sense of something set up, or produced, by things, nor in the sense that something is added to him by things, but in this sense only, that he is attained by things."[63] Nor are actions done for the sake of a human being, oneself or another, necessarily or always directed to that person's use or pleasure. The most commonplace examples are acts of courtesy, which may well neither be useful nor pleasing, nor believed to be, but be done and accepted wholly out of mutual respect. Actions of abstaining from injuring or offending others are also of this kind: they are neither pleasing nor useful (for refraining from harming somebody does him no good); but they are morally obligatory, as done out of respect for an already existing being whom practical reason recognizes as an end in itself.

Kant's and Aquinas's versions of the primary common principle that humanity is to be loved for its own sake, although they converge, do not coincide. For while most acts of respecting human nature as an end in itself are also acts of respecting certain fundamental human goods as to be promoted and never violated, not all are. For example, respecting as an end in itself one human being who attacks the life of another, who is innocent, does not appear to exclude using deadly violence on him, if only so is the life or fundamental well-being of his innocent victim to be safeguarded. A man is not degraded to a mere manipulated means by being forcibly prevented from degrading somebody else to a mere manipulated means. But respecting every human life as an inviolable fundamental good does exclude using deadly violence on anybody, even to safeguard innocent lives. Hence Aquinas's version of the *principium communissimum* can only be reconciled with the received Christian doctrine that killing in self-defence or in defence of the innocent is licit, by such devices as confining its application to direct actions and drawing a distinction between direct and indirect killing (see 5.3).

There are three reasons for preferring Kant's interpretation of the primary and common principle to Aquinas's. First, it is simpler. If the principle that one is to love one's fellow human beings as oneself is to be understood as a principle of respect, as it must be to play the part it does in Jewish and Christian moral thinking, then it is most straightforwardly read as ordaining respect for human beings, not for fundamental human goods. Second, as the examples of self-defence and the safeguarding of innocent lives show, received Jewish and Christian moral conclusions are derivable more directly from the principle as Kant interpreted it. And finally, although the question itself will not be investigated until the final chapter, the principle appears to be more defensible in its Kantian form than in its Thomistic one.

In what follows, therefore, I take the fundamental principle of that part of traditional morality which is independent of any theological presupposition to have been expressed in the scriptural commandment, "Thou shalt love thy neighbor as thyself," understanding one's neighbor to be any fellow human being, and love to be a matter, not of feeling, but of acting in ways in which human beings as such can choose to act. The philosophical sense of this commandment was correctly expressed by Kant in his formula that one act so that one treats humanity always as an end and never as a means only. However, Kant was mistaken in thinking this formula to be equivalent to his formula of universal law, in which he captured the philosophical truth underlying the inaccurately stated Golden Rule.

Since treating a human being, in virtue of its rationality, as an end in itself, is the same as respecting it as a rational creature, Kant's formula of the fundamental principle may be restated in a form more like that of the scriptural commandment that is its original: *Act always so that you respect every human being, yourself or another, as being a rational creature.* And, since it will be convenient that the fundamental principle of the system to be developed be formulated in terms of the concept of permissibility analysed in the preceding section, the canonical form in which that principle will hereafter be cited is: *It is impermissible not to respect every human being, oneself or any other, as a rational creature.*

2.5   The Structure of the First-Order System

The structure of any system of morality whose sole first principle is that which has been identified in the preceding section must be logically very simple.

It cannot be an axiomatic system; for in axiomatic systems a body of theorems is rigorously derived from a small set of unproved propositions, the "axioms," which are stated by means of a few primitive terms. Except for additional terms introduced as abbreviations, and which therefore could be dispensed with, neither theorems nor demonstrations contain any term not mentioned in the axioms. The primitive terms remain uninterpreted at the end, as they were at the beginning. Such systems explore what follows on the assumption that their axioms hold true for everything that satisfies their primitive terms.

The structure of the fundamental principle is itself simple. It contains only one concept peculiar to moral thought, that of (moral) permissibility. And its sense is that no action which falls under the concept of not respecting some human being as a rational creature can fall under the concept of being permissible. The second concept it contains, that of (not) respecting some human being as a rational creature, is not peculiar to moral thinking. It has a place in descriptions of human conduct in anthropology and psychology, and of course in everyday descriptive discourse.

Of those precepts derivable from the first principle which are needed for the solution of serious moral problems, virtually all turn on the concept of respecting a human being as a rational creature, and virtually none on the concept of permissibility. There are, indeed, serious problems about the construction of formal systems in which "it is permissible that" figures as a modal operator, and which are investigated in deontic logic; but their philosophical interest is logical rather than moral. The problems that will occupy us in what follows all have to do with what falls under the concept of respecting a human being as rational, and what does not.

None of these problems can be solved by means of the logical operation of substituting for one expression another that, by definition, is synonymous with it. The concept of respecting a human being as a rational creature is not usefully definable for our purposes. Thus to define it as treating a human being, by virtue of his rationality, as an end in itself, while perhaps clarifying, does not furnish us with a useful substituend. Yet it does not follow that the process of deriving specific precepts from the fundamental principle is arbitrary and unreasoned.

The formal character of such derivations is uncomplicated. Consider the three schemata of specific moral precepts that were listed in 2.3 above: namely,

(1) It is always permissible to do an action of the kind K, as such;
(2) It is never permissible to do an action of the kind K;
(3) It is never morally permissible not to do an action of the kind K, if an occasion occurs on which one can be done.

Now let us ask what are the simplest additional premises by which precepts satisfying these schemata can be validly inferred from the fundamental principle

(P) It is impermissible not to respect every human being, oneself or any other, as a rational creature,

and a truth about the system of common morality being investigated, namely,

(S) The principle (P) is the sole first principle of common morality.

Precepts falling under schema (1) require a proposition derivable from (P) and (S), namely,

(1a) No action of a kind which, as such, does not fail to respect any human being as a rational creature, is impermissible as such,

and an additional premise, namely, one satisfying the schema

(1b) No action of the kind K, as such, fails to respect any human being as a rational creature.

Precepts satisfying the schemata (2) and (3) are each directly derivable from the fundamental principle (P) together with one additional premise. Thus precepts satisfying (2) follow from (P) and a premise satisfying

(2a) All actions of the kind K fail to respect some human being as a rational creature;

and those satisfying (3) follow from (P) and a premise satisfying

(3a) If an occasion occurs on which an action of the kind K can be done, not to do it will fail to respect some human being as a rational creature.

Premises satisfying the schemata (1b), (2a), and (3a) may be called "specificatory premises," because they each identify a species of action as falling or not falling under the fundamental generic concept of action in which every human being is respected as a rational creature.

Although simple derivations of these three kinds raise no serious logical questions, the question of how specificatory premises satisfying the schemata (1b), (2a), and (3a) are obtained is both serious and difficult. Nor has it been much studied by philosophers. Of processes analogous to those that are required, perhaps the closest are those by which courts apply legal concepts to new cases.

In common law, as Edward H. Levi has observed, a "circular motion" is perceptible in the reasoning by which concepts are first elicited from cases and then applied: in the first stage, a legal concept is created by comparing and reflecting on cases; in the second, that concept, more or less fixed, is applied to new cases; and in the third, reasoning by example with new cases goes so far that the concept breaks down, and a new one must be created.[64] Those who accept traditional morality, without necessarily believing that it originated in a divine command, can hardly escape concluding that its concepts were created by just such a "circular" process; and they will read both Hebrew and Greek literature as containing evidences of it. But they must go further. To accept traditional morality is to accept its fundamental principle as true, and hence to be confident that the concepts in terms of which it is formulated are not liable to break down when applied to new and unforeseen cases. With regard to that principle, although not to the more specific of the specificatory premises by which it is applied, they must hold that a point has been reached beyond which only reasoning of the kind found at the second of Levi's stages is called for. And this has been accepted by some common lawyers, for example Lord Atkin, who pointed out, in an opinion which dislodged a number of entrenched legal concepts, that the common law of tort is an application of the moral principle that you are to love your neighbor, interpreted restrictively, because of the practical difficulty of providing legal remedies, as "You must not injure your neighbor."[65] Quite evidently, Lord Atkin would have dismissed any suggestion that the concept of injuring your neighbor might break down and have to be replaced.

Legal reasoning, in which a concept is applied to new cases, presupposes that the concept has a content which in part is comprehended by members of the law-abiding community and in part remains to be determined by reflecting on cases to which it and related concepts have been applied. And it further presupposes that the determination of that concept, and its application to new cases, is not arbitrary: that, even though up to a point bad judicial decisions must be allowed to stand, according to the doctrine of *stare decisis*, there is an objective distinction between correct judicial opinions and incorrect ones. The rational processes by which such opinions are arrived at can be pronounced sound or unsound, although they cannot be usefully formalized, because they depend in large measure on weighing likenesses and differences between cases on principles which, although received, are acknowledged to be corrigible.

The analogy to legal reasoning of the unformalized reasoning by which specificatory premises in morals are established has recently been made much of by Hare, although he has not taken the same view as I of the analogue.

If a normative or evaluative principle [Hare wrote] is framed in terms of a predicate which has fuzzy edges (as nearly all predicates in practice have), then we are not going to be able to use the principle to decide cases on the borderline without doing some more normation or evaluation. If we make a law forbidding the use of wheeled vehicles in the park, and somebody thinks he can go in the park on roller skates, no amount of cerebration, and no amount of inspection of roller skates, are going to settle for us the question of whether roller skates are vehicles 'within the meaning of the Act' if the Act has not specified whether they are; the judge has to decide whether they are *to be* counted as such. And this is a further determination of the law. The judge may have very good reasons of public interest or morals for his decision; but he cannot make it by any physical or metaphysical examination of roller skates to see whether they are *really* wheeled vehicles.[66]

The chief difficulty in Hare's argument is that he considers only one feature of the predicates in terms of which the moral principles in question are formulated, namely, whether they have fuzzy or nonfuzzy edges; and that feature is itself fuzzy. He does not make clear whether or not he takes the mere fact that it is disputable whether a predicate applies to a certain species of case to be a sufficient condition of its having fuzzy edges; or whether, in addition, he demands that disputes about its application be intrinsically irresoluble.

Suppose that a child is directed to sort toy building-blocks of various shades of blue and green into two boxes, putting the blue into one and the green into another. Of some bluish-green (or greenish-blue) blocks he complains that he has not been told which box to put them in; for as bluish they are not green and as greenish they are not blue. Somebody more theoretically minded may have added that the predicates "green" and "blue" have fuzzy edges; that in order to decide in which box to put the blocks that lie within the fuzzy region, he must make further determinations of what is to be accounted green or blue; and that neither further scrutiny of the blocks nor cerebration about the meanings of "green" and "blue" can settle the matter. Within the terms of what he was directed to do, it is intrinsically irresoluble.

Hare's case of the roller skates, as far as can be told from his sketch, is not of this kind. He rightly remarks that nothing in it turns on differences about what roller skates are, as to which all parties may be expected to agree, although he does not point out that cases having to do with complex machines may well be different. (In the moral case to which he applies his example, that of abortion, questions about the nature of a foetus more resemble those about the nature of a complex machine than those about the nature of roller skates.) But on what ground does Hare conclude that no amount of "cerebration" by a judge about the nature of wheeled vehicles "within the meaning of the Act" could settle the question whether roller skates are wheeled vehicles? While the predicate "wheeled vehicles within the meaning of the Act" has fuzzy edges in the superficial sense that disputes can arise about what it applies to, it does not follow that it has fuzzy edges in the deeper sense that those disputes can be resolved only extrinsically: that is, by considerations, whether of public interest or of morals, which according to received canons of statutory interpretation are not implicit in the words of the Act.

It is true that positivist legal systems are possible in which questions about what an expression in a legal instrument applies to, when that is not explicitly settled either in that instrument or in some other pertinent enactment or ruling, are expressly required to be settled by additional acts of "normation or evaluation" by judges. But only a tiny minority of students of the law consider that a logically coherent legal system must be of that kind, much less that British and American common or statute law is. Any British or American bench, called upon to determine whether the words of an Act forbidding the use of wheeled vehicles in a public park apply to roller skating, the Act itself specifying neither that it does nor that it does not, would normally be able to do so by the ordinary process of statutory interpretation. It is almost unthinkable that it would have to legislate under the guise of giving judgement.

The respects in which moral reasoning is not analogous to legal, of which the chief are that it is not confined to questions of rights which courts can practically enforce, and of wrongs which they can remedy or punish, and that it is not practically obliged to accord authority even to bad precedents, in no way impair the objectivity with which in moral reasoning general concepts are applied to specific cases. The fundamental concept of respecting every human being as a rational creature is fuzzy at the edges in the superficial sense that its application to this or that species of case can be disputed. But among those who share in the life of a culture in which the Hebrew-Christian moral tradition is accepted, the concept is in large measure understood in itself; and it is connected with numerous applications, as to the different weights of which there is some measure of agreement. This is enough for it to be possible to determine many specificatory premises with virtual certainty and others with a high degree of confidence.

The moral system that may be derived from the fundamental principle in this way may with equal truth be described as a "simple deductive" system according to Robert Nozick's classification,[67] or as an informal analytical one. The structure consisting of fundamental principle, derived precepts, and specificatory premises is strictly deductive; for every derived precept is strictly deduced, by way of some specificatory premise, either from the fundamental principle or from some precept already derived. But that structure is not the whole of the system. For virtually all the philosophical difficulties that are encountered in deriving that structure have to do with establishing the specificatory premises; and that is done by unformalized analytical reasoning in which some concept either in the fundamental principle or in a derived precept is applied to some new species of case. As with the legal reasoning to which it is analogous, many specimens of thinking of this kind are beyond dispute. Others, however, especially those having to do with the more specific and complicated cases, are not. And a further difficulty is that different thinkers sometimes do not agree about what is seriously disputable.

One strategy for indirectly establishing specificatory premises, which will be adopted in a number of the cases that follow, ought to be described in advance. Often direct analysis is not the most effective way to establish a specificatory premise; for the problem is that, while it is evident that certain kinds of action in most cases fall under a certain concept (for example, killing people in most cases is failing to respect them as rational beings), in some cases they do not, or are thought not to (for example, killing in self-defence is not failing to respect the person killed). How is a moralist to determine what the fundamental principle requires with respect to such kinds of action?

A natural approach is to begin by showing that it is impermissible to perform actions of that kind at will, and then to go on to determine the kinds of cases in which it is permissible. Accordingly, with respect to killing human beings, one would begin by establishing that:

(K1) To kill another human being *merely at will* is not to respect every human being (in particular, the one killed) as a rational creature.

This would not be denied by any Jewish or Christian moralist. And now an attempt is made to find in what kinds of cases killing another human being is legitimate. For example, it might be argued that:

(K2) To kill another human being who is attacking you, and concerning whom you reasonably judge that he may well kill or seriously injure you, and that his attack can only be stopped by killing him, is not to fail in respect to another human being as a rational creature, even to the one killed.

To the extent that it is possible to be assured that a complete list of such cases has been found, it will be possible to infer that:

(K3) To kill another human being, except under the circumstances specified in (K2) and the other propositions obtained from the search, is to kill him merely at will.

From (K1) and (K3) it follows that, except under specified circumstances, killing a human being is impermissible. And this conclusion is equivalent, as an appropriate definition will show, to a prohibition of murder.

The chief weakness of this strategy is that it is seldom possible to eliminate all doubts of the completeness of the survey. How can we assure ourselves beyond doubt that no significant case has been overlooked? Nozick goes so far as to state that many who have ceased to assent to "any or very many exceptionless moral principles" although at one time they did so—by which I take him to refer, among others, to the many who have repudiated the traditional morality in which they were brought up—have done so because "more and more complicated cases" forced them into what seemed an interminable process of revision.[68] And he ventures the suggestion that such a history would be common among lawyers, who know by experience how difficult it is to devise, in advance, rules adequate to "all the bizarre, unexpected, arcane, and complicated cases which actually arise."[69]

This misplaces the difficulty by comparing a moralist's task to that of a legislative draftsman, to which its resemblance, despite Hare, is slight. The task of legislative draftsmen is seldom to formulate specific precepts derived from a fundamental legal principle: almost always it is to contrive a set of regulations to further the complex and politically determined objects of public policy. Thus they attempt to solve such problems as how to frame legislation by which the rich will not be able to escape income tax, but also by which municipalities may continue to raise money by selling bonds at low interest, given that the established method, exempting such interest from income tax, enables the rich to avoid income tax. Moralists and judges do not have tasks of this kind. Their business is not to contrive ways of furthering a variety of ends, many of them hard to reconcile, and all of them subject to change; they have only to work out what rationally justifiable moral and legal principles really do require, however disconcerting the result may be.

The difficulties that arise for moralists in any tradition mostly consist of discrepancies between precepts derived by established methods from their first principle or principles, and what seem to be intuitively evident applications of those first principles to cases falling under those precepts. To invert the example given above: it is an established doctrine in the Hebrew-Christian tradition that it is permissible to kill another human being in self-defence; but to some, for example Quakers, killing another human being seems to be quite evidently incompatible with respecting his humanity. Such problems have arisen, as a matter of history, far less often from "bizarre, unexpected, arcane, and complicated cases," than from deeper reflection on cases already considered in what is now a very long tradition. And that is why Nozick seems to have exaggerated as well as misplaced the difficulty of surveying all the possible kinds of circumstances in which an action, impermissible if done merely at will, is permissible. Unusual and unexpected cases are unlikely to make much difference. The chief source of doubt is the suspicion of having overlooked the significance of some feature of a case already known.

3

First-Order Precepts

3.1 The Classification of First-Order Precepts

In proceeding to determine what system of specific first-order precepts follows from the principle that has been identified as fundamental to common morality, two reminders may not be out of place. First, the precepts to be derived, like the fundamental principle itself, have to do only with that part of what the Hebrew-Christian tradition takes to be common morality which does not presuppose any theological doctrine. That part, however, is large; and it comprises almost everything those who are not theologically minded treat as belonging to morality. Second, while the derivations to be presented are mine, in that I think them valid, almost none will be original. Most of them will be critically selected from the writings of the moralists whose work has shaped traditional morality.

Although the first-order precepts to be derived may be classified in a number of ways, for reasons to be given I have divided them into three groups, according as they have to do with: (1) the duties of each human being to himself or herself; (2) the duties of each human being to other human beings as such; (3) duties arising out of participation in human institutions. Those of the third group are further subdivided, according as the institutions giving rise to them either (*a*) are among the varieties of purely voluntary contract or (*b*) are in one way or another imposed on individuals by the civil or noncivil societies of which they are members. To the last of these groups belong the precepts arising out of possession of property and out of membership in a family or in a civil society.

3.2 Duties of Human Beings
to Themselves

That each human being has duties to himself follows immediately from the fundamental principle; for if it is impermissible not to respect every human being as a rational creature, it is impermissible not to respect oneself as such. As we shall see, the relations which human beings can have to one another are more complex than those they can have to themselves. But they can injure or hurt themselves; and they can take care of themselves, and cultivate their various capacities. Their duties to themselves are classifiable by reference to these powers.

The worst physical injury anybody can do to himself is to kill himself, that is, to commit suicide. Yet there are reasons for which people do kill themselves; and an important question in common morality is whether it is permissible to do so. A possible view, which the Stoics maintained with respect to sages, is that any human being may quit life as he or she pleases. So stated, it is untenable. It seems evident that if one is to respect oneself as a rational creature, one may not hold one's life cheap, as something to be taken at will. Here the Jewish and Christian repudiation of the Stoic position is plainly correct. Conceding, then, that *it is impermissible for any human being to take his own life at will*, it is necessary to inquire whether there are any circumstances at all in which it is permissible.

An opinion sometimes advanced is that the precepts with respect to killing oneself are exactly parallel to those with respect to killing others: so that killing oneself is impermissible only when it is self-murder. And, presuming murder to be killing the objectively or materially innocent, most of the circumstances in which killing another is not murder cannot hold for killing oneself; for nobody need kill himself in order to defend himself, or others, or his society, against an attack from himself—all he need do is call off the attack. However, one circumstance traditionally acknowledged by Jews and Christians to be a justification for killing another, namely, that one be an executioner carrying out a lawful capital sentence, would seem to justify suicide also: at least in a jurisdiction in which, sentence of death having been passed, the culprit is permitted to carry it out.

Yet both Jews and Christians have been reluctant to draw this conclusion. In the case of Jews, the reason has been religious. For, as David Daube has pointed out,[1] rabbinical authority held suicide to be forbidden, not by the prohibition of murder in the Mosaic

Jewish view
David Daube - rabbinical authority

decalogue, but by a revelation to Noah, "Surely your blood of your lives I will require,"[2] which was read as implying that it was for God to determine when a man should die, and not for the man himself. It was on this ground that the martyr Rabbi Hanina ben Teradion refused to shorten his sufferings when he was being tortured to death.[3]

Nor can the traditional Christian denial that it is ever permissible to kill oneself be rationally justified on any other ground.[4] Consider Kant's unqualified declaration:

> Man cannot renounce his personality so long as he is a subject of duty, hence so long as he lives. . . . To destroy the subject of morality in one's own person is to root out the existence of morality itself from the world; and yet morality is an end in itself. Consequently, to dispose of oneself as a mere means to an arbitrary end is to abase humanity in one's person.[5]

Here the *ignoratio elenchi* is patent. For to carry out a lawful judicial sentence upon oneself is not to dispose of oneself as a mere means to an arbitrary end. What Kant wrote is only intelligible as expressing the religious conviction that to take one's own life is to repudiate one's existence as a divine creation.

Setting aside religious considerations of this kind, and confining ourselves to those that are purely moral, there are clear reasons for concluding that there may be circumstances in which suicide would be permissible but in which killing another would not. For suicide cannot be against the will of the person killed, whereas killing another can. To kill another for his own good, but against his will, fails to respect him as a rational creature, because respecting a being as a rational creature is respecting him as autonomous—as having the right, subject to the moral law, to decide for himself what his own good is, and how to pursue it. The purely moral question, then, reduces to this: Are there circumstances in which a human being would not fail to respect himself as a rational creature by killing himself? If there are, it will be permissible in those circumstances for him to kill himself, and for another to help him, although not to kill him against his will.

A preponderance of Jewish discussions of this subject acknowledge the permissibility of killing oneself when an external force one is powerless to resist either (1) imposes on one a choice between denying one's fundamental practical allegiance (in particular, one's religious faith) and suffering death or unendurable torture,[6] or (2) credibly threatens to force one into a life unfitting to a rational creature, such as a life of enforced prostitution, or of any other form of dehumanizing slavery.[7] There appears to be no reason to conclude that, in circumstances of either kind, killing oneself would fail to respect oneself as a rational creature. On the contrary, not to kill oneself would be either heroic or cowardly.

Suicide has also been held to be permissible when it is either (1) to ensure the lives or the fundamental well-being of others, or (2) to escape a condition of natural dehumanization.

Three kinds of case in which suicide appears to be necessary to ensure the lives of others may be mentioned. (i) Those represented by the memorable Stoic example of an overloaded boat, which will sink unless some of its load is jettisoned but the entire load of which is innocent human beings.[8] If nobody can be saved unless somebody goes overboard, and if to go overboard would be suicide,[9] then suicide in such circumstances would certainly not be contrary to the respect due to humanity as such. (ii) Those in which a disease makes a man dangerous to others, whether by infection or by making him insanely violent. Kant describes a case of the latter kind.

A man who had been bitten by a mad dog already felt hydrophobia, and he explained, in a letter he left, that since, so far as he knew, the disease was incurable, he killed himself lest he harm others as well in his madness, the onset of which he already felt.[10]

While Kant was presumably sceptical of the assertion that only by suicide could the hydrophobic have secured others from harm, situations seem perfectly possible in which there would be no other way; and others could obviously occur in connection with infectious diseases. (iii) Those in which suicide relieves others of a duty which they cannot carry out and survive. The suicide of Captain Oates, in Scott's antarctic expedition, in order not to retard his companions as they struggled back to their depot, is rightly considered an act of charity as well as of courage.

In addition, suicide has been justified simply as sparing others excessive burdens. For example, the care of a relative who has contracted an illness or suffered an injury, which incapacitates him for normal life, may call for very great sacrifices by whoever undertakes it. Suppose the sufferer to know that, although those sacrifices are supererogatory, somebody will either make them cheerfully or be coerced by family pressure into making them resentfully. In circumstances of either kind, to describe his suicide

Hydrophobia – final ground upon which suicial might held to be permissible

as wanting in the respect due to humanity would be questionable.

Kant's example of hydrophobia incidentally illustrates a final ground upon which suicide may be held to be permissible: namely, to obtain release from a life that has become, not merely hard to bear, but utterly dehumanized. Supposing hydrophobia to be incurable and its inevitable course to be one of extreme torment, culminating in madness and death: does respect for himself as rational compel a man to submit to it, and not escape by suicide? Or suppose that a man is trapped in a burning vehicle, without hope of getting out: does respect for himself as rational require him to let himself be burned to death, rather than commit suicide?[11] In my own judgement, suicide is in both cases entirely legitimate. The problem is to draw the line between despairing of human life in adversity and perceiving that, owing to illness or injury, the possibility of a genuinely human life will cease before biological death. When that line is crossed, the case for the permissibility of suicide is strong.

Since a man is a rational creature who is a rational animal, respect for man as the rational creature he is implies respect for the integrity and health of his body. Hence *it is impermissible,* according to the first principle, *for anybody to mutilate himself at will, or to do at will anything that will impair his health.* It may be doubted whether anybody has ever mutilated himself for the sake of the thing; but Kant was distressed by the thought of people selling their teeth, and appears to have believed that there were those who had themselves castrated "in order to make a more comfortable living" as singers.[12] Setting aside such cases, on the ground that those who offer inducements to anybody to submit to mutilation commit a grave wrong, the only conditions on which most people would be inclined to submit to it coincide with those in which it is permissible according to the first principle to do so. Surgical operations such as amputation, for example, are permissible for the sake of the health of the body as a whole. And, despite Kant, it is generally and reasonably allowed to be legitimate to give a bodily organ such as an eye or a kidney for transplantation, in order to save a faculty, or the life, of another. Yet this must not be at the cost of that faculty in the giver, or of his life. One may not blind oneself to save another from blindness.

Ex's why.. Suicid Not pemiss ible.

As for impairment of health, the requirements of common morality are much less stringent than those of the respectable part of contemporary culture. For morality, the conditions of human life are to be accepted: risk is a part of normal life, even risks taken solely for the sake of enjoyment and recreation. As the history of both Judaism and Christianity shows, horror at the use of drugs and intoxicants as such is characteristic of fanatical sects rather than of orthodoxy. It is not inspired by common morality. Nor, as the tolerance of tobacco by both Judaism and Christianity shows, has addiction to a drug been traditionally considered unfitting to a human being. Inasmuch as the relief and enjoyment afforded by a drug compensate for any ill effects it may have, then it is permissible to use it. But it is contrary to the precept forbidding the impairment of health so to use drugs as to incapacitate oneself for the ordinary business of life. And, perhaps more importantly, it is contrary to the fundamental principle itself to allow the use of a drug to become the main point of life. For anybody to place any kind of drug-induced enjoyment before the full use of his capacities as a rational creature, is a plain case of failure to respect himself as the kind of being he is. The objection is not to the enjoyment in itself but to the inordinate value set upon it. It was on this ground, as involving *concupiscentia inordinata*, that Aquinas condemned the vice of drunkenness as a species of gluttony. [13]

In addition to the precepts forbidding anybody to kill or injure himself, except in certain specifiable situations, common morality demands of every human being that he *adopt some coherent plan of life according to which, by morally permissible actions, his mental and physical powers may be developed.* Not to adopt such a plan is impermissible, as wanting in respect to himself as a rational creature capable of developing such powers.

Adopting Paton's term for its Kantian equivalent, I shall refer to this precept as the "principle of culture." [14] Obviously, it entails certain prohibitions, such as that *it is impermissible for anybody to neglect his health or his education.* But in what it requires to be done, it allows large scope for choice. Most human beings are capable of mastering, to some degree, any one of a number of different branches of knowledge and skill, but not of mastering more than a few of them together. As long as a man does not neglect the fundamentals of mental and physical development, without which he cannot follow any coherent plan of self-cultivation, it is up to him to decide which of the different possibilities open to him he will choose: whether, say, to be a farmer, or a soldier, or a philosopher. Given that he has the capacity to be any one of the three, and the opportunity, common morality leaves the choice to him. And having chosen, say, to be a soldier, he does not violate the principle of culture by not developing his powers as a philosopher as far as he might have done had he chosen philosophy as his profession.

The principle of culture, as has been remarked, entails that a man must not neglect his health. This subordinate precept must be interpreted in the light of the principle itself, which requires that a man live according to some coherent plan of life. Most plans of life demand, at various junctures, that risks be taken, or that physical and emotional resources be spent. A man does not violate the principle of culture by risking his life in the pursuit of his calling, or by undermining his health with hard work and with anxieties inseparable from his responsibilities.

3.3   Noninstitutional Duties to Others

Duties to others correspond with duties to oneself only up to a point. A man can injure or look after others as he can injure or look after himself; but there are things he can do to himself which he cannot do to others, and things can do to others which he cannot do to himself. For example, he can develop his mind by study, and his physique by exercise; but he cannot develop anybody else's mind or physique. Hence there is no precept of duty to others corresponding to the principle of culture. On the other hand, he cannot, strictly speaking, give help to himself, inform or misinform himself, or transfer property from himself to himself, although he can do all those things to others.

In investigating duties to others, it is convenient to begin with those that can arise between one man and another independently of any institution with which either may be associated. By an institution, following John Searle, I understand any system of constitutive rules according to which anything of a certain kind, in situations of a certain kind, is counted as something of a certain kind.[15] The most familiar institutions, like those of civil society, such as parliament and the legal system, invest certain official positions with certain rights, duties, and immunities; specify certain kinds of action as impermissible and others as permissible; and provide for the adjudication of whether the rules have been violated, and for the imposition of penalties if they have.[16] However, I shall consider any system of constitutive rules whatever to be an institution, even that for a game of patience played by a solitary man, which he has invented and has divulged to nobody else.

The first set of noninstitutional duties to others to be considered are those having to do with force and violence. Since respect for human beings as rational creatures entails, in general, treating every normal adult as responsible for the conduct of his own affairs, to interfere by force with anybody else's conduct of his life, unless there is a special and adequate reason, is not to respect him as a rational creature. The principle may therefore be laid down that *it is impermissible for anybody at will to use force upon another.*

Not all human beings are normal, however, and not all are adult. The insane, who cannot wholly take care of themselves, must be looked after; and, if it is necessary for their well-being, may be constrained to do various things they would not do if they had their own way. The question of how far a man's insanity gives those charged with looking after him the right of coercion is a difficult one, which I shall not pursue. The general principle, however, is clear: since a madman is a rational creature whose reason is impaired, he is entitled to the respect due to a normal rational creature except to the extent that the impairment of his reason makes it necessary to prevent him from harming himself or others, and to bring him to undergo treatment which it is reasonable to think may benefit him, provided that it is neither cruel nor offensive.

Children also are rational creatures, whose reason is in process of development. Although it must be recognized that the power of normal children to look after themselves is constantly growing, while they remain children they are not fully capable of doing so: and, in a measure as they are not, those in charge of them may forcibly prevent them from harming themselves or others, and may compel them to submit to education reasonably thought to be of benefit to them.

The question of when a given human being's life as an individual begins is of great importance in the Hebrew-Christian system. The duties of human beings to others are duties to them as human beings, that is, as rational creatures of a certain kind. The forms which may be taken by the fundamental moral duty of respect for a rational creature as such will vary with the degree to which that creature is actually in possession of the reason a mature creature of that kind would normally possess; but such variations in no way annul the duty. In simpler ages, it was practically sufficient to treat duties to others as beginning with their birth. However, as medical knowledge has grown, and as techniques have been developed by which the unborn can be both benefited and injured, the theoretical issue cannot be set aside on the ground of practical unimportance. The question of when the life of a human being begins is a biological one, since human beings are rational *animals;* and biology answers it simply and unequivocally: a human life begins at conception, when the new being receives the genetic code.[17] Although a zygote does not, even when made visible through a microscope, look like a human being, and although adult human beings cannot have the kind of relations with it that they can have to other adults, or even to children, its status as a rational creature is in no way compromised. Attempts to deny the humanity of zygotes, by declaring that humanity begins at birth, or at viability (that is, at the point when an unborn child, extruded from the womb, could be kept alive) are scientifically obscurantist. An eight-month-old premature baby is biologically less mature than an eight-and-three-quarter-month-old unborn one; and viability has no biological significance. Whether an unborn child is viable or not depends on the state of medical technology. It is reasonable to forecast that, in a century or so, a zygote will be viable.

It follows that the principle *it is impermissible for anybody at will to use force upon another* applies to adult and child alike, to born and unborn. However, just as it is legitimate to use force on children for purposes for which it would not be legitimate to use it on adults, so very difficult questions are raised about the extent to which it is legitimate to use force upon an unborn child. Since these questions bring into doubt the consistency of Hebrew-Christian morality, they will be deferred for special consideration when its systematic structure will have been made clearer (see 5.4).

Three precepts are readily derivable from the general prohibition of the use of force: that *no man may at will kill another;* that *no man may at will inflict bodily injury or hurt on another;* and that *no man may hold another in slavery.*

Only the third of these precepts is unqualified. Although nobody may kill or injure another at will, there are circumstances in which it is legitimate to kill or injure others. Yet there are no circumstances in which the enslavement of another can be reconciled with respect for him as a rational creature. Whewell has stated the point forcibly. A slave is a human being who is entirely at the disposal of another, a condition to which no normal adult can be reduced except by violence. As institutionalized, slavery treats certain human beings as "chattels personal" of their masters. In Whewell's words, "The slave is the property of the master, in the same manner as a horse or a cart is"; and this is "contrary to the Fundamental Principles of Morality," because

> it neglects the great primary distinction of Persons and Things; converting a Person into a Thing, an object merely passive, without any recognized attributes of Human nature. A slave is, in the eye of the State which stamps him with that character, not acknowledged as a man. . . . [Yet] all men are moral beings, and cannot be treated as mere brutes and things, without an extreme violation of the Duties of Humanity. [18]

The justification of slavery as an institution, on the ground that slaves are descended from criminals or captives, who purchased their lives by giving up their liberty, was exploded by Dr. Johnson, when he pointed out that nobody can forfeit or bargain away the liberty of his descendants. [19] And Johnson might have added that penal servitude and contractual servitude are *not* slavery. The point of criminal justice is that the criminal be treated as a rational creature and not as a chattel; and, since a man may not give up his rights and duties as a rational creature, any contract by which he purported to do so would be invalid (cf. 3.4).

Although slavery violates the fundamental principle of Hebrew-Christian morality, early Christianity had no choice but to accept it as an institution. Jewish law also accepted it, while modifying it for Jews by forbidding the permanent enslavement of any Jew without his consent and enjoining Jewish masters to care for their slaves, remembering that their ancestors had been bondmen in Egypt. Yet, despite this inglorious record of acquiescence, individual Christians and Jews, like the Stoics before them, from the beginning perceived the fundamental immorality of slavery. And it was as contrary to common morality that it was abolished by a Europe still formally Christian.

Although there are no circumstances in which slavery is sanctioned by the Hebrew-Christian first principle, there are circumstances in which the use of force upon others is. Violence—the exercise of physical force so as to inflict injury on persons and damage to property[20]—is common among human beings, even though respect for man as rational forbids using force at will upon others. Yet the immunity to violence to which everybody consequently has a moral right is obviously conditional; and perhaps its most obvious condition is that one not further one's own ends by resorting to violence or threatening it. If anybody, in furthering his own ends, resorts to violence or threatens it, he ceases to satisfy the condition of his right to immunity and may be forcibly withstood. By violating the immunity of others, he forfeits his own. In general: *It is permissible for any human being to use force upon another in such measure as may be necessary to defend rational creatures from the other's violence.*

In this matter, common morality is not content with a permissive precept. But to appreciate the nature of its mandatory precept, it is necessary first to consider the general precept from which it is derived, and which I shall refer to as the "principle of beneficence." If a man respects other men as rational creatures, not only will he not injure them, he will necessarily also take satisfaction in their achieving the well-being they seek, and will further their efforts as far as he prudently can. In short, he will observe the general precept: *It is impermissible not to promote the well-being of others by actions in themselves permissible, inasmuch as one can do so without proportionate inconvenience.*

The duty to promote the well-being of others derives from their character as rational creatures, not from their desert. However, human well-being is a matter of human flourishing: that is, of the development and exercise of human potentialities. In a reasonably just society, human adults in good health normally can and do support themselves, either independently or in families. Hence the well-being of others can be successfully promoted only if they do their part: little can be done for the well-being of anybody who will not cultivate and exert the powers he has.

Promoting the well-being of others most conspicuously consists in: (1) contributing to the upbringing and education of those who are not adults, especially of orphans; (2) helping those who have duties which, owing to bereavement, injury, illness, or desertion, they can perform only with help; (3) restoring to a condition of independence those who have been incapacitated by illness, accident, or injury; and (4) caring for those who are crippled, deaf, or blind, or are chronically ill or senile. But it also comprises such less conspicuous activities as preventing what might harm others or frustrate their permissible projects, and abstaining from actions that would foreseeably elicit responses by which others would be injured.

There are two conditions upon the duty of promoting the well-being of others: one mandatory and one permissive. The mandatory condition is that it is absolutely impermissible to promote the well-being of others by any action that is impermissible in itself. This condition is implicit in common morality as a system (cf. 5.2). Accordingly, it is impermissible to secure a benefit for some (say, a legacy that will enable a physician to open a free clinic for the poor) by doing wrong to others (say, by killing the testator who has bequeathed that legacy). The permissive condition is that nobody is morally obliged to promote the well-being of others at disproportionate inconvenience to himself. One does not fail to respect another as a rational creature by declining to procure a good for him, if that good can be procured only by relinquishing an equal or greater good for oneself. Hence, except for special institutional duties, for example those of a parent, to promote the well-being of others at the cost of one's life or fundamental well-being would be supererogatory.

Like the principle of culture, the principle of beneficence ordains, not any specific actions, but the policy of promoting a certain end, provided that the means are in themselves permissible (cf. 5.2). In large measure, it leaves it to each human being to contrive how to carry out that policy, and the plans he makes will to some extent determine what benevolent actions he can conveniently do. On the other hand, should he encounter another who then and there needs help which only he can give without disproportionate inconvenience, the principle of beneficence calls on him to give it. This is the foundation of an important precept, which Maimonides formulated as follows:

> If one person is able to save another and does not save him, he transgresses the commandment, *Neither shalt thou stand idly by the blood of thy neighbor* (*Lev.* 19:16). Similarly, if one person sees another drowning in the sea, or being attacked by bandits, or . . . wild animals, and although able to rescue him . . . does not rescue him; or if one hears heathen or informers plotting evil against another . . . and he does not call it to the other's attention . . . ; or if one knows that a . . . violent person is going to attack another, and although able to appease him on behalf of the other and make him change his mind, he does not do so; or if one acts in any similar way—he transgresses in each case the injunction.[21]

It is therefore not merely permissible but a duty to employ force against the violent if their victims cannot otherwise be protected. Allowing for the impracticability of nice calculation, only necessary force is sanctioned.[22] But if it is reasonably believed necessary to kill the attacker in order to save the victim, the attacker not only may be killed but ought to be.

Two extensions of this line of thought must be mentioned. The first has to do with combatants in war. Given that each side reasonably holds its cause to be just, as we shall see, it is legitimate for both to make war. It is also plausible that the danger to be apprehended from the enemy's armed services may be such that attacks on the members and installations of those armed services are permissible at any time; and that the deaths of noncombatants who are killed in direct attacks on military installations are to be deemed accidental, on the ground that it is the enemy's fault that noncombatants are there. Accordingly, in a just war it is accounted permissible to kill and disable enemy combatants who are not at the time attacking anybody, and to bombard installations even when it will result in the deaths of noncombatants. What is forbidden is directly to attack noncombatants or nonmilitary installations.

The second extension has to do with abortion. It is stated clearly by Maimonides, and is accepted by most Protestants as well as by Jews. Until recently, however, it was rejected by most Catholics.

... the Sages have ruled that if a woman with child is having difficulty in giving birth, the child inside her may be taken out, either by drugs or by surgery, because it is regarded as one pursuing her and trying to kill her. But once its head has appeared it must not be touched, for we may not set aside one human life to save another human life, and what is happening is the course of nature.[23]

Without for the present exploring these questions further (that of abortion will be resumed in 5.4), it is evident that the concept of defending other human beings, and the correlative concept of attacking other human beings, have developed beyond the straightforward concept of defending somebody against an immediate physical assault. Yet a cardinal concept of Hebrew-Christian morality, that of murder, turns on this extension.[24] Murder is commonly defined as killing the innocent, understanding "the innocent" in a material sense, as referring to those who are neither attacking other human beings nor have been condemned to death for a crime. According to the Hebrew-Christian tradition, the only grounds on which it is permissible to use force on a responsible adult human being are those from which it follows that that human being is not innocent. A fortiori, it is impermissible to kill an innocent human being in this sense: that is, *it is absolutely impermissible to commit murder.* However, the precise scope of the class of the innocent is still in dispute.

Some injuries are not bodily; in particular, loss of property, or of honor or reputation. As to property, since in established societies it is a socially regulated institution, consideration of the precepts relating to it will be deferred (see 3.5). The precepts having to do with honor and reputation are simple. Respect for a man as a rational creature includes showing him courtesy in dealing with him, respecting his legitimate pursuits, and, generally, not thinking ill of him. Blunt reproof or even ridicule are permissible when there is clear evidence of wrongdoing; but it must be genuine wrongdoing. And even when a man knows something genuinely to another's discredit, he may not divulge it except as far as is necessary to prevent a wrong. Anybody who, except to prevent a wrong, has insulted, or ridiculed, or disparaged another, must make appropriate reparation.

Relations between human beings are largely carried on by means of language; and much of what is communicated in language consists of expressions of opinion about what is the case. Unless it is required by a specific moral precept, nobody has a right to know another's opinion. The respect owed to other human beings includes respect for their liberty to withhold their thoughts when it is not their duty to divulge them; but, if anybody chooses to divulge his thoughts, the respect he owes to his audience requires that the thoughts he communicates must really be his. Judaism and Christianity agree in condemning with peculiar vehemence any lie (*mendacium*), that is, any free linguistic utterance expressing something contrary to the speaker's mind.[25] A lie is not necessarily false in the sense of being contrary to fact: its falsity is that it misrepresents what is in the liar's mind. Even for a good end, *it is impermissible for anybody, in conditions of free communication between responsible persons, to express an opinion he does not hold.*

Many moralists have justified the duty of veracity on the ground that lying violates an understood pact. Thus, in his *Lectures on Ethics,* Kant declared that

> Every lie is objectionable and contemptible in that we purposely
> let people think that we are telling them our thoughts and do not
> do so. We have broken our pact and violated the right of
> mankind.[26]

And, as we have seen, Whewell believed that there is "a Universal

Understanding among men, which is involved in the use of language, and according to which understanding, each may depend upon the representations of the others."[27] Yet, the duty of veracity appears to be independent of the institution of contract and to rest simply on the fact that the respect due to another as a rational creature forbids misinforming him, not only for evil ends, but even for good ones. In duping another by lying to him, you deprive him of the opportunity of exercising his judgement on the best evidence available to him. It is true that the activities of a lying busybody may sometimes bring about a desirable result; but they do it by refusing to those whom they manipulate the respect due to them.

The duty of veracity is not unrestricted. It applies only to free communications between rational creatures who are fully responsible. For benevolent purposes, it is sometimes permissible to dupe children, madmen, and those whose minds have been impaired by age or illness. Yet even with regard to them, the weight of Jewish and Christian opinion is on the side of veracity, except where it is beyond doubt that a truthful statement or evasion will cause unjustifiable harm. Dr. Johnson's objection to the licence to lie to the sick that is often usurped by physicians is characteristic.

> I deny the lawfulness of telling a lie to a sick man for fear of alarming him. You have no business with consequences; you are to tell the truth. Besides, you are not sure what effect your telling him that he is in danger may have. It may bring his distemper to a crisis, and that may cure him. Of all lying, I have the greatest abhorrence of this, because I believe it has been frequently practised on myself.[28]

Of the casuistical problems about veracity, many, like the ancient problem of whether you may lie to a would-be murderer who threatens your life if you will not tell him where his quarry has gone, are solved by a correct formulation of the precept of veracity. As Kant pointed out in his *Lectures,* although he was to retract it in his *Metaphysik der Sitten,* such a criminal "knows full well that [you] will not, if [you] can help it, tell him the truth and that he has no right to demand it of [you]."[29] The principle of respect for man as a rational creature does not require that the truth be told in such a case.

The casuistical problems about veracity that are usually considered most difficult arise out of responsibility for keeping secrets. No doubt recollecting an obiter dictum of Johnson's about the concealment of the identity of Junius, that "a man ... questioned, as to an anonymous publication, may think he has a right to deny it,"[30] Boswell once asked Johnson, "Supposing the person who wrote *Junius* were asked whether he was the authour, might he deny it?" In the course of his reply, Johnson said this:

> But stay, Sir; here is another case. Supposing the authour had told me confidentially that he had written *Junius,* and I were asked if he had, I should hold myself at liberty to deny it, as being under a previous promise, express or implied, to conceal it. Now what I ought to do for the authour, may I not do for myself?[31]

This problem, however, evaporates on investigation. Admittedly, through earlier indiscretions, a man may be trapped into a position in which he might be unable to conceal his knowledge except by lying; but such cases may be disregarded. That one wrong may give rise to a situation in which other wrongs are inevitable is not a defect in morality. If, however, the man who is asked the improper question has been previously discreet, without betraying anything he may reply either by expostulating at the impropriety of the question or by an evasion: for example, by asking, "How can we make up our minds on the evidence that has been made public?"

May not such expostulations or evasions lead the questioner to the truth? Certainly, he may jump to the true conclusion. But the obligation to keep a secret cannot oblige anybody to prevent anybody else from drawing an unwarranted conclusion. Since a man who is discreet on principle would never in conversation divulge or allude to any confidential information he may have, he would expostulate or be evasive whenever *possible* confidential information was in question. Indeed, a habitually discreet man would be more likely to betray his knowledge by a lie than by a truthful evasion: that he should say anything on a matter about which he could be taken to have confidential knowledge would be suspicious.

Most of the precepts that follow from the prohibition of lying do so obviously: for example, that *no man may calumniate another,* calumny adding the wrong of lying to the wrong of detraction; and that *no man may defraud another,* that is, persuade him by false representations to give up his property. The Mosaic commandment, *Thou shalt not bear false witness against thy neighbor,* prohibits lying about another in connection with a dispute.

3.4   Contracts

The most elementary institution that gives rise to moral obligations is that of contract. A contract exists when two parties, each of which must be a rational creature or an organized group of rational creatures, enter into the following relation: one of the parties, the promiser, addresses to the other a statement that he will do a certain thing, intending his statement to be understood as binding him to do that thing, provided that the party addressed should understand it as intended, and accept it; the other, the promisee, understands the promiser's statement as it was intended to be understood, and indicates his acceptance of the promiser's utterance as binding him to do what he said he would. These conditions imply the existence of an institution, because they imply that the utterance by the promiser of a statement that he will do a certain thing is accepted by both parties as the creation of a bond. Taken literally, what is uttered is a statement about the future, a statement that may turn out to be either true or false. That there is a contract consists in the fact that both parties accept that utterance, not as a statement about the future, but as the giving of the utterer's word to see to it that his statement proves true.

What a promiser gives his word to do may be either conditional or unconditional; and the conditions may be either expressed or unexpressed. Obviously, the normal conditions of the existence of a contract are not fulfilled if the promisee misunderstands what the promiser intends. With regard to legally enforceable contracts, different conventions are adopted in different legal systems. Apart from legal contract, a promiser is morally bound to perform whatever he believed his promisee to have understood him to promise. He cannot reasonably do less; for he should have corrected any misunderstanding he was aware of. And not even his promisee can fairly claim that he has knowingly bound himself to do more.

It may be objected that this description of the institution of contract attributes a false belief to promiser and promisee alike: namely, that merely by uttering certain words a man can directly create a moral bond.[32] Moral bonds cannot be directly created, since they exist, when they do, by virtue of a moral agent's situation and his nature as a rational being. Nobody is morally bound to do anything merely because he decides or declares that he is. As F. S. McNeilly has pointed out, there is nothing intrinsically moral about the institution of contract.[33] This is shown by the fact that it is possible to promise to do wrong. It would be absurd to suppose that, by promising to commit a murder, a member of a criminal gang can place himself under a moral obligation to commit it, or even give himself a *prima facie* reason for committing it. Yet the institution of contract may be held in high regard by members of criminal gangs: a man's reputation as a member of the team may depend on his keeping his word to the others; and for him to break it may be considered not merely to be shameful but to be a serious grievance to the promisee.

The moral question, then, is this. Given that the nonmoral institution of contract exists, and given that contracts can be made, and are made, which have no moral force whatever, does the institutional bond between promiser and promisee ever constitute a moral bond?

The chief premise of the answer to this question is that, although contracts may be made which it would be wrong to keep, in itself the institution of contract is morally legitimate. And, given that the institution is legitimate, then to break a freely made promise to do something morally permissible would be wrong for a reason related to the reason why it is wrong to lie.

Yet a man's promising to do a certain thing must not be confounded with his expressing the opinion that he will do it. It is an undertaking, not a prediction. Such undertakings, like predictions, may be lies: like predictions, they are lies if they falsely represent the minds of their makers when they make them. A lying promise falsely represents its maker's intention, as a lying prediction falsely represents its maker's opinion: and lying promises are wrong for exactly the same reasons as lying expressions of opinion. Hence breaking a promise must be distinguished from lying in making it. A promiser breaks a promise only if he fails to fulfil it, even though it is in his power to fulfil it. But a lying promise is not necessarily broken; for, circumstances not having turned out as the lying promiser expected, he may change his mind and do what he promised.

Breaking a promise nevertheless resembles lying. The institution of promising enables a moral agent to make himself responsible for his failure in the future to do what it will be in his power to do. It thereby extends from the past and present to the future the range of his acts of will, and hence of his voluntary actions, about which a man can give assurances to others. It also extends his power to deceive. For by not keeping his word he will deceive the promisee about what he will choose to do, even if he had no intention of deceiving him when he gave it. Such a deception, of a promisee who has forfeited no rights, plainly fails to respect him as a rational creature. *It is* therefore *impermissible for anybody to break a freely made promise to do something in itself morally permissible.*

That promises are not usually formulated with regard to extraordinary and improbable circumstances has caused much theoretical confusion. For example, in a familiar passage in *The Right and the Good*, Sir David Ross correctly pointed out that "If I have promised to meet a friend at a particular time for some trivial purpose, I should certainly think myself justified in breaking my engagement if by doing so I could prevent a serious accident or bring relief to the victims of one." However, he misdescribed this situation as one in which "besides the duty of fulfilling promises, [he] ha[s] and recognize[s] a duty of relieving distress," and in which he thinks the latter duty to be "in the circumstances more of a duty." [34]

If a man accepts an invitation to dinner, it would be absurd for his host to understand him as having promised not to prevent a serious accident, or not to bring relief to the victims of one, if to do these things would prevent him from dining. It is a promiser's duty to express any condition to his promise which the promisee might misunderstand; but there would be no misunderstanding in such a case, and to demand that the promiser stipulate all the emergencies on which his obligation would be annulled would be vexatious as well as superfluous. To any relatively trivial promise there are a host of tacit conditions, all of which will normally be satisfied, which both promiser and promisee must and do understand; and when, as occasionally happens, such a condition is not satisfied, the promiser treats his obligation to the promisee as annulled. He has no need to consider himself as having a responsibility to fulfil it that is outweighed by a heavier responsibility.

It would be unjust to Ross not to record that, in his *Foundations of Ethics*, he treated a number of casuistical problems about promising on these traditional lines. [35] However, he did not see that such a treatment deprives his theory in *The Right and the Good* of its raison d'être.

On the whole, the Hebrew-Christian tradition has held that a contract is null and void if exacted by violence or by credible threats of death or serious injury. Notwithstanding this, some moralists have maintained that certain contracts, involving an exchange of promises, are valid even though they are forced. Cicero records a Stoic example of a forced contract of this kind: pirates capture a trader, and undertake to release him in return for an undertaking that, after release, he will send them a ransom. Cicero's own view of such cases was traditional: after being released, the trader is not bound to keep the promise exacted from him, because anybody who exacted a promise in such a way would be the common enemy of all, *Cum hoc nec fides debet nec ius iurandum esse commune.* [36]

To this both Hobbes and Whewell demurred. Holding that even a forced contract is void only if one of the parties has reason to suspect that the other will not fulfil his part, Hobbes argued that, since in releasing the trader the pirate had done his part, the trader was bound to do his, "till the civil law discharge [him]." [37] Directly controverting Cicero, Whewell added that in such cases "we keep our word, not as what is due to robbers, but as what is due to ourselves, and necessary to our character as truthful men." [38]

Here Hobbes and Whewell have fallen into error through mistaking the ground of the moral obligation to keep promises. Hobbes's mistake was to confound the institutional bond created by a contract for a bond under the "law of nature." Whewell's mistake was to confound what some nineteenth-century Englishmen thought due to themselves as Englishmen with what was in truth due to themselves as rational creatures. In exacting a promise by violence or threats of violence, a promisee forfeits his right as a rational creature to its fulfilment. A forced contract is morally void; and the promiser morally owes it neither to himself nor to anybody else to fulfil it. That his self-esteem, or the mores of some group to which he belongs, should demand that he fulfil it, is of no moral significance.

3.5 Property

The second human institution which, according to the Hebrew-Christian moral tradition, gives rise to moral duties is that of property. The institution of property in a given society is, at bottom, the system of rules agreed upon by its members as to rights to dispose of the various material things individually and collectively under their control, and the distribution among them of those rights. The variety of specific forms taken by the institution is enormous, ranging from the almost complete "communism" of some communities of primitive food-gatherers or of highly sophisticated religious devotees, to the capitalism of mid-nineteenth-century Europe and America, in which almost all rights to use or otherwise dispose of things were parcelled out among individuals or groups of individuals. This variety must not be exaggerated: even in a Shaker community each individual presumably had the exclusive right to use a certain toothbrush; and even in Mr. Gladstone's England there were public roads and public buildings.

Like contract, property is not in itself a moral institution. In the Hebrew-Christian tradition, many forms of it are considered morally permissible, and many not. The moral questions that arise with respect to it are: "What species of the institution are morally permissible, and what not?" and "What moral duties, if any, arise out of its morally permissible species?"

Since the institution of property in a given community consists not only of a set of rules or laws specifying the various rights recognized in it to dispose of things, and how those rights may pass or be passed from one proprietor to another, but also a distribution of those rights, any specific institution of property must be judged morally with respect to both.

Strictly, all rights of property are rights of disposal. However, when a given thing is considered to be at the disposal of a given person or group of persons in all except certain specified respects, with understandable looseness the thing itself is said to be his property, and he is said to be its owner or proprietor. Such property is called "tangible," and is contrasted with the "intangible" property constituted by a right to dispose of something only in a specified way. When a farmer has the right to dispose of a field in every way he wishes, except that he must yield a certain right of way through it to a neighbor, the farmer is said to have the field itself as his tangible property, his neighbor merely to have the intangible property of a certain right or use. Tangible property, in turn, is classified as movable or immovable. Movable property can be taken hold of, carried about, and consumed—clothes, food, tools, livestock. Immovable property, or land, cannot.

When the proprietor of a given piece of property, tangible or intangible, is the community at large, that piece of property is said to be "public"; when the proprietor is some individual or set of individuals, in the community or out of it, it is said to be "private." In general, the ownership of property of all kinds may be transferred from one proprietor to another on whatever terms they may agree upon. This imposes a limitation on the transfer of public property to private ownership; for, since a community is, in Burke's words, "a partnership of those who are living, those who are dead, and those who are to be born," any transaction by one generation that is disadvantageous to its successors is apt to be declared invalid for want of proper consent.

In the Hebrew-Christian tradition, the fundamental principle governing man's relation to the earth he inhabits is expressed in the great myth of Genesis 1:26.

> And God said, Let us make man in our image, after our likeness: and let them have dominion over the fish of the sea, and over the fowl of the air, and over the cattle, and over all the earth, and over every creeping thing that creepeth upon the earth.

This myth is reasonably interpreted as an affirmation that the earth and all that is on it exist for the sake of the rational beings who live in it; that is, for the sake of man. Yet mankind at large, like any limited human society, is a partnership of the living with the dead and the unborn. The right of the living to use the earth does not entitle them to despoil it. They must respect those who come after them, and not their contemporaries only.

A generation's respect for its successors will restrict its right to use the earth in two ways. First, it may not exploit natural resources in such a way as to deprive its successors of the power to provide for themselves. Second, in the Hebrew-Christian tradition, the earth is not merely a source of raw materials and fuels, but something to be contemplated and enjoyed. When God had completed the six days of creation, he looked upon his handiwork and saw that it was good. No generation of men has the right to disfigure the earth as an object of contemplative enjoyment for its successors. Of course those restrictions must be interpreted liberally. It is possible to farm the soil without exhausting it, but not without altering the landscape as an object of contemplation. And it is not possible to work a mine without doing both. A generation has discharged the duty it owes to its successors to preserve the earth, if it has taken care, as it has exhausted supplies of traditional raw materials and fuels, so to develop its technology as to be able to use other available things in their place; and if it has altered the face of the earth neither wantonly nor in such a way that the result is hideous to contemplate.[39]

As well as by the duty of preservation, which each generation of mankind owes to its successors, the permissible forms of the institution of property are limited by the duties every man owes to his fellows. Obviously, if it is impermissible for any man to enslave any other, no institution of property in which property in human beings is recognized can be morally legitimate. No social institution can create or destroy moral rights or duties. Hence the establishment of an institution in which, by the law of civil society, a human being is a piece of property neither confers any moral right to use him as such nor gives rise to any moral duty with respect to such things as the restitution of property. It was because they failed to perceive these consequences of their position that Christian moralists like Whewell, clearly though they understood that slavery was morally wrong, nevertheless mistakenly held that anybody in the antebellum United States was morally obliged to obey such laws as the Fugitive Slave Act, even though, by doing so, they would violate the moral rights of the slaves.

Some moralists have maintained that at least some private property exists by nature, that is, purely by moral law, independently of any human institution, and that no human institution is morally entitled to interfere with it. They are, I think, mistaken. It is true that private property can exist without civil society, as it has done on the frontiers of human settlement, where no system of civil or criminal justice has been established. Yet it does not follow, because there is no civil society, either that there is no society or that there are no institutions. For example, the institution of contract is only in small part regulated or upheld by civil society. The thesis that some private property exists by nature goes beyond the thesis that it may exist without civil society.

What that thesis comes to is this: although the right to use the earth is vested in mankind at large, under the moral law each human being has certain rights of appropriation; and what he appropriates by the exercise of those rights cannot morally be taken from him. Those rights of appropriation may be specified as follows. (1) Things may be appropriated only if they are by nature susceptible of it (as, say, the air we breathe is not), if appropriating them would not be contrary to the common good (as appropriating the only running water in a region inhabited by a number of people would be), and if they are not already somebody's property, whether naturally or by legitimate institution. (2) The appropriator must carry out some external action with respect to what he proposes to appropriate, which signifies his intention to others of putting that thing to his exclusive use, and he must confirm that action by, within a reasonable time, putting that thing to use. (3) What is appropriated in this way must be usable by the appropriator without spoiling. (4) Enough and as good must be left for others to appropriate. Appropriation under these conditions does not infringe upon the right to use the earth vested in mankind at large, because the earth will be adequately cultivated for the general good if the individual to whom it falls to cultivate a given piece of it is also its proprietor.

The essential element in an act of appropriation, according to this view, is labor. And the reason why such appropriation has been thought to give a moral title has been well expressed by Pope Leo XIII, in a passage reminiscent of Locke:

> when man ... turns the activity of his mind and the strength of his body towards procuring the fruits of nature, by such act he makes his own that portion of nature's field which he cultivates— the portion on which he leaves, as it were, the impress of his individuality; and it cannot but be just that he should possess that portion as his very own, and have a right to hold it without any- one being justified in violating that right. [40]

I do not question that simply to dispossess a man who has occupied and improved a previously vacant and unclaimed piece of land would violate the respect due to him as a rational creature. Yet it does not follow that he has the same moral right to the exclusive disposal of that land as to his life and liberty. He has only improved the land, not made it. And his right to appropriate it presupposes that, in general, land will be adequately used for the general good if owned by its cultivators. But what if the form of cultivation an owner chooses is not the one required by the general good? Is an original occupier who uses land as a cattle run entitled to obstruct its conversion to agriculture? Or an agriculturalist to forbid its being mined for needed minerals?

These questions arise because the happy situation in which, in appropriating something, the appropriator leaves as much and as good to be appropriated by those who come after, almost never exists. Even in societies with a moving frontier, in which it is believed to exist, it is usually an illusion. During the European expansion, from the sixteenth to the nineteenth centuries, in the Americas, Africa, and Australia, the illusion of unoccupied land was created by treating the original occupiers as nonpersons.

As soon as it is manifestly impossible for anybody who needs some natural resource to move to the frontier and appropriate it, the rights of those who are in possession of the needed resources are called in question. And inevitably, when such questions arise, civil society claims authority to decide them. For the most part, the Hebrew-Christian tradition has allowed this claim. Aquinas, for example, scrupulously refrained from asserting that there was a natural right to private property (*proprietas possessionum*), and maintained rather that, while not contrary to natural law, private property is superadded to it by human institution (*iuri naturali superadditur per adinventionem rationis humanae*).[41]

What form of the institution of property will be established in a given civil society will be determined by the political processes of that society. But specific forms of the institution of property may fall short morally in a variety of ways. Two have already been encountered. A form of proprietorship which permits owners to violate the duty of preservation they owe to future generations would be defective. And no form of proprietorship in human beings is tolerable at all, whether open or concealed. Open proprietorship in human beings, or chattel slavery, is absolutely impermissible for reasons set out in 3.3 above. Concealed proprietorship in human beings, or forced labor, while less obviously intolerable, must be condemned on the same grounds. Duties of beneficence, since they are not owed to particular individuals (see 3.3 and cf. 5.2), generate no enforceable rights; and, apart from duties of beneficence, no innocent person has any obligation to contribute to the well-being of others, except as he may freely undertake.

Property in natural resources, and in chattels other than human beings, may take forms in which labor is forced. A human being born in a society in which all land is already distributed, and in which he commands neither natural resources nor capital, cannot independently provide for his own needs. Hence it has been argued that society must compensate him for depriving him of the right to use, with others, the natural resources common to all, by affording him the opportunity to earn, by no more labor than the productive capacity of that society makes necessary, the necessities of a fully human life.[42] This has been rejected as excessive, on the ground that nobody is entitled to be compensated for more than he has lost;[43] and that very few, turned out to forage on the most fertile virgin land, would contrive even to stay alive. But that is fallacious. A society, under the system of property described, deprives every propertyless person of access to natural resources, whether or not such access would enable him to make a living. Nothing can compensate for such a deprivation short of an opportunity, within the society, to earn a living in a nonservile way.

Besides depriving the propertyless of the means of living without servitude, systems of property may be impermissible as preventing individuals from nondestructively exercising their productive powers, or as confiscating what they produce. In both these ways, and with innumerable variations, all existing civil societies abuse their authority to regulate the access of their members to natural resources. By that abuse, they have brought into question their own legitimacy.

Yet nobody can live a full human life except as a member of a morally tolerable civil society. Solitude and civil anarchy are both human evils. Hence a man owes it both to himself as a rational creature and to others, to obey even the defective laws of his civil society, while doing what he can to rectify defects and to prevent abuses. Only in extreme cases can direct disobedience, or general civil disobedience and rebellion, be justified (see 3.7).

It follows that, except in the extreme cases alluded to, the institution of property established in a civil society is to be accepted, while it lasts, by those who live under that society. Hence the familiar Mosaic prohibitions of *stealing, whether violently (robbery), or furtively (theft)*, are part of common morality. The various forms of fraud and cheating fall under precepts already considered, against lying and breach of contract; but they are considered especially evil because by them others are not only deceived, but also deprived of their property.

3.6   The Family

An institution, as I have described it in 3.3, is a system of constitutive rules. Some institutions constitute what I shall call "societies": that is, entities consisting of human beings (their members) participating in some common enterprise by virtue of their joint activity as rational agents.[44] The institutions hitherto considered are not of this kind. The existence of property sets up no society, because it requires no joint enterprise. Nor do contracts necessarily bind their parties to engage in any common enterprise, although some do. That is why human beings who are largely solitary, living in frontier conditions, may recognize one another's property and now and then make contracts with one another, without forming any society.

Of the kinds of society instituted by contracts, most are limited, and give rise to no duties that are not contractual. One kind, however, is exceptional: the family. For, while families are brought into existence by contracts between adults, they give rise to duties between those adults and their children, who are not parties to the contracts between their parents. And there is a further kind of society, namely, civil society, which is not instituted by a contract at all, but which claims to regulate all other human institutions, including those of contract, property, and the family.

The family, as traditional morality understands it, is essentially a matter of relations having to do with parenthood.[45] It is a society instituted by an agreement between male and female human beings to enter into relations from which children may be expected to be born, and to join in bringing up any children who are born or adopted. However, since any natural or adopted children are members of the family that was instituted by the joint agreement of their parents, it is not a pure society; for it has members who belong to it whether they will or no. The family, so conceived, is not the family as it is now usually conceived in sociology: as a household, the members of which are not necessarily connected by the relation of potential or actual parenthood, real or adoptive.

The chief traditional moral precepts relating to the family derive from the respect due to children as human beings. Those who voluntarily enter into sexual relations from which a child is born are reasonably held to fail to respect the child as a rational creature if they refuse to provide for its upbringing. During childhood, nobody can live a genuinely human life unless he is protected, fed, and educated; but, although human beings at large have a duty to care for abandoned children as far as they can, if they cannot, they cannot be reproached with failing to care for a helpless human being whom they have brought into existence. If these considerations are sound, the fundamental principle of morality yields a precept of parental responsibility: *It is impermissible for human beings voluntarily to become parents of a child, and yet to refuse to rear it to a stage of development at which it can independently take part in social life.* This precept presupposes that *it is impermissible for human beings voluntarily to become parents of a child they cannot rear.*

The traditional view of the permissible variety of family structures is largely derived from the precept of parental responsibility, by way of specificatory premises about what is necessary for rearing a child until it can take its independent place in social life. The chief of these premises is that a child's upbringing is impaired unless the ultimate authorities in charge of it are its natural parents, joined in a stable marital union. For a child whose natural parents cannot assume this authority, for any reason from death to temperamental unfitness, other arrangements must be made, for example, adoption; but they are considered to be intrinsically inferior. This has implications both for the permissible varieties of marriage and for their permissible duration.

Logically, there are four varieties of marital union: monogamy (one female with one male); and the various forms of polygamy—namely, polyandry (one female with more than one male), polygyny (one male with more than one female), and finally, a variety which exists only in primitive societies divided into exogamous clans and in experimental communes, more than one female with more than one male.

In the vast majority of civilized societies, the only varieties found are monogamy and polygyny. Polyandry is very rare; and the traditional moral objection to it is that, since in polyandrous families the natural father of a given child often cannot be known, polyandry makes it impossible for natural fathers to take the part they ought to take in the upbringing of their children.[46] This objection does not apply to polygyny, which was sanctioned by ancient Judaism and still is by modern Islam. The moral objection to polygyny is that it fails to respect, not the children, but the wives. In a polygynous family, as Aquinas pointed out, it is normal for wives to be reduced to a position of servitude (*uxores quasi ancillariter habentur*).[47] Hence, even in societies which permit polygyny, growth of respect for women as human beings has gone with the supersession of polygynous marriage by monogamous. Both Jewish and Christian moralists now agree that only monogamous marriage is morally permissible.

Granting its assumption that a child not brought up under the authority of its natural parents is at a disadvantage, the traditional doctrine that only monogamous marriage is permissible is well founded. But, partly because the principal form of it they considered was the manipulative one devised by Plato in *Republic*, V, 457C–461E, traditional moralists did not take sufficiently seriously the possible forms of marital union between more than one male and more than one female.[48] Consider a possible form in which a group consisting more or less equally of males and females make a compact that they will have sexual relations exclusively with one another as they may agree, that when a female intends to have a child she will ensure that its natural father is known by cohabiting only with him in the period of conception, and that authority for bringing up any child born within the group shall be shared equally between those who agreed to form it. This libertarian variation upon Plato sufficiently resembles experiments in some communes and kibbutzim for there to be some reason to think it practicable. If it is, no doubt the psychological characteristics of children reared in such a family would differ in various ways from those brought up in monogamous families; but, although most Jewish and Christian moralists would consider those differences disadvantages, it is not obvious that they are right. It is at least thinkable that children brought up in such a communal family would not fail to be respected as rational creatures.

The possibility that there may be more than one permissible family structure is confirmed by considering structures which differ with regard to the duration of the marital union. A monogamous marriage endures as long as it is impermissible for either spouse to contract another. In both Judaism and Christianity, a marriage as a rule endures until the death of either husband or wife. But, as an institution, Jewish marriage differs from traditional Christian marriage in that it contains provisions for dissolution. Since most Jewish moralists agree that those provisions may be wrongly invoked, their nature is of less moral interest than the grounds on which it is held that they may be permissibly invoked: namely, the wilful refusal or the unfitness of either party to carry out the joint agreement both made in marrying. Quite evidently, these are serious grounds, and much undeserved suffering is avoided by permitting divorce upon them. In traditional Christian marriage, by contrast, if we except the view of the Eastern church that adultery is a valid ground of divorce, such grounds have been held sufficient only for separation, not for dissolution. And there is a serious reason for the Christian institution, although nowadays few except Roman Catholic moralists acknowledge it: namely, that in many cases, to dissolve a marriage will not make the party who seeks it any happier, but will make the other party, who opposes it, much less happy.

In most investigations of divorce by moral philosophers and

theologians, it is assumed without examination that common morality must either permit the dissolution of marriage on certain grounds or forbid it. But that assumption is unfounded. The institution of dissoluble marriage (as in Judaism, Islam, and most modern post-Christian societies) and that of indissoluble marriage (as in Roman Catholicism) each cause great and avoidable suffering which the other does not. And there is no way to find out which causes the greater suffering. Accordingly, it can be pleaded on behalf of each that for the suffering it causes there is proportionate reason. Hence, since the only objection to the permissibility of either is the suffering it causes, neither can be condemned as failing to respect every human being as a rational creature. As far as common morality goes, both are permissible.

Most moralists (Whewell was a happy exception) have failed to perceive that, while it is their business to criticize institutions, it is not their business to design them. Even when, as with the bringing up of children, common morality requires that a certain human activity be carried on only within an institution of a certain kind, there may be a variety of specific forms of that institution between which it does not pronounce. Without attempting to ascertain what the variety of permissible forms of the family is, even this brief examination has given reason to think that there is a variety of them. It follows that no ground on which any specific form of the family may reasonably be held to be mandatory can be moral—can, that is, be a ground upon which that form is mandatory for human beings merely as rational creatures. Those who accept the Jewish or the Christian religious revelation, and wish to have children, are obliged to find a partner with whom to found a Jewish or Christian family; but the obligation is religious, not moral.

When a certain human activity can permissibly be carried on only in an institution of a certain kind, but in any one of several specific forms of that institution, is it permissible for civil society, or for public opinion, to deny legitimacy to any of those forms? Is it, for example, legitimate for the Republic of Ireland to deny legitimacy to morally permissible forms of dissoluble marriage? Apart from mistaken arguments to the effect that no form of dissoluble marriage is morally permissible, the usual defence of such prohibitions is that not to impose them would endanger the stability of the legally sanctioned institution. And it may be conceded not only that the stability of Roman Catholic marriage is endangered by civil laws according to which it can be dissolved with respect to all its civil effects, but also that Roman Catholics have a legitimate political interest in opposing such laws. Yet for a Roman Catholic majority to prohibit those who are not Roman Catholics from instituting their own morally permissible forms of marriage would be oppressive. Cannot the legitimate interest of any group in safeguarding its own form of marriage be met by making that form legally enforceable on the petition of either of the parties to the marriage contract?

As religions, Judaism and Christianity not only impose on their adherents a specific family structure but also prohibit them from seeking sexual gratification of any kind except in courtship with a view to founding a family, and afterwards in sexual relations between husband and wife the end of which is nondeviant, that is, genital, heterosexual intercourse. Consequently they forbid both nonfamilial heterosexual acts, such as fornication and adultery, and all deviant sexual practices, such as sodomy and bestiality. Although, as religious, these prohibitions do not concern us, most Jewish and Christian moralists have considered them to be not only religious but moral also. Can any case be made out for this?

The familiar arguments are remarkably weak. Kant, for example, put into words the horror of irregular sexual activity that appears to underlie both Jewish and Christian condemnations of it. In seeking extramarital sexual gratification, he argued, a man degrades himself to a mere means of satisfying his animal instincts, and so abandons his status as a rational creature (*seine Persönlichkeit dadurch (wegwerfend) aufgiebt*).[49] But, there is nothing impermissible per se about a man, as animal, gratifying his animal instincts; and it is incomprehensible why he should be said thereby to degrade himself to a mere means of their satisfaction, unless in satisfying them he violates some duty to himself or others. To follow Kant in describing, say, the erotic adventures of Propertius with Cynthia as "surpass[ing] even self-murder in . . . viciousness", and as a "complete abandonment . . . to animal inclination, [which] makes man not only [a mere] object of enjoyment but, still further, an unnatural thing, i.e. a loathsome [*ekelhaften*] object," would be to verge upon hysteria.[50]

The more dispassionate Thomist argument is no more persuasive: namely, that since sexual gratification is obtained from procreative acts, the natural end of which is to produce children, and since it is impermissible to produce children except in a monogamous family, anybody who seeks sexual gratification except in nondeviant intercourse as husband or wife in such a family violates the fundamental human good of procreation.[51] Two faults in this argument are patent. First, even allowing that the natural end of nondeviant intercourse is procreation, and that procreation is a great good, the argument does not show that it violates that good to engage in intercourse outside marriage in circumstances, contrived or not, in which that good cannot be attained. And second, with regard to deviant sexual acts which do not lead to procreation, it does not seem to follow, merely because sexual gratification is obtained from them as well as from nondeviant intercourse, that to seek sexual gratification in them *eo ipso* violates the human good of procreation.

Many philosophers, struck by the weakness of the traditional arguments as they are customarily formulated, have urged that, contrary to traditional morality, acts giving rise to sexual gratification, being in themselves harmless physical events in the participants' bodies, cannot as such fail to respect every human being as rational, although they may have remote harmful physical or psychological effects in virtue of which they would so fail. Sexual acts in which any participant is coerced or intimidated are of course impermissible, but as contrary to the precepts against violence. Apart from this, sexual acts are impermissible only if their physical or psychological effects are harmful. And so, acknowledging that "the sexually promiscuous life may fall far short of one's ideal," Ronald Atkinson has declared that "it need not be immoral, in a narrow but possible sense of the term, in that it need not involve harming others or treating them unjustly."[52] He takes a similar view of the homosexual life.[53]

Such reactions to the errors of the traditional moral position fall into an opposite error. Kant was wrong in thinking that to seek sexual gratification for its own sake was dehumanizing as such, and Aquinas was wrong in thinking that nonfamilial or deviant sexual acts are as such offences against the human good of procreation; but it is equally wrong to think of the sexual gratification obtained from physical acts as deriving from them solely as physical. One's imaginative awareness of the other, of the emotional response to the other expressed in one's actions, and of the other's expressive response to those actions, not only partly determines one's nonvoluntary physical reactions but makes a difference to the intensity of one's pleasure, as well as to its moral significance. And this imaginative awareness is largely nonsensory and nonphysical. In consequence, whether or not a sexual act fails to respect oneself or another as human depends not on its physical character alone, or on whether it causes physical or psychological harm, but also on its imaginative significance for those who participate in it: on what they are aware of themselves as expressing in it.

Reflecting on the intense joy he took in robbing a neighbor's pear tree with some fellow youthful delinquents, St. Augustine decided that what mattered was not the pears they stole, which they threw away, but the very act of stealing itself, done in company. "[W] hat I stole did not rejoice me, but that I stole; and it would not have rejoiced me to do it alone, nor would I have done it." [54] It appears probable that the intense, even orgastic, pleasure taken by those who engage in some perverse sexual acts, such as certain sado-masochistic ones, springs from a similar source: from abasing, in a ritual act, one's hated humanity. And if that is so, then those sado-masochistic acts are impermissible, not because of their physical character, and not because they are physically or psychologically harmful, but because they degrade humanity. Kant's insight that by sexual acts one can repudiate one's humanity is therefore vindicated, although not in the ways he described, or for his reasons.

The imaginative significance of a form of sexual activity cannot but be affected by its relation to the forms I have called "nondeviant," which, when carried on in any permissible form of marital union, are characteristically both life-affirming and nonexploitative. Hence it is probable that the imaginative significance of any sexual act will be either life-affirming, as being analogous to that of nondeviant sexuality, or life-denying. Nonsignificant "purely physical" sexuality is virtually inconceivable. Hence the general precept of common morality relating to sexual activity will be: *Sexual acts which are life-denying in their imaginative significance, or are exploitative, are impermissible.* Some specific precepts can be derived from this with fair assurance; for example, the impermissibility of certain sado-masochistic acts, or of prostitution, as life-denying; and of casual heterosexual seduction, as exploitative. On the other hand, it also seems probable that some forms of sexual activity that have been traditionally condemned need not be either life-denying or exploitative, and may therefore be permissible.

3.7   Civil Society

When human beings live together as neighbors they need to institute means whereby disputes between them may be settled according to known rules, and the settlements enforced. This is recognized in the sixth Noachite commandment, that men are to set up courts of justice. Moreover, human potentialities cannot be cultivated to the full except in association. Their associations may be societies in the strict sense: bodies set up by the joint will of their members for specified enterprises. But in addition to such pure societies, in all human civilizations that have existed, a unique and impure form of society has established itself, which is traditionally called "civil society."

The distinctive mark of a civil society is that it has territorial boundaries, within which it asserts and enforces its authority not only to determine the system of justice but also to define the terms on which all other associations, including the voluntary pure societies, shall exist. Both Judaism and medieval Christendom were exceptions to this in one respect: in them certain functions were recognized as religious, and were assigned to a priesthood, or a rabbinate, or a church; and those functions were not subject to civil authority.

General acceptance within its boundaries, whether active or passive, is essential to the existence of a civil society. Since the Middle Ages, both Jewish and Christian moralists have tended to advocate forms of civil society in which the social order is actively rather than passively accepted, and in the functioning of which as many of the inhabitants of its territory as possible participate. However, a civil society may be legitimate even though these conditions do not obtain.

Rousseau and Hegel distinguished civil society (*bürgerliche Gesellschaft*), which Hegel described as "the external state [*äusseren Staat*], the state based on need, the state as understanding thinks of it," from the true state (*Staat*), "the actuality of concrete freedom" in which "personal individuality and [the citizens'] particular interests not only achieve their complete development" but also "pass over of their own accord into the interest of the universal" and "know and will the universal."[55] The Hebrew-Christian tradition has no theory of the state, in this sense, because it dismisses as a delusion the notion that such a thing could exist. No actual state is more than *ein äusserer Staat*—a civil society.[56]

As Karl Marx pointed out, no civil society can be stable unless its structure is harmonious with the system of property instituted within it. A large part of any system of public justice has to do with laws, civil and criminal, about property. And if the political system of a given society is not in harmony with its economic system, inevitably a struggle will take place and one system or the other be modified to remove the cause of strife. However, Marx's view that the outcome of such struggles is always determined by the economic system is probably false.

All members of a civil society are morally at liberty to work for what they take to be desirable changes in it, whether in the established system of property, or in its political-legal system. Few political questions of either kind can be decided on moral grounds alone. With respect to the political struggles by which decisions upon such questions are reached, common morality requires only that those who take part in them treat their adversaries honestly and without violence. *Given that neither the established system of property nor the legal-political system seriously violates anybody's moral rights,* since the possibilities of human life can be much more adequately realized in even an imperfect civil society than in a state of anarchy, the principle of culture and the principle of beneficence alike imply that *it is impermissible for anybody within a civil society to disobey its laws.*

Even when a civil society, either in the system of property established in it or in its legal-political system, does infringe somebody's moral rights, disobedience ought generally to be passive. It is a simple deduction from the very nature of morality that *it is impermissible to obey any law of civil society, if such obedience would contravene the moral law.* But active disobedience, or *rebellion, is permissible* according to the principles of culture and of beneficence *only if the moral wrong done by the civil society rebelled against is great, and if it can reasonably be predicted that the rebellion will succeed in righting the wrong, and that what is gained by the change will compensate for the sufferings and unintended moral wrongs that occur even in a just rebellion.*

Civil societies have various relations with one another which can give rise to quarrels. During the whole of recorded history such quarrels have been numerous, and most of them have been sordid on one or both sides. The profound horror with which Christianity has traditionally regarded the world is abundantly justified in the history of relations between civil societies, and especially in the history of their wars. In many wars, perhaps in most, both sides act so foolishly and wickedly that it is, in Dr. Johnson's phrase, difficult to settle the proportion of iniquity between them. In some, however, most obviously in those in which a major power intervenes in the affairs of a minor one, or resorts to military force to sustain a hegemony gained in the past by violence, there is a just as well as an unjust side. The precepts which permit, or even require, that in certain circumstances one may resort to force against another, are not suspended when those circumstances arise in relations between civil societies.

Where one civil society infringes the rights of another, whether by invading its territory, or molesting its members, or in any other way that interferes seriously with its existence as a peaceable society, it is morally permissible for a society whose rights are thus infringed to defend itself by force of arms, and for other societies to go to its help, provided that the force employed is no more than is needed for its defensive purpose. One consequence of Christianity has been that professedly Christian states bent upon wars of aggression usually manufacture pretexts which, were they true, would justify wars of defence. They stand condemned, because a just cause for a defensive war cannot excuse a war of conquest.

Jewish and Christian moralists are generally agreed that, *in a just war, a civil society may impose military service on its members.* Some Christians, it is true, maintain that no war may be just and that all service in war is morally wrong. However, most Christians (rightly in my opinion) consider those opinions to be erroneous, and not justified by the Hebrew-Christian fundamental principle. What is due to those whose consciences, in all sincerity, are mistaken in this way, will be considered in the next chapter.

How must a member of a civil society act, if his society embarks upon a war claiming that it is just, and if he is not convinced that that claim is true? It is generally agreed—in view of history nothing else is possible—that nobody is entitled simply to accept his society's word on such a matter. It is his duty to try to establish the truth for himself. His attempt to do so may either, in his own judgement, succeed or fail. What if it fails? What, that is, if he cannot, to his own satisfaction, determine whether the war is just or not?

Moral theologians generally agree that nobody may rightly

volunteer to serve in a war unless he is convinced that it is a just one. If, however, his society requires him to serve, under threat of death (the usual sanction) or other severe penalty (in most English-speaking countries, it is a long term of imprisonment), it is generally agreed that it is not wrong for him to comply, provided that he honestly believes that the cause may be just. He is in duty bound to obey lawful civil authority, and he may not reject a command of civil authority as morally unlawful in a case which he acknowledges to be doubtful. [57]

His doubt, however, must be genuine. Perhaps nothing has brought more discredit upon the various branches of organized Christianity than the readiness of their leaders to act as recruiting officers, and their extreme reluctance to denounce wars that are plainly unjust. War is so horrible an evil that only a very clear and great cause can justify it; and when such a cause exists, it should not be difficult to show it. One difficulty is that in most civil societies the reputation of the authorities for veracity is so low that the evidence they present may be suspected of being fabricated, even when it is not.

When, as will usually be the case, a member of a civil society can to his own satisfaction determine whether a given war is just or unjust, his duty is clear. *If it is just, it is permissible to volunteer to serve* in it, provided that no other duty prevents it; *and it is impermissible not to accept lawful conscription to serve. If it is unjust, it is impermissible to serve under any circumstances.* As Richard Baxter put it:

> In a bad cause, it is a dreadful thing to conquer, or to be con-
> quered. If you conquer, you are a murderer of all that you kill;
> if you are conquered and die in the prosecution of your sin, I need
> not tell you what you may expect. [58]

4

Second-Order Precepts

4.1 Voluntariness and Moral Responsibility

Having determined the principal precepts concerning the permissibility or impermissibility of nonjudicative actions, it is now time to take up second-order questions about acts of blaming or not blaming their doers for doing them. Our analysis in 2.3 has shown that a prescription of practical reason that somebody not do an action of a certain kind does not entail a prescription that he be blamed if he does it. A deed may be impermissible, and yet its doer be inculpable; and a doer may be culpable even though his deed is permissible.

In what follows, much of the analysis of 2.2 will be assumed. In particular it will be presupposed that a human being is the agent-cause of his actions. Agents will be held to cause only: (1) what they do, and (2) what follows in the course of nature from their intervening in what is going on. When what they do is to abstain from intervening, they will be held to allow to happen whatever follows in the course of nature from their abstention, but not to cause it. And since it is often possible to foresee (although not by calculations according to laws of nature) how others will react to situations brought about by a certain action, it will be held that an agent may do something, foreseeing that something will follow which he neither causes nor allows.

The senses of the words "action" and "act" are not discriminated in the same ways by all philosophers. Father Eric D'Arcy, in *Human Acts*, to which my debt will become obvious, takes "action," with respect to human beings, to stand for any movement of a man's body, or in it, whether that movement is ascribable to him as doer (as his action in running is) or not (as his heartbeat is not).[1] By contrast, he takes "acts" to stand for actions that are ascribable to a man as doer. Hence he takes human actions to be a genus, divisible into acts (processes of a man's body or in it that are ascribable to him as doer) and nonacts (processes of a man's body or in it not ascribable to him as doer). A man's running is an action that is also an act; his heartbeat is an action that is not an act.

Unfortunately, this distinction is not fine enough for our purposes. First, it excludes the possibility of purely mental acts. Multiplying 364 by 73 in one's head is as good a specimen of something done by a human being as running or jumping. Yet although some philosophers make bold to assert that mental acts are brain processes, partly relying on the well-established neurophysiological hypothesis that different mental acts have different processes in the central nervous system as counterparts, whether or not multiplying numbers in one's head is a genuine act seems in no way to depend on the truth or falsity of the mind-brain identity theory.

Once the existence of mental acts is conceded, a further division becomes necessary. Consider the various verbs of sensation, such as "sees," "hears," and "tastes." All can be used in saying what, in some sense, human beings "do." So can verbs of emotion, like "loves," "fears," and "hates," although we need not become entangled in the complexities to which, as Ryle has shown, they lead. Yet what a man does in seeing the table laid, hearing the kettle whistle, or tasting his tea is very different from what he does in working a sum in his head, in that it does not involve full agency. What a man sees, hears, or tastes is partly a matter of what he looks at, listens to, or puts in his mouth; but given that he is in a certain place, looking at something, or listening to something, or with something in his mouth, what he sees, hears, or tastes is simply the natural actualization of a sensory power, in no way under his control as agent. Acts which are natural actualizations of bodily, sensory, imaginative, or emotional powers are ascribable to human beings as things they "do," but human beings do not "do" them as agents. In working a sum in his head, a man does something as an agent; in seeing the teacups on the table, he does not.

This classification can be generalized and extended. Actions, in the sense of processes consisting in movements of human bodies or in them, are divisible into acts and nonacts. There appears to be no parallel division of the processes that go on in human minds. Even passive processes like feeling dejected, are things I "do" in the wide sense, and are therefore acts. Both bodily and mental acts, however, are in turn divisible into acts in which the doer is an agent and acts in which he is not. Clearly, it is desirable to register this distinction in our terminology. One way of doing so (adopted by Wilfrid Sellars, among others)[2] is to refer to human acts in which the doer is an agent as "human actions." An obvious objection is that "action" is already in use, in a generic sense, as standing for all bodily processes, whether or not they are even ascribable to the individuals in whose bodies they occur. However, this objection is not decisive. There are virtually no contexts in which the use of the word "action," qualified or not by the epithet "human," as referring to acts in which the doer is agent, would be misunderstood as referring to bodily processes as such. Nor are observations about the action of the liver or the pancreas likely to be taken to be about anything done as agents by the possessors of those organs. Accordingly, in what follows, acts done by a human being as an agent, as opposed to acts that are natural actualizations of bodily, sensory, imaginative, or emotional powers, will be referred to as "(human) actions."

Whatever a human being does as an agent, he does as a rational creature. Hence, in his classical analysis of human action, which underlies much traditional moral theory, Aquinas described human actions as *operationes rationales*,[3] and maintained that every *operatio rationalis* is a *voluntarium*, or voluntary act, which he followed Aristotle in defining as an act originating within the doer and done knowingly or wittingly.[4]

The nonoccurrence of a human act that is not an action cannot be an act. Since acts that are not actions are the natural actualizations of such human powers as the power of sight, the nonoccurrence of a certain act of seeing in a creature with the power of sight is the nonactualization of that power, and so not an act. With actions it is otherwise. Whether or not a man sees a teacup, given that he is capable of seeing one and that he is looking at a tea-table, depends solely on whether a teacup is on the table; but whether he picks up a teacup from the table, given that he is capable of it and in a position to do it, depends solely on himself. Whether he picks it up *or not* is something of which he is agent-cause. Consequently, his not picking it up is as much an exercise of his power to pick it up as his picking it up would be. In general, agency is exercised in omitting to do something, or in abstaining from doing it, as well as in doing it. And so Aquinas defined as a *voluntarium* everything which proceeds from the will, whether *directe sicut ab agente* or *indirecte sicut a non agente.*[5]

Many acts, such as for example a cough, may be either full human actions, and so voluntary, or not. Acts which are not voluntary are either nonvoluntary or involuntary. When a man coughs deliberately, to attract attention, he has performed an action—a voluntary act. When he coughs simply as a bodily reaction to an irritation in his throat, without caring whether he does so or not, he has performed a nonvoluntary act. When, however, he coughs as an uncontrollable reaction to an irritation in his throat that he has tried to suppress, his act in involuntary. This traditional classification is technical and does not accord with the colloquial use of the English adverbs "voluntarily" and "involuntarily," which has been investigated by Gilbert Ryle, J. L. Austin, and others.[6]

One striking way in which the traditional technical sense of "voluntary" and its cognates diverges from the colloquial use has to do with duress. In the technical sense, except for cases in which his body is moved or prevented from moving by external physical force, as when he is dragged or pushed, or imprisoned or fettered, or when extreme pain has deprived him of the power to determine what he will do, as when he has accidentally dipped his hand in boiling water, neither a man's moving nor his not moving can be rendered involuntary by violence, fear, or desire. Colloquially, a man is said not to have joined the army voluntarily if he was conscripted; but in the technical sense, what a man does even under threat of death or torture is voluntary: it depends wholly on him what he does in that situation. As Aquinas observed with reference to an example of Aristotle's, when a ship's captain orders the cargo to be jettisoned for fear of foundering, his act is voluntary, because it orginates with him (*principium eius est intra*).[7] In what follows, "voluntary" and its cognates will be used in these technical senses, and not colloquially.

The Hebrew-Christian conception of action as voluntary, in the sense defined, traverses the most familiar contemporary psychological paradigm for the explanation of human behavior, to which Goldman has given the name "want-and-belief causation."[8] According to that paradigm, every human action is explicable as the causal outcome of the agent's wants and beliefs at the time of acting. Roughly, wanting something to come about is conceived as a tendency, of a certain strength, to do what will bring that thing about, given the belief that it is feasible to bring it about without frustrating any stronger want. Whether a want in fact gives rise to any action at all thus depends on the agent's beliefs and the nature and strength of his other wants. Obviously, this rough model may be developed in several different ways. But one thing is common to them all: that every human action is as simply a function of its agent's wants and beliefs at the time of acting as the path followed by an iron ball rolled on a table between several electromagnets is a function of its initial velocity, of the resistance offered by the air and any unevenness in the table's surface, and of the attractive forces of the various magnets.

By contrast, the conception of action as voluntary in the traditional sense treats wants (or desires, as moralists usually prefer to say) as motives for action, not as causal determinants of it. Motives, so understood, are not forces of which actions are resultants but rather considerations in view of which an agent acts.[9] If an agent were to do no more than try to satisfy the desires he finds himself to have, then his actions would of course accord with the want-and-belief paradigm. However, it is open to every agent to conceive a variety of ideal possibilities, as to what he himself, his household, his neighborhood, or anything else might be made to be; and, whether or not he finds in himself any desire to realize any of those possibilities, if he chooses, he can attempt to realize some of them. In making the attempt he will as a consequence find himself wanting all the things necessary for their realization; but those wants will be, in Thomas Nagel's useful word, "motivated."[10] That is, they will arise solely from his attempt to achieve certain ends he has set himself; and his setting himself those ends need not be determined by further unmotivated wants and desires, and seldom seems to be.

The most important thing to be said about these opposed conceptions of human action is that they are paradigms: that is, conceptual systems in terms of which the empirical facts of human behavior are interpreted. Empirical evidence certainly bears upon the question whether either is true, but not in any direct way. However, prejudice in favor of the want-and-belief paradigm is so strong that its *prima facie* empirical weakness should be pointed out. It appears to have arisen from observation, not of human life, but of human and animal behavior in simple situations susceptible of laboratory study: in particular, of choice situations in which the task is to choose between different desired objects or different ways of obtaining the same desired object. Yet serious human decisions, such as what professional career to follow; or whether to join a political party, and if so which; or, more important still, whether to continue to practise the religion in which you were brought up, when you find it hard either to believe its tenets or to disbelieve them, are none of them at all like deciding which cake to take from a plate offered to you, or whether to take the train or the bus to town.

One obvious difference is that when a man considers even so straightforward a question as what professional career to follow, the various options will not as a rule present themselves to him as more or less to his taste, as cakes on a plate do. It is quite possible that he will have no inclination to any. Yet he will, if he is intelligent, recognize that the decision is important. He may ask himself: What in the long run will satisfy me most deeply? And then he may be struck with the thought: Could I be deeply satisfied with the result of any choice founded on such a calculation? Wouldn't it be better to ask what is most worth doing; for, if I choose that, I shan't waste my life? It is gratuitous to represent such an inner debate, in which a man is making up his mind what ends to set himself, as merely a process of calculating the different outcomes of his various possible choices, prudently preparing for the moment of decision, when his strongest desire will have its way.

A motive is not a causal determinant of an action, but rather, in Roy Lawrence's convenient approximation, a circumstance because of which a man may take action.[11] One is apt to overlook this if one confines one's inquiry to the motives people have in doing what they do, and neglects cases, familiar in detective fiction, in which several people have motives for doing something but only one of them in fact does it. When the police are compiling their list of suspects, they may even find a man who had a motive for committing the crime—the victim, say, had seduced his daughter—but who protests that he did not know that he had.

Motives have been variously classified. Anscombe drew attention to the difference between forward-looking motives—consequences of contemplated actions seen as desirable; and backward-looking motives—circumstances in the past seen as calling for some action in one's present situation. Motives of ambition and greed are of the first kind, those of gratitude and revenge are of the second. Another classification is into apparent and ulterior. When an action is of such a kind that it is natural to take it as being done from a certain motive, forward-looking or backward-looking, the question may arise as to whether it really is being done from its "apparent" motive, or from some less obvious "ulterior" one.[12]

However complicated the preceding analysis has been, and however much at certain points it affronts contemporary prejudices, most of it has been worked out by others, and all of it has been derived from traditional philosophical sources. But now we must turn to matters calling for novel treatment, and of which no novel treatment yet proposed satisfies anybody. As traditionally conceived, a human act is an action, and hence voluntary, if it is the bringing about of something by a human agent, or the omission to bring it about, the agent being aware of what he is doing. But if, as I have presupposed, human actions are individual events, there is a difficulty. Since there is no end to the possible true descriptions of any individual, only an agent capable of infinite knowledge can know everything there is to know about any of his actions. Man is emphatically not such an agent. How, then, can any of his acts be voluntary, or even, strictly speaking, actions?

The obvious way out of these difficulties is to treat the predicable " . . . is voluntary" as signifying what some logical theorists call an "intensional function." Most predicables, like " . . . is red" or " . . . is to the left of . . . " signify extensional functions: that is, if they yield a proposition having a certain truth-value when their blanks are filled up with designations of certain individuals, they will yield propositions of the same truth-value under any substitution of one designation of the same individual for another. The designations "my earliest copy of *The Concept of Mind*" and "my earliest copy of Ryle's masterpiece" are different designations of the same individual object. And therefore, since a true proposition results when the blank in " . . . is red" is filled up with one of them, namely, "My earliest copy of *The Concept of Mind* is red," a true proposition also results when the other is substituted for it, namely, "My earliest copy of Ryle's masterpiece is red." By contrast, intensional functions, among which are numbered all functions signified by predicables whose sense has to do with the relation of a mind to its objects, do not necessarily yield propositions of the same truth-value when a given blank in them is filled up with different designations of the same individual. To use William Kneale's classical example in *The Development of Logic*: Oedipus chose to kill the haughty stranger who ordered him to give way on the narrow road from Delphi to Phocis, but he did not choose to kill his father, although the haughty stranger was in fact his father.[13] The two action-descriptions, "the killing of the haughty stranger who ordered him to give way on the narrow road from Delphi to Phocis" and "the killing of his father," are both true definite descriptions of one and the same action performed by Oedipus; but propositions of different truth-values are generated when one of those designations is substituted for the other in the blank of the predicable "Oedipus chose to attempt...."

Intensional functions like that signified by "Oedipus chose to attempt ...," therefore, in Kneale's words, "cannot be satisfied by an object as such, but only by an object considered as falling under a certain description."[14] Some philosophers disapprove of Kneale's conclusion, on the ground that whether a predication is true or false would be indeterminate if it should vary with how an individual referred to by its subject-term is described. They are mistaken. When its terms are changed, a predication is itself changed; but its truth or falsity in its original form is unaffected. The predicable "Oedipus chose to attempt ..." is truly predicated of the killing of the haughty stranger who ordered Oedipus to give way on the narrow road from Delphi to Phocis, inasmuch as it truly falls under that description. No redescription of that event as "the killing of Oedipus's father" can affect that truth in the least. Nor can anybody's choice of descriptions affect the truth of any proposition not about that choice, although it can limit the range of the true propositions he can express.

Another way of expressing Kneale's conclusion would be to say that certain intensional functions cannot be satisfied by any object as such but only by an object inasmuch as it has certain properties, or only by an object *qua* having certain properties. Purely for reasons of convenience, I have followed Kneale's way of putting it, which Anscombe anticipated for the intensional functions "X performs ... with the intention ..." and "X intentionally performs...."[15]

If, following this line of thought, the predicables "X voluntarily performs ..." and "... is voluntary" are taken to signify intensional functions, it is possible to solve the problem of how an act can be voluntary, given that there is no end to the possible true descriptions of it, and that a man can only voluntarily do what he is aware of doing. An act will be said to be voluntary only as falling under the descriptions which its agent is aware it falls under.

But there is a further difficulty. According to the traditional analysis, every human action is, as such, voluntary. Does it follow that an act is a human action only as falling under such descriptions as its agent is aware it falls under? Certainly this is not how traditional moralists spoke of human actions, or how they are spoken of colloquially. In the familiar Aristotelian example, which Aquinas refers to, a man who, thinking himself to be shooting at game, shoots and kills his enemy, is colloquially said to have killed his enemy accidentally, and in the traditional terminology is said to have done so nonvoluntarily;[16] but, both colloquially and traditionally, what he thus accidentally and nonvoluntarily did is recognized as having been a genuine human action. It is not like a heartbeat, an act of sensation, or an involuntary cough. It therefore seems to follow that the predicable, ". . . is a human action," both colloquially and traditionally signifies an extensional function. But if ". . . is a human action" is extensional, and ". . . is voluntary" is intensional, it is impossible that "X is a human action" should entail "X is voluntary" under all substitutions for X of another designation of the same act.

Davidson has proposed a way in which this difficulty can be removed. Instead of saying that if an act is a human action then it is voluntary *simpliciter*, what must be said is that if an act is a human action then there is a true description of it such that it is voluntary as falling under that description. Thus, "although the criterion of agency is, in the semantic sense, *intensional*, the expression of agency is itself purely *extensional*."[17] That certain events are human actions, deeds of certain agents, is true no matter how they are designated, even though those events can only truly be said to be voluntary as falling under certain descriptions.

The distinctions drawn in 2.2 all hold for the descriptions under which an action is voluntary. If somebody knows his circumstances to be C, and what he is doing to be of kind A, then his action is voluntary under the description "doing A in C." And if he knows that a consequence of kind E would follow in the course of nature on his doing A in a certain situation, then his doing A in that situation is voluntary under either the description "causing E" or the description "letting E happen," according as doing A is an intervention or an abstention. On the other hand, if in voluntarily doing A he divines that E will come about, not in the course of nature, but as a causal consequence of the reactions of others who are not his agents, his action is not voluntary under either the description "causing E" or the description "letting E happen."

Since an individual action is impermissible if and only if it falls under some description such that any action falling under that description is impermissible, and permissible if and only if it falls under no such description, the criterion of permissibility is intensional, although, like that of agency, its expression is extensional. This has consequences for the application of the fundamental principle to second-order questions. When a human being does something, he does not know, with respect to many of the descriptions his action in fact falls under, that it does fall under them. Inasmuch as it falls under them, his action is at best fortunate and at worst unfortunate; for, in his situation, no act of will on his part to abstain from an action falling under any of those descriptions can as such affect what he does. Even if, as he was about to strike the haughty stranger, Oedipus had called to mind the evil of parricide, and had willed neither then nor ever to commit it, his so willing could not, as such, have stayed his hand: how could willing not to kill his father have made, as such, any difference to his striking somebody he did not even suspect to be his father?

If an action under a certain description is such that its agent would have done it even had he, in doing it, willed not to, then an action under that description is one from which, as such, he cannot abstain at will. He may, it is true, abstain from it under other descriptions. Oedipus could not have abstained at will from an action under the description "killing his father"; but he could have abstained from killing his father by abstaining from any action falling under the description "using potentially deadly force on another human being." Now blaming somebody for an action is, in part, holding him answerable for it. Hence, since a rational agent, as such, controls his actions in the light of his knowledge of what they are, to hold him answerable for his actions under descriptions he does not know they fall under is to demand that he answer for something for which, as a rational agent, he cannot answer. And that would be to refuse to respect him as a rational creature.

And so we arrive at the principle: *It is impermissible to blame anybody for an action except as falling under a description under which it is voluntary, that is, done knowingly.* Or, in abbreviated form: *Actions are culpable only as falling under descriptions under which they are voluntary, that is, done knowingly.* This explains the importance of deliberateness in traditional moral thought. Of acting deliberately, J. L. Austin has written that

> I act *deliberately* when I have deliberated—which means that I have stopped to ask myself, 'Shall I or shan't I?' and then decided to do X, which I did. That is to say, I weighed up, in however rudimentary (sometimes almost notional or fictional) a fashion, the pros and cons. And it is understood that there must be some cons, even when what I do deliberately is something unexceptionable, such as paying my taxes. . . . Deliberation is not just any kind of thinking prior to action.[18]

An action is deliberate only if there are considerations against it, and it is done after they have been weighed. Unless they deliberate, agents often cannot know what they do.

4.2 Intention and Purpose

In the Hebrew-Christian moral tradition, a moral agent is held answerable not only for what he voluntarily does but also for what he intends. And this has given rise, in the last hundred years or so, to various proposals to simplify the traditional position by treating permissibility and impermissibility as, strictly speaking, properties of what is intended, not of what is voluntarily done. These proposals have not been made with the same motives. Within the Hebrew-Christian tradition itself, the scope of what an agent intends is held to be in certain respects narrower than that of what he voluntarily and knowingly does; and the usual intention is to restrict what he is answerable for. Outside this tradition, the proposal is commonly made in conjunction with Sidgwick's further proposal "to include under the term 'intention' all the consequences of an act that are foreseen as certain or probable";[19] and the foreseen consequence has been enormously to enlarge the bounds of moral responsibility.

In J. L. Austin's persuasive analysis, what is central to the concept of intention is that intended actions are, "as it were," done according to plan, "only of course nothing necessarily or, usually, even faintly, so full-blooded as a plan proper."[20] His characteristic example is that of a cashier who dips into the till for the purpose of playing the ponies but with the intention of putting the money back. In the traditional analysis, as found in Aquinas for example, the plan "as it were" is to accomplish an end; and intending is consequently identified with willing an action for the sake of an end.[21] This suggests a modification of Austin's analysis. An action may be "as it were" done according to several concomitant plans. Such plans fall into two classes: they are plans either to accomplish an end by means of the action in question, or they are plans to bring something about in view of that action but not by means of it. Plans of the first class are plans to accomplish a purpose, except when what is planned is done for its own sake, and wantonly.[22]

An agent's purpose is a state of affairs the coming about of which is the (an) end to which the plan of action is directed; his intention is so to act that his plan will go into effect and not miscarry. Austin summed up the distinction well: "I act for or on (a) purpose, I achieve it; I act with the intention, I carry it out, I realize it."[23] I purpose that something shall come about, I intend so to act that it will come about.

Because intending and purposing often go with calculating the effects of actions, some philosophers have jumped to the conclusion that to every intention that is carried out there corresponds a causal consequence of an intentional action. But that is a mistake. It is true that, like causal chains, intentions may be ordered serially. A man may (ultimately) purpose that G_3 come about; and he may intend so to act that G_2 will come about, because he calculates that, if it does, the coming about of G_3 will be its effect; and he may further intend so to act that G_1 will come about, because he calculates that, if it does, G_2 will be its effect. Suppose that his calculations are correct, and that he also correctly calculates that, by doing X, he will cause G_1 to come about. Then, if he does X, his action will be correctly describable also as the causing of G_1, the causing thereby of G_2, and finally as the causing thereby of G_3. And this causal order will correspond to the order of his intentions: he did X with the intention of causing G_1, he caused G_1 with the intention of causing G_2, and he caused G_2 with the intention of causing G_3. In such a case, as G. E. M. Anscombe has pointed out, "the last term we give in such a series gives the intention *with* which the act in each of its other descriptions was done, and this intention so to speak swallows up all the preceding intentions *with* which earlier members of the series were done."[24] But from none of this does it follow that the intention with which an agent does something must correspond to what he can cause, or believes he can cause.

Consider the following example. Smith is playing stud poker with Jones and Robinson. His hole cards give him a hand that is probably stronger than Jones's, whose face-up cards are stronger than his. At the second round of betting, he checks, foreseeing that Jones will raise heavily and that Robinson, who has marked Jones as a bluffer, will stay in the game. Jones does raise, and Robinson stays, enabling Smith to achieve his purpose, of winning a large pot. Now there is no natural science, existing or in prospect, according to the laws of which, given the situation, Jones's and Robinson's actions must follow Smith's; and if Hebrew-Christian presuppositions about the nature of human action are sound, there can be no such laws. Their actions, then, are not causal consequences of his. Yet there can be no doubt that he acted as he did with the intention of creating a situation in which they would act as they did, and thereby of achieving his purpose; or that he carried out his intention. Hence an agent can intend, not only to cause certain events to come about, but to create situations in which others will act as he foresees, even though he neither can cause their reactions nor believes that he can.

It has already been remarked (2.2) that, as colloquially used, expressions of the form "consequence of doing X" are not confined to the *causal* consequences of doing X, but are applied to any event that would not have come about had something else occurred. Hence, speaking colloquially, Jones's and Robinson's actions in the poker game may be described as "consequences" of Smith's. In this wide sense of the word "consequence," Sidgwick's proposal to include under the term "intention" all the consequences of an action that are foreseen as certain or probable would entail, as in our example in 2.2, that a Christian who, given a choice between apostasy and martydom, refuses apostasy, intends his own death and persecution. Such a result seems to me intolerable.

An agent's intentions are involved in the plans (often less than full-blooded) according to which he acts; and in following a plan, he may foresee many consequences, in the wider sense, that lie outside it. Thus a Christian may foresee that by following his plan of avoiding apostasy, his death will result; but he does not plan that it should result. And since, except in the case of wanton actions, the plans according to which an agent acts will be in terms of means and ends, his intentions will be to promote various proximate or ultimate ends by means of various actions: whether by causing them to come about or by causing situations to come about in which the reactions of others will promote them. An action is intentional if and only if it is done with an intention: either of doing it for its own sake or of promoting some other end by doing it. But it will be done for its own sake, or for the sake of promoting some other end, only by virtue of possessing certain characteristics. And, since it is an individual event, those characteristics will not be all it possesses. Inasmuch as it possesses other characteristics—those which are irrelevant to its being done for its own sake or for the sake of something else—it does not fall within its agent's plan or within his intention. Hence it follows that, like "... is voluntary," the predicables "... is intentional" and "... is done by A with the intention that X come about by means of it" signify intensional functions. They are true of a given action only under certain descriptions.

It should also be evident that descriptions under which a given action is voluntary are sometimes not descriptions under which it is intentional. Austin has given the following example. By exacting the payment of a debt, a creditor foresees that he will cause the ruin of his debtor. He does not desire to ruin him; but, on the other hand, he has calculated that, if he is not repaid, he himself will suffer severely. So, with a heavy heart, he exacts repayment. There can be no doubt that, under the description "ruining his debtor," the creditor's action is voluntary: the exaction of repayment originates with him, and he is well aware that it will cause his debtor's ruin. But, ruining his debtor is no part of the plan according to which he acts. He would cheerfully agree to anything, except nonpayment, that would save his debtor. Therefore, under the description "ruining his debtor" his action is not intentional.

Can it be maintained, as some would like to maintain, that because the creditor's action is not intentional under that description, then, even if it should be morally impermissible to ruin his debtor, he would not be culpable for doing so? I do not see how it can. In choosing to act according to a certain plan, a man chooses thereby to bring about *all* the causal consequences of doing so, whether or not they fall within the plan. He cannot escape responsibility for his choice by pleading that he did not desire or intend to do what he voluntarily did. And this is the traditional Hebrew-Christian position. The distinction drawn by some post-Reformation Roman Catholic casuists between the directly and the indirectly voluntary, corresponding to what is intended as opposed to what is brought about voluntarily but unintentionally, is therefore untenable. It is not drawn by Aquinas.[25]

Yet intentions have a distinctive place in common morality. For just as many voluntary actions are not intentional, so many intentions miscarry and are not realized in action. As we have seen (in

4.1), it is impermissible to blame somebody for a voluntary action except under a description under which it is done knowingly. That it falls under other descriptions is his good or bad fortune. By parity of reasoning, since the miscarriage of an intention is not something of which the person who makes that intention can know as he makes it, that it miscarries is his good or bad fortune. But an agent is not answerable for his good or bad fortune. Hence he must answer for his intentions to do wrong, even if by good fortune they miscarry. And so it is a general rule that if an action of a certain kind is impermissible, then it is impermissible to intend to do it, even if that intention miscarries.

Yet there is a difficulty in this. If it can be impermissible to intend something, as well as voluntarily to do it, an apparent contradiction arises in applying certain moral precepts. As we have seen (3.1-2), it is permissible to cause certain human evils (for example, pain, mutilation, even death) as a byproduct of actions that are required by respect either for oneself or for other human beings (for example, self-defence, the defence of others, or saving oneself or others from worse evils), even though it is impermissible to cause those evils under other circumstances. In addition, as we have also seen (3.3), not only doing what it is one's duty to do, but declining an unreasonable burden, may make it permissible to allow some evil to come about, or to act foreseeing that the reaction of others will bring it about, even though it would be impermissible to do so under other circumstances. Now, if intending something can be impermissible, it will be possible to do something it is one's duty to do, say to defend an innocent from violence, but with no other intention than to do something impermissible, say, to harm the violator. Are these not cases in which it is both impermissible not to do an action (say, not to stand idly by while violence is done to another) and yet impermissible to do it (say, to do violence to the violator for some reason not sanctioned by morality)?

Abelard gave this memorable illustration:

> [T]he same thing is often done by different people, justly by one and wickedly by another, as for example if two men hang a criminal, one out of zeal for justice, and one out of hatred arising from an old enmity. Although it is the same action of hanging, and although they indeed do what it is good to do and what justice requires, yet, through difference of intention, by the different men, the same thing is done by one badly, by the other well.[26]

The solution of this difficulty is that every rational agent has the power to determine his intentions. A man may have a motive to do wrong (as had Abelard's hangman, whose victim was an old enemy), but it is in his power not to intend to act on it. Abelard's hangman may, despite temptation, hang the criminal as his duty requires—namely, humanely; and thàt intention will naturally show itself in various ways.

It is, therefore, *impermissible to do what it is impermissible to intend*: one may not do even the right deed for the wrong reason. And there was no error in our earlier conclusion, that *it is impermissible to intend what it is impermissible to do*: that a bad intention miscarries does not excuse it.

4.3   Ignorance: Culpable and Inculpable

The second-order precepts of common morality all depend on the principle that actions are culpable only as falling under descriptions under which they are voluntary, that is, done knowingly. A stronger principle is sometimes advanced, which makes use of Aquinas's doctrine that ignorance makes involuntary those actions which would not have been done without it (*ignorantia de se habet quod faciat actum quem causat involuntarium esse*):[27] namely, that impermissible actions are inculpable only if they are involuntary, that is, would not have been done but for the ignorance of their doers. However, our previous argument shows it to suffice for inculpability that an action be nonvoluntary, that is, that it be possible that it would not have been done but for its doer's ignorance.

Two kinds of ignorance are pertinent to culpability: ignorance that an action falls under a nonmoral description, that is, a description which does not involve the concept of moral permissibility; and ignorance that it falls under a moral description. The first kind of ignorance is exemplified by a man striking another in the face, not knowing that other to be his father and hence being ignorant that what he does is to dishonor his father. Such ignorance is described by Aquinas as *secundum scientiam particularem*, and is known to jurists as *ignorantia facti*. The second kind of ignorance is exemplified by a man who strikes his father in the face and does not know that dishonoring one's parents is wrong. Ignorance of this kind, which Aquinas described as *ignorantia universalis principii*, is known to jurists as *ignorantia iuris*. [28]

In jurisprudence, the distinction between *ignorantia facti* and *ignorantia iuris* is crucial, because it is deemed to be everybody's duty to know what the law is, inasmuch as it applies to himself, and hence it is a legal principle that *ignorantia iuris neminem excusat*. In common morality, however, as D'Arcy has pointed out, it is otherwise.

> In the ordinary language of day-to-day moral evaluation, we speak as if ignorance (or error, or oversight, or forgetfulness, and so on) excuses or fails to excuse, not according as it bears upon matters of moral rule, law, or principle, or upon matters of relevant fact; but according as the ignorance itself is or is not culpable. [29]

In order to render an action inculpable, ignorance must be genuine. A man who holds a jug over a carpet, announcing that he is going to upend it, and interrupts a companion who protests, "You can't do that, it contains ..." with "I don't want to hear it," cannot be said not to act voluntarily when, by upending the jug, he pours ink on the carpet. In refusing information about what was in the jug, he makes himself culpable for any wrong he would wittingly have done had he been possessed of the information he refused. Such ignorance is commonly known as "affected" (*ignorantia affectata*). [30]

In the same way, if a superior directs a subordinate to carry out a task and interrupts his subordinate's expostulation "Very well, but in order to do that I must ..." with "I don't want to hear how you are going to do it," he cannot plead that he involuntarily issued what his subordinate took to be a command to commit a crime: by affecting ignorance of the means that his subordinate thought necessary, and by not qualifying his command, he voluntarily intimated that his subordinate was to do whatever he took to be necessary.

Affected ignorance is spurious. But a man may be genuinely ignorant of the nature of what he is doing, and yet be culpable for doing it.

Aristotle distinguished two ways in which an act may be done ignorantly: either the ignorance may be the cause of its being done or it may be merely an accompaniment. In the former case, the act is said to be done *because of* ignorance; in the latter, *in* ignorance. [31]

In turn, there are two ways in which what is done may be done in ignorance. In the first, what is done is less than a full action, because the doer has no idea at all of what he is doing, as when he is in a fit of insanity, or under the influence of a drug, or in a genuinely blind rage. In such cases, both the doer's acts and his ignorance of them are parallel effects of the same cause: his madness, his intoxication, or his rage. Such acts are not culpable, because they are not voluntary; and so the doer's culpability is a matter of his culpability for their cause. Was his madness, or his intoxication, or his rage, voluntary? The answer turns on whether or not he could have helped falling into it. If he could not, he is not a fully responsible moral agent and is subject to restraint by others for the common good. If he could, he is culpable for not having taken proper precautions to prevent himself from becoming mad, or intoxicated, or enraged. And culpability for falling into a state in which one may well do grave wrongs in ignorance is commonly greater than culpability would have been for what one actually does in that state. A fighting drunk who gets drunk and then merely insults somebody is far more culpable for getting drunk than a sober man would have been for the same insulting behavior. That is why, in certain jurisdictions, being drunk in charge of a motor vehicle is a serious offence, even when no harm in fact comes of it.

The second way in which a man may do a wrong in ignorance, but not because of ignorance, presupposes that he is in full possession of his wits. It is that, although culpably or inculpably he does not know that what he is doing has whatever character makes it wrong, it would make no difference to him if he did. Taking parricide to be a more serious crime than murder, Aquinas sketches an example of the following sort: a cutthroat murders his father for his purse, not knowing that his victim is his father but not caring either.[32] Such a man cannot be said to commit parricide because of ignorance; for he would have committed it even had he not been ignorant. Another example is that of revolutionaries who blow up a prison wall to release the inmates, thereby unwittingly causing the death of a man who, unknown to them, is sleeping by the wall and is killed by its fall. Since they would have blown up the wall even had they known the man was there, they do not cause his death because of ignorance but only in ignorance. In such cases, it is clear that the doer is fully culpable for his deed.

Wrongs done through recklessness approximate to wrongs done in ignorance but not because of ignorance. A man who does a wrong through recklessness, who may well not know that he is doing it, is aware that what he does may involve wrongdoing, but does not reck it. It is true that there is a difference in culpability between doing something you know is wrong and doing something you think probably or possibly wrong; but it is not a great one. You voluntarily take the risk.

When a wrong is done because of ignorance, it follows that, if the doer had not been ignorant, he would not have acted as he did. How, then, would he have acted? Were his intentions such that he would have done a different wrong? It seems reasonably clear that only if they were not—only if, given the intentions he had, he may well have done no wrong at all—can ignorance exculpate; and even then it exculpates only if it is itself inculpable. In general: a wrong done *solely* because of ignorance is culpable in a measure as the ignorance from which it is done is culpable.

Ignorance of fact (that of moral principle will be treated in 4.4) *is culpable if and only if it springs from negligence—from want of due care*. A man may fail to take due care in using his brains or his senses; or, for want of due care, he may fail appropriately to use his brains or his senses.[33] He may, for example, be culpably ignorant that the check he is writing will not be honored by his bank, because in computing his balance he carelessly misread some figures in his check book, or because he carelessly added up the figures he read correctly, or because he did not compute his balance at all—either from general idleness or from some infatuated notion that his bank owed him a living.

When is a misobservation, or a miscalculation, or an omission to observe or think, a want of due care? A human being shows his respect for himself and others as rational creatures by using his wits and intelligence to see to it that he does not fail in what is due to them, in particular under those cardinal precepts I have called the principles of culture and beneficence. Not to do so would fail in what Whewell called "the duty of consideration": the duty to do "all that is in our power" to free our actions from the defects of ignorance and error.[34] In those jurisdictions which recognize the concept of negligence, an attempt is usually made to specify an objective standard applicable to all legally responsible persons.[35] Everyone is held to be obliged to take the care a man of ordinary prudence and intelligence would, or the care a reasonable man with ordinary capacities would. Morally, this is a minimal standard. Anybody who fails to consider what he is doing to the extent that a reasonable man of ordinary capacities would, certainly fails to do what is required of all morally responsible agents; for a morally responsible agent is at least of ordinary capacities. More, however, is required of men of superior capacities. They should reproach themselves if they do wrong through failure to give the consideration to a matter it is in their power to give, even though it is not in the power of a man of ordinary capacities. Of course, in determining what consideration it is in a man's power to give, heed must be paid to other demands upon his consideration. A man may inculpably make a mistake which he would not have made if he had had more time for consideration.

Finally, a man may do wrong because of ignorance, but his intentions may be such that, if he had not been ignorant, he would have done a different wrong: perhaps a lesser wrong, as when a burglar shoots a watchman, because he mistakenly thinks he is armed; or perhaps a greater one, as when he clubs the watchman on the head, but would have shot him had he known that he wore an armored hat. In all such cases the wrongdoer at least voluntarily attempts to commit a wrong and is culpable for that. His ignorance has no part in his attempt, but only in the particular form it takes. The general rule holds: he is culpable for any wrong he voluntarily did; and for any wrong he did that was not voluntary, he is culpable in a measure as his ignorance was culpable. A burglar who voluntarily shoots a watchman he does not know to be unarmed is culpable for the shooting and culpable for his ignorance, even though, as falling under the description "the shooting of an un-armed man," his action is not voluntary.

4.4   Conscience and Conscientiousness

In a well-known passage in *Huckleberry Finn*, Mark Twain describes the state of mind of a Missouri boy of the 1840s after he has found he cannot bring himself to betray his guardian's runaway slave.

> Conscience says to me, "What had poor Miss Watson done to you that you could see her nigger go off right under your eyes and never say one single word? What did that poor woman do to you that you could treat her so mean?"[36]

It is now a commonplace that Huckleberry Finn's conscience was, on this matter, erroneous. Yet it was not merely sincere but was an instructed conscience in a professedly Christian society. Can so profoundly erroneous a deliverance of conscience—if you will, so profoundly erroneous a putative intuition—be inculpable? And, if conscience can be inculpably erroneous, what is one's duty with respect to its deliverances?

First, let us examine the concept of conscience (Latin, *conscientia*; Greek, *syneidesis*) more closely.[37] "Properly speaking," Aquinas observes, "conscience is not a power, but an act."[38] It is the act of applying one's moral knowledge to one's own conduct. The pre-Christian Roman moralists had thought of *conscientia* as backward-looking—as passing judgement on what one has done; but St. Paul pointed out that it may be forward-looking also—the passing of judgement on what one contemplates doing. Whether forward-looking or backward-looking, however, the verdicts of a man's conscience are confined to his own actions. Ryle spoke for tradition when he remarked that it is absurd to say, "My conscience says that *you* ought to do this or ought not to have done that."[39]

Under the influence of St. Jerome's commentary on Ezekiel, the scholastic moral theologians agreed that the verdicts of conscience proceed from something called *synderesis*. But they bitterly disputed whether or not *synderesis* is a distinct power in the soul. In postscholastic writings, in which "conscience" is often used as the scholastics used *synderesis*, the dispute has continued under a different name.

St. Jerome himself insisted that *synderesis* is a special faculty, distinct from the three Platonic faculties of reason, spirit, and desire, and superior to them. This view is the ancestor of Bishop Butler's description of conscience as "a faculty in kind and nature supreme over all others, and which bears its own authority of being so,"[40] which Cardinal Newman echoed when he attributed to Protestants as well as Catholics the doctrine that conscience is "a constituent element of the mind, as our perception of other ideas may be, as our powers of reasoning, as our sense of order and the beautiful, and our other intellectual endowments," and that this constituent element of the mind is "the internal witness of both the existence and the Law of God."[41]

By contrast, Aquinas maintained that *synderesis* is not a power or faculty at all, but a disposition (Latin, *habitus*; Greek, *hexis*)[42] of ordinary practical reason: namely, a disposition consisting in the understanding of principles (*intellectus principiorum*).[43] The corresponding disposition in the speculative intellect is the understanding of the principles of the theoretical sciences, for example, of the principles of logic. This disposition does not consist in the contemplation of formulations of those principles; it is a *habitus scientiae quo potest considerare etiam cum non considerat.* [44] I think that Aquinas's remarks about degrees of possession of knowledge [45] commit him to the view that a man may possess *intellectus* of, say, the law of contradiction even though all his life he never formulates it; it is enough that he can recognize certain self-contradictions as absurd. It is the same with *synderesis*, or *intellectus* of the principles of morality: a man possesses it in some degree if he can recognize certain kinds of treatment of human beings as contrary to what is due to them as human.

In this dispute, although like Newman he was a professed admirer of Butler, Whewell took the side of Aquinas. The distinction between right and wrong, he wrote,

> must be one *not* immediately apprehended by any *peculiar sense* or faculty, which belongs to each individual . . . ; but must be a distinction discerned by some use of the faculty of Reason which is common to all mankind. [46]

According to the traditional definition of morality as a law binding upon every rational creature as rational, a faculty for making moral judgements that is distinct from reason would be theoretically superfluous. And in view of the variety of human moral judgements, to claim that one's own moral judgements proceed from such a faculty is something worse. It is sheer matter of fact that, as Whewell put it,

> actions which the Conscience of man in one century or nation determines to be odious vices or atrocious crimes, Conscience at another time and place has regarded as innocent and even laudable. [47]

Now, if the verdicts of a power distinct from human reason are irreconcilable, human reason must condemn that power as a source of error. And if the possibility of irreconcilable verdicts of conscience is excluded by laying it down that no genuine verdict of conscience may be logically incompatible with any other, the problem is raised as to how, when two putative verdicts of conscience collide, it can be ascertained whether either is genuine, and if so which.

True, there are cases in which the claim of one of the parties that his conscience testifies in such and such a manner may be dismissed as hypocrisy; but the hypothesis that whenever alleged verdicts of conscience collide, one of the parties must be a hypocrite, is itself fraudulent. The verdict of Huckleberry Finn's conscience, that he did wrong in not informing on Miss Watson's runaway, would have been corroborated with perfect sincerity by most adults of his time and place; yet neither were the abolitionists hypocrites, when they protested that the verdict of their consciences was otherwise.

Once it is acknowledged that genuine verdicts of conscience may be in conflict, the theory must be abandoned that the power from which those verdicts proceed is distinct from reason and superior to it. And the only plausible alternative is that put forward by Aquinas: that the verdicts of conscience derive from a disposition of ordinary human reason. They can be in conflict with one another because they can err; and there are two possible sources of such error. First, the disposition from which they derive, which Aquinas called *synderesis*, is not developed equally in all human beings. Everybody has some understanding of the principles of morality and, inasmuch as he has it, cannot be mistaken about them. In this sense, *synderesis* cannot err. But it can fail; that is, a man's understanding of the principles may be limited, and naturally, when he judges what lies beyond the limits of his understanding, the verdicts of his conscience will be defective. Second, even when he does understand the principles applying to a given case, that application often calls for an act of subsumption, in which the case is brought under the principle by one or more specificatory premises. Although this process is not as a rule explicit, especially when the conscience in question is uninstructed, the verdicts of conscience nevertheless presuppose it. And error is possible about specificatory premises, as it is about any outcome of nontrivial conceptual analysis.

Ignorance, whether of the principles of morality, or of precepts derived from them by means of specificatory premises, is culpable or inculpable according as it proceeds from negligence—from want of due consideration. Many Jewish and Christian authorities, although fewer now than formerly, have succumbed to the temptation to reprobate all error about the main precepts of morality as negligent and therefore culpable. It may well be that no human being can reach normal adulthood, in any society which is not totally corrupt, without some notion of the respect owed to rational creatures as such. But that notion may be defective and distorted.

There are almost no societies which do not teach their members to think of themselves as owing duties to others, and as having duties owed to them, in virtue of being what they are. But how clearly a man's notion of himself as agent will be connected with the notion of rationality, and with what other notions both it and the notion of rationality will be mixed, will vary from society to society. In a given society, whether individuals or generations can be held culpable for their errors about moral principles depends on a number of factors. Were the moral principles in which they were brought up erroneous? How thoroughly were they indoctrinated with error when they were too young to make critical resistance? Were they brought up in bad mental habits; and, if they were, how thoroughly were those bad habits inculcated? Finally, how easy or difficult would it have been for somebody brought up in that society to detect the errors in the moral principles accepted in it, and how easy or difficult would it have been for him to correct them? A graduate of Sandhurst or West Point who does not understand his duty to noncombatants as human beings is certainly culpable for his ignorance; an officer bred up from childhood in the Hitler *Jugend* might not be.

In passing from opinions about principles to judgements in specific cases, the probability of inculpable human error increases. Its sources are the same: sheer intellectual failure and inadvertence to the need to scrutinize accepted and plausible propositions and inferences. But the opportunities for it are more numerous: besides fundamental conceptual analysis, we are now called upon to consider analogies between specific cases, to recognize all the characteristics of a specific case that fall under any moral precept, and to employ information about man and his world correctly. Errors on any of these matters may vitiate a verdict of conscience.

It therefore follows that, even though he makes no error about the facts of his particular situation, a man may make an inculpable error about what it is permissible to do. He may inculpably think that a certain kind of action is permissible or even obligatory in a certain kind of situation, when in fact it is impermissible. And so he may act from an erroneous conscience, not merely from an error of fact.

In the Christian tradition, a very strong position has been taken about the authority of an erroneous conscience. It goes without saying that, if conscience is inculpably in error, impermissible actions done in accordance with it are also inculpable. As Jeremy Taylor reasoned:

If the conscience be weakly and innocently misguided, there is no sin either in the error, or in the consequent action. Because no man is bound to do better than his best; if he hath no sin in the principle of his error, it is certain he did his best, that is, he did all his duty. [48]

But Christian moral theologians were not content with allowing the inculpability of impermissible actions done at the behest of conscience; they also ruled that *an action done against conscience is always culpable.* A man is not merely held inculpable if he does something impermissible in accordance with his conscience, he is held culpable if he does not. The reason is simple. In acting against conscience, a violation of the moral law must be intended; and such intentions are always culpable, even though, because of the agent's erroneous conscience, nothing materially wrong is done.

It follows that the position of a man with a culpably erroneous conscience is a terrible one. If he acts in accordance with his conscience, he does something materially wrong for which he is culpable, because, although he acts from ignorance, his ignorance is culpable. Yet if, against his conscience, he does what is materially right, he is still culpable, because he has fallen foul of the second-order precept that an action done against conscience is always culpable. As Richard Baxter sombrely ruled, the verdict of a culpably erroneous conscience

is neither to be obeyed nor disobeyed without sin: it can make you sin, although it cannot make you [do your] duty: it doth ensnare, though not oblige. [49]

In recent moral philosophy, for want of a clear distinction between first-order and second-order moral questions, these issues have become badly muddled: most notably by Prichard in his lecture "Duty and Ignorance of Fact," and by Ross in *The Foundations of Ethics.* [50] Although they speak of "subjective" and "objective" right and wrong where moral theologians usually say "formal" and "material," Prichard and Ross accepted the theologians' doctrine that an action may be materially or objectively one thing, and formally or subjectively another. But, because they did not perceive that these two descriptions have to do with questions of different orders, they propounded questions in terms of them that are strictly unintelligible, as being assignable to no order at all. "Is the subjective or the objective view of the basis of obligation correct?" inquired Prichard. Ross was more blunt: "Ought a man," he asked, "to do the subjectively or the objectively right act?"

Kurt Baier has largely restored matters to rights by insisting that attention be paid to the contexts within which questions arise about right and wrong, guilt and innocence.[51] When an agent and his moral counsellors are considering the moral permissibility of a proposed action, the first question to arise is, "Is it (materially, objectively) permissible?" Until they have settled this, no question of formal or subjective permissibility can arise at all. And, when they have settled it, a question of formal or subjective permissibility can arise only if it has been decided that the proposed action is materially permissible. There is no way in which a man can inculpably do what he believes to be materially wrong. But even if an agent is convinced that a certain action is materially or objectively permissible, and perhaps obligatory, he may, like Abelard's malicious hangman, have reason to be troubled about his intentions: "Would I," he may ask, "in my present state of mind, do this materially right action with a morally permissible intention?" For a Christian, to whom the last temptation is "To do the right deed for the wrong reason,"[52] such questions are serious.

Yet he cannot rightly ask, "If I, in my present state of mind, would do what I acknowledge to be materially obligatory with an impermissible intention, ought I to refrain from doing it?" If the action is materially obligatory, he must do it; and if in his present state of mind he would not do it with a right intention, he can and must change that state of mind.

Prichard's and Ross's confusion is hardest to disentangle with respect to backward-looking questions. Looking back on a deed which he now sees to have been materially wrong, a conscientious man asks in distress, "I did my best to find out what was right, and I honestly thought that what I did was right; now I know it was wrong; but what, given my state of mind at the time, ought I to have done?" Supposing that his error of conscience was inculpable, the only correct reply is to reject his question as an unintelligible hybrid, in which two different questions are conflated into one. The two are: "What was the materially right thing to do?" and "What, given his inculpable conscientious judgement, would he have been to blame for not doing?" By imagining that the different answers to these two questions may both be considered plausible candidates for the true answer to his hybrid, he has (like Prichard and Ross) conjured up a spurious and insoluble problem.

The second-order precept that it is always culpable to act against conscience imposes a limitation on the criminal law of civil society. Since any law commanding an action contrary to a citizen's conscience, even if his conscience is misguided, can be complied with only at the price of falling foul of a second-order precept of common morality, any society which promulgates such laws without grave reason acts immorally.

What reasons can be grave enough for a society to coerce citizens into acting against their consciences?

The first, and most obvious, is that sometimes the innocent can be protected in no other way. Although the Thugs of early nineteenth-century India thought themselves obliged in conscience to waylay, rob, and murder travellers with whom they had ingratiated themselves, the British government in India rightly suppressed Thuggee, according to the precept, *Thou shalt not stand idly by the blood of thy neighbor.* And it properly suppressed Suttee, the orthodox Hindu practice according to which wives submitted to being burned to death on the funeral pyres of their husbands, on the ground that they were subject to coercion.

Second, a civil society may coerce its members to perform certain services for the common good, even though to perform those services would be against the consciences of some of them. The most controversial case is of compulsory military service in a just war. If a conscription law is enacted, it must be upheld, like all coercive laws, by punishing those who will not comply with it. However, the barbarous penalties which can be imposed in most nominally civilized countries for refusal to serve (either death or a long period of imprisonment) are morally indefensible. If a large majority of the members of a civil society at war both reject pacifism and accept the war as just, barbarous punishments for refusal to serve will be unnecessary; and unless they do both, military conscription will be either ineffective or wrong.[53]

4.5   The Corruption of Consciousness

Despite the persuasiveness of the traditional doctrine that it is always culpable to act against conscience, the example with which our inquiry into conscientiousness began shows that, beyond a certain point, it is unacceptable. In not informing on the runaway, Huckleberry Finn acted directly against his conscience.

"Good-by, sir," says I; "I won't let no runaway niggers get by
me if I can help it."
They went off and I got aboard the raft, feeling bad and low,
because I knowed very well I had done wrong, and I see it warn't
no use for me to try to learn to do right; a body that don't get
started right when he's little ain't got no show.[54]

Yet Huck's action was right, not only materially, but formally also.
Twain's art shows that for Huck to have played the informer would
have been culpable as well as wrong. For it makes clear that his
belief that the runaway was not a being to whom he owed respect,
although not insincere, was false to his deepest consciousness.

In his *Principles of Art*, R. G. Collingwood worked out a theory of
the phenomenon imaginatively presented by Mark Twain. The
foundation of that theory is that at any level of consciousness, from
simple sensory awareness to the most self-conscious abstract
thought, a man will be aware or not aware of what is presented to his
consciousness according as he pays attention to it or not, and that it
is in his power to withdraw attention from most of what is presented
to him—violent and immediate feelings being the chief exception.
Without the power to direct their attention largely where they
choose, human beings would not be able to think effectively at all.

Yet they can abuse their power to direct their attention. A man
may avert his attention from something presented to him, not
because it is irrelevant to the subject at hand, or insignificant in
itself, but because it is disturbing. To think about it would call in
question things he does not want to question, usually from vanity,
shame, or fear. Merely to divert attention from something disturbing to something undisturbing is not in itself objectionable:
there are times when what is disturbing must be confronted, and
others when it need not be. But for a man utterly to exclude from his
attention some disturbing object does give rise to error: the error of
disowning what he cannot bring himself to face. As Collingwood put
it:

Whenever some element in experience is disowned by consciousness, that other element upon which attention is fixed, and which
consciousness claims as its own, becomes a sham. In itself, it does
genuinely belong to the consciousness that claims it; in saying
"This is how I feel," consciousness is telling the truth; but the
disowned element, with its corresponding statement "And that is
how I do not feel," infects this truth with error. The picture which

consciousness has painted of its own experience is not only a selected picture (that is, a true one so far as it goes), it is a bowdlerized picture, or one whose omissions are falsifications. [55]

The most elementary cases of this sort of falsification are by individuals of the character of their own actions. The classic scriptural example is in 2 Samuel, chaps. 11–12. King David, having adulterously begotten a child by the wife of Uriah the Hittite, one of his officers, arranged to have Uriah sent into battle and treacherously left unsupported to be killed by the enemy; thereafter, he married the widow. How he represented these abominable actions to himself we are not told, but presumably it was not as being the filching, by a great and powerful man in want of nothing, of the thing most dear to one of his dependents; for when Nathan the prophet pretended to report an action of the same general kind, in which a man with many flocks and herds robbed a poor dependent of a lamb, we are told that

David's anger was greatly kindled . . . and he said to Nathan, As the Lord liveth, the man that has done this thing shall surely die: and he shall restore the lamb fourfold, because he did this thing, and because he had no pity.
And Nathan said to David: Thou art the man (2 Sam. 12:5–6).

The corruption of David's consciousness was not inveterate: although he did not at first recognize the applicability of Nathan's example to himself, he did not deny it when it was pointed out.

Corruption of consciousness reaches a further stage when it becomes inveterate: when a man is unable to recognize his deed or his situation for what it is, even when it is pointed out to him. And it is not necessarily confined to individuals. A whole society may refuse to face plain facts, not only about its own actions as a society, but about its institutions. Thus an institution such as slavery can exist in a society whose members are not utterly depraved only at the price of moral ignorance or of corruption of consciousness. The antebellum South was not morally ignorant. Its inhabitants professed to believe that all men are created equal, and are endowed with certain inalienable rights, among which is liberty. They therefore paid the price of a corrupt consciousness: they would not face the undeniable evidence of the humanity of their slaves.

The moral significance of Mark Twain's presentation of Huckleberry Finn is that it shows somebody struggling to confront a fact which is in a way obvious, yet which is screened from him by the moral system of his culture—a system which has partly vitiated the very language he speaks. When asked whether anybody was hurt in an accident he has told of witnessing, he finds it natural to reply, "No'm, killed a nigger," and to accept the response, "Well, it's lucky because sometimes people do get hurt." On the other hand, when rebuked by his runaway friend for a silly and humiliating practical joke, he finds himself responding as to another person: "It was fifteen minutes before I could work myself up to go and humble myself to a nigger; but I done it, and I warn't sorry for it afterward either."[56]

The state from which Huckleberry Finn struggles, largely success-fully, to free himself, is neither one of vice nor one of disease. Under the pressure of his culture, his consciousness presents to him a bowdlerized or falsified picture of the negro slaves he knows, but he is not a hypocrite or liar. Yet neither are the facts needed to correct his bowdlerized picture hidden from him, as the intentions behind his symptomatic acts are hidden from a neurotic. In serious mental illness, a man cannot bring to consciousness the intentions under-lying his symptomatic behavior, even when he honestly directs his attention to why he is engaging in it. He is genuinely ill, because he has lost part of his normal capacity for self-awareness and can recover it, if at all, only by the aid of special therapy.

The diversions of attention that are characteristic of a corrupt consciousness, while voluntary and intentional, are not intentional falsifications. In diverting his attention from what disturbs him, the man whose consciousness is corrupt acts as it were on a premonition. He does not know what the danger is or even, strictly, that there is danger; but he divines that he must not look. In Collingwood's words:

> The untruthful consciousness is not making a bona fide mistake, for its faith is not good; it is shirking something which its business is to face. But it is not concealing the truth, for there is no truth which it knows and is concealing. Paradoxically, we may say that it is deceiving itself; but this is only a clumsy effort to explain what is happening within a single consciousness on the analogy of what may happen between one intellect and another.[57]

The art of Mark Twain and the theoretical analysis of Colling-wood converge upon the same point: that the moral conscience may be vitiated by a corrupt consciousness. They enable us, without calling in question the received doctrine that it is always culpable to act against conscience, to understand why, hypocrisy apart, conscientiousness has an equivocal name in the world: why it suggests officiousness, busybodydom, and obstinate insensibility, as well as straightforwardness and disinterestedness. And so they dispel the mystery in the fact that many conscientious men are more detestable than any rogue. Collingwood may have exaggerated when he declared that the corrupt consciousness—not the bad will—is "the true *radix malorum*," but not by much; and he did not exaggerate at all in the reason he gave for it, that "[a] truthful consciousness gives intellect a firm foundation on which to build; a corrupt consciousness forces intellect to build on a quicksand."[58]

One misleading association should perhaps be anticipated. Collingwood's remark about the corrupt consciousness, "its faith is not good," whether or not it owes anything to Heidegger's distinction between the authentic (*eigentlich*) and the inauthentic life, or to Sartre's between *bonne foi* and *mauvaise foi*, has nothing whatever to do with the existentialist doctrine that authenticity, or good faith, consists neither more nor less than in seeing through the pretense that anything is required of man as such, other than that he act in full awareness of the fact that he is mortal and that nothing is required of him. On the contrary, moral nihilism is but one more of the innumerable devices by which a corrupt consciousness may disguise from a man what he is, and how he is called to live.

In his *Letter to the Duke of Norfolk* on papal infallibility, Cardinal Newman remarked that, were he obliged to bring religion into after-dinner toasts, he would drink to the Pope, but still "to Conscience first, and to the Pope afterwards."[59] Were we obliged to bring morality into toasts, we should not refuse to drink to conscience; but we should beg to drink to a truthful consciousness first.

5   Consistency

5.1   Moral Perplexity

The system of morality elaborated in the preceding chapters invites questions of two kinds: internal ones about its coherence as a system, and external ones about whether things are in fact as it says they are.

The only serious question of the first kind is whether the system is consistent. For, while it is all too probable that I have made mistakes both about what specific precepts are derivable from the fundamental principle, and in constructing derivations of precepts that really are so derivable, the work of traditional moral philosophers and theologians leaves little doubt that my bad workmanship can be repaired without major alterations in the conclusions arrived at.

But how can the consistency of the system be in question? Is it not placed beyond doubt by the derivation of the whole of it, by simple logical operations, from a single fundamental principle? Not at all. For, although the specificatory premises are not independent of the fundamental principle, inasmuch as they purport merely to make explicit the content of a concept in that principle, namely, that of respect for every human being as being a rational creature, the controversial character of much of the informal reasoning by which those premises are reached calls in question the consistency both of the concept they unfold and the principle that incorporates it.

When the suspected source of inconsistency in the fundamental principle of a system is a rich concept which is never more than partly analysed, the consistency of that system cannot be proved in the same way as can that of some formalized axiomatic systems—as, for example, can that of some systems of deontic logic. Hence no formal proof of the consistency of traditional common morality is possible.

Nor does its long and widespread acceptance in practice ensure consistency. For not all of those who accepted it believed it to be consistent. Rabbis for the most part appear to have had no doubt of the consistency of the Mosaic Torah, but not all Christian theologians followed them. It was a respectable theological opinion that the devil could bring about situations in which common morality prescribes that a certain kind of action both be done and not done. A mysterious remark in the Book of Job (40:12) about Behemoth, who was taken to symbolize Satan, was thought to imply it: namely, *Nervi testiculorum eius perplexi sunt* ("the sinews of his stones are wrapped together," or, in Knox's primmer rendering, "the sinews of his groin are close-knit"). St. Gregory the Great expounded it as follows:

> But the sinews of these testicles are close-knit, because the suggestions which [Satan] puts to us are linked together by cunning devices, so as in the following way to make many sin: inasmuch as it happens that they make an effort to escape a sin, they avoid that one only by [falling into] another snare of sin.[1]

That such entrapment should be possible was terrible to the early faithful. Now it would serve only to discredit the common morality they tried to follow.

St. Gregory's three examples of moral perplexity led Aquinas to an important clarification of what it is for a moral system to contradict itself. Two of the examples are of persons who have made injudicious vows, in one case of secrecy, and in the other of obedience, and who find themselves bound by their vows to do what they have a moral duty not to do. The third is of an ecclesiastic who has obtained a cure of souls through simony, and must either exercise a wrongful authority or wrongfully desert his flock.[2] Aquinas classified all such examples as cases of perplexity *secundum quid*, that is, of perplexity conditional upon some misdeed; and he distinguished them from cases of perplexity *simpliciter*, which are not conditional upon wrongdoing. He then denied that a moral system is inconsistent merely because cases of perplexity *secundum quid* arise in it.[3] "It is not *inconveniens*," he remarked, "that [a person in mortal sin] be perplexed";[4] for it is a logical consequence of some sins that they entangle the sinner in situations in which he cannot but commit others. A moral system is inconsistent only if it allows the possibility that, without any wrongdoing on his part, a man may find himself in a situation in which he can only escape doing one wrong by doing another: that is, only if it allows the possibility of perplexity *simpliciter*. And Aquinas protested that common morality, as Christianity understands it, does not allow that possibility. Kant, as was to have been expected, followed him: "Since duty and obligation in general are concepts which express the objective practical necessity of certain actions," he argued, "and since two opposite rules cannot be necessary at the same time . . . it therefore follows that a conflict of duties and obligations is inconceivable [*obligationes non colliduntur*]."[5]

Precepts having to do with situations that are perplexing *secundum quid* are a subspecies of what Chisholm has paradoxically called "contrary-to-duty imperatives."[6] Morality, Chisholm points out, must lay down not only what we ought to do absolutely, "but also what we ought to do after we fail to do some of the things we ought to do";[7] and common morality does so, in familiar first-order precepts about confession, restitution, and reparation, and equally familiar second-order ones about blame, repentance, and punishment. Theoretically, there is no difficulty in deriving such precepts from the fundamental principle; but since their derivation would have prolonged this study intolerably, except for the main principles of blame, they have been mentioned only allusively. Recent studies of contrary-to-duty conditionals have followed Chisholm's in taking the important problems about them to be logical rather than moral. For systems of deontic logic are variations upon systems of the logic of necessity and possibility, according to which, given that it is necessary that a certain event occur, it follows that it does occur. But it is morally uncontroversial that no system of deontic logic is satisfactory according to which, given that a certain action is morally necessary, it follows that it is performed.[8]

The questions with which we are concerned are moral; and whether or not, as I think, moral questions about contrary-to-duty conditionals are important and just as controversial as those about absolute duty, they will not be settled by logical innovations. As will be seen in the subsequent section (5.2), not even problems arising from contrary-to-duty situations that are perplexing *secundum quid* present any special logical difficulty. Yet our original problem remains: acknowledging that the possibility of perplexity *secundum quid* does not show common morality to be inconsistent, were Aquinas and Kant right in flatly denying the possibility, within common morality, of perplexity *simpliciter?*

Moral theologians as sympathetic to Aquinas as Bishop Kirk have doubted it. However, their doubts appear to spring from general logical considerations rather than from specific moral difficulties. Those which troubled Kirk are representative.

[T]he number of clearly-defined principles of which it can be said that in no *conceivable circumstances* may the breach of them be thought of as in any degree allowable must at the best be very small. Indeed, if we followed out this line of thought to the end (as has rarely been done in Christian ethics) there could strictly speaking be only one such principle. For if any principle had an inalienable right to be observed, *every* other principle would have to be waived if the two came into conflict in a given case. It is only because such conflicts between primary moral principles [that is, such things as the precepts of the Mosaic decalogue] are in most cases almost inconceivable that we are able to speak loosely of a *number* of laws whose breach would be "wrong in itself." But the conception *is* a loose one.[9]

Kirk here assumes that if more than one "clearly defined" (presumably nonequivalent) principle should be laid down as admitting no exception, then circumstances would be conceivable, although perhaps barely so, in which they would come into conflict. And that presupposes that a plurality of nonequivalent exceptionless precepts cannot be validly derived from a single consistent first principle. It is, however, difficult to believe that, on reflection, Kirk would have persisted in an assumption so false and foolish.

It is not hard to imagine systems of mores, each consisting of several nonequivalent exceptionless principles, which can be informally exhibited as admitting no conflict. A system consisting of two absolute prohibitions, one of killing human beings and one of lying, would be an example. It seems evident that the two prohibitions are each self-consistent: there is no way in which not killing one human being can be represented as killing another, without improperly extending the concept of causing a human death; and there is no way in which not lying on one matter is lying on another, unless it is improperly supposed that the person in question must speak, that what he says will be understood differently by different hearers, and that he cannot explain the ambiguity. And it seems equally evident that there is no room for either of the two prohibitions to contradict the other. Unless "killing" is given an extended meaning which it does not have, there is no way in which not lying can, as such, be killing. It is conceivable that X may kill Y in reaction to Z's not lying; but Z does not thereby kill Y. Nor is there any way in which a man can be *perplexus simpliciter* because not to kill would be a lie. One can imagine a tyrant whose sign language for answering certain questions is to have the questioner decapitated if the answer is "That is not true," and to refrain if the answer is "That is true." Such a tyrant could indeed lie by not killing somebody; but he could not be *perplexus simpliciter* in doing so, because he could at any time abandon his murderous sign language.

Hence it does not follow, simply because a moral system lays down a plurality of exceptionless precepts, that perplexity *simpliciter* is possible in it, notwithstanding that a surprising number of Christian moral theologians have disarmed themselves against the onslaught of "situation ethics" by imagining, with Kirk, that it does.[10] However, it is not enough to explode fallacies like Kirk's; for there have been Christian moralists who were never taken in by them, but who have nevertheless hesitated to follow Aquinas and Kant in maintaining that, within the system of common morality, perplexity *simpliciter* is impossible.

One of the most interesting of them is Peter Geach. His position rests, not on general logical considerations, but on his view about how the moral law is known. Briefly, it is this. The major precepts of morality, such as the prohibitions of murder, stealing, and lying, which are exceptionless, prohibit actions that are known to be generally objectionable by all persons of sound understanding. It is open to such persons to advance, by way of natural theology, to perceiving their rational knowledge that such actions are generally undesirable as "a promulgation of the Divine law *absolutely forbidding*" them.[11] It is because of the limits of human understanding that the moral law is promulgated to mankind in this way. And, since it is logically possible that actions that are objectionable only in general may in special circumstances be permissible or even required, it follows that circumstances in which one divine law can be obeyed only by disobeying another are logically possible. But it does not follow that divine law is inconsistent. For "if God governs all events by his providence, he can see to it that circumstances in which a man is inculpably faced by a choice between forbidden acts do not occur."[12]

Within Geach's conception of morality as divine positive law, our knowledge of which rests on premises drawn from natural theology, there is no valid internal objection to his argument that morality is consistent because, although perplexity *simpliciter* is logically possible, natural theology assures us that it never occurs. Unfortunately, the consistency of common morality, as it has been presented in the preceding chapters, could not be demonstrated in this way, even if (and I do not wish to dispute them) all Geach's conclusions in natural theology were true. For the precepts of common morality as presented above purport to have been derived rationally from a rationally defensible fundamental principle, without at any point resorting to premises drawn from natural theology. If Geach is right about natural theology, some at least of the precepts of common morality are also part of divine positive law; and of those that are, we can assert on theological grounds that no situation will arise in which, through no fault of the person in it, obeying one would be disobeying another. But it would not follow that they are consistent as precepts of common morality—that is, as precepts required by reason independently of theology, whether revealed or natural. To establish that, it must be shown that in no possible world of the sort with which common morality has to do can a situation arise, except through wrongdoing, in which some moral precept can be observed only by violating another.

Nor can that be established by recourse to a device of which advantage is legitimately taken by contractarian moralists, following Rawls: namely, that of ordering the precepts of morality in a series, and adding to each the proviso that when it can be observed only by violating some precept higher in the series, it is not to be observed. [13] Such serial ordering, while perfectly proper in contractarian systems, is incompatible with the very nature of deductive systems. To number the precepts in the first-order system expounded in chapter 3, for example, and to lay it down that precept (3) is not to be observed if its observance would without wrongdoing entail violating either precept (2) or (1), would be as absurd as to lay it down that, in Book I of Euclid, proposition (32) is true in a given case provided only that it would not follow that either proposition (29) or (27) is false.

Since there are a number of rationalist or "natural law" systems of morality, like those of Aquinas and Kant, the precepts of which are well defined, it is surprising that those who object that all such systems must be inconsistent, have seldom attempted decisively to prove their objection by producing specific cases of perplexity *simpliciter* that are possible in those systems. Hard cases, of course, are familiar: that is, cases in which the ruling of Thomist or Kantian morality will be considered by many to be objectionable. The most difficult cases I have encountered will be examined in the sequel; but I know of no specific case of perplexity *simpliciter* that has plausibly been alleged to arise in any competently formulated traditional moral system.

However, if the system of common morality presented in the preceding chapters is consistent, even though its consistency does not admit of formal proof, something better should be possible than disposing of alleged cases of inconsistency as they appear. Has it no structural characteristics from which it is at least plausible to infer that its precepts cannot come into conflict?

It has. Moreover, they are reflected in familiar principles, which, although they appear to be merely external, like the contractarian device of serial ordering, are in fact implicit in the various precepts of the system themselves, as they are derived from its fundamental principle. Of these principles, as we shall see, by far the most important is: *It is impermissible to do evil that good may come of it*, to which, because of St. Paul's much-quoted formulation of it in Romans 3:8, I shall refer as "the Pauline principle."

5.2 Doing Evil That Good May Come

The precepts of common morality divide into first-order ones about what kinds of action are permissible in themselves, or materially permissible, and second-order ones about the conditions under which an agent is culpable or inculpable for doing something.

The chief difficulties about the consistency of the second-order precepts have been anticipated in deriving them. They are derived from three major principles: (1) that actions are culpable only as falling under descriptions under which they are voluntary (4.1); (2) that ignorance is culpable inasmuch as it springs from negligence (4.3–4); and (3) that it is culpable to do what you believe to be impermissible, but not what you inculpably do not (4.4). Our investigation of the relations between first-order and second-order precepts has shown that there is no inconsistency in the same action's being either materially permissible and culpable or inculpable and materially impermissible: that is, that no second-order precept can be incompatible with a first-order precept (2.3). Hence the second-order precepts of common morality are inconsistent only if, according to them, without being in any way at fault, a man can find himself in a situation in which he must be blamed whether he does a certain kind of action or whether he does not.

Fortunately, it is fairly easy to show that the second-order precepts of common morality cannot be a source of inconsistency independent of the first-order ones. For according to our analysis of the second-order precepts, they prescribe that a man is to blame for acting or intending to act in a certain kind of way, only if he either believes that acting in that kind of way is wrong, or is culpably ignorant of it (4.4). It follows that nobody can find himself in a situation in which he is to blame whether he acts or intends to act in a certain kind of way, or whether he does not, unless he either believes that it would be wrong to act in that kind of way and wrong not to, or is culpably ignorant of it. Hence the second-order precepts of common morality can generate perplexity *simpliciter* only if the first-order precepts either generate it and are culpably not thought to, or are believed to generate it.

But any set of first-order precepts according to which situations can arise in which it would be both wrong to act or intend to act in a certain kind of way, and wrong not to, is inconsistent and therefore false. Hence it would be preposterous to describe ignorance of its specific inconsistencies as ignorance, culpable or otherwise, of right and wrong. And it would be equally preposterous for anybody who believes that people can inculpably find themselves in situations in which, according to common morality, it would be both wrong for them to act or intend to act in a certain kind of way, and wrong not to, to be prepared to blame them for it. If the first-order precepts of common morality are as he takes them to be, then common morality can provide no grounds for any second-order conclusions whatever.

In short, the second-order precepts of common morality cannot give rise to perplexity *simpliciter* if the first-order ones are consistent; and, if the first-order ones are inconsistent, it is irrational to invoke the second-order ones at all. The question of whether or not common morality, as presented in the preceding chapters, is consistent therefore turns wholly on whether or not its first-order precepts are consistent: that is, on whether or not they can give rise to perplexity *simpliciter*.

Its first-order precepts, as we have seen, are divided into (1) those of duty to oneself and (2) those of duty to others; and each of these species is in turn divided into (a) prohibitions of actions of certain kinds as violating the respect owed to human beings as rational and (b) commands that policies be adopted for promoting the good of human beings as rational, whether one's own (1b) or that of others (2b). Finally, precepts forbidding actions violating the respect owed to others (2a) divide into prohibitions of actions that do not, as such, presuppose institutions (2ai) and the prohibitions of actions that do (2aii).

It will be convenient to begin by surveying the various species of prohibitory precept, namely, (1a), (2ai), and (2aii).

The prohibitions of actions as violating the respect owed to oneself all have to do with self-injury; and it is evident that abstaining from one kind of self-injury cannot be committing or permitting another, in view of the fact that actions in which a human function is impaired are not injuries if, like surgical operations, they are for the sake of one's well-being as a whole (see 3.2). As for the prohibitions of actions violating the respect owed to others, the noninstitutional ones are: of injuring others; of not helping others in grave need, when one can; and of the various forms of lying. The institutional ones are: of breaking faith; of injuring or neglecting a member of one's family as such, whether spouse (e.g. by adultery), or parent (e.g. by active disrespect), or child (e.g. by miseducation); of the various forms of stealing; and of breaking the morally valid laws of a civil society of which one is a member. It is not too much to say that, once the limits of such institutions as contract and property and civil society are made explicit, especially those implied in the condition that no morally permissible institution can annul existing moral duties, and once the distinction between perplexity *simpliciter* and perplexity *secundum quid* has been drawn, no apparent case of conflict between these prohibitory precepts is found in the voluminous literature of casuistry that cannot be easily solved. Just as there is no way in which not lying can be murder, or in which not murdering can be lying, so there is no way in which refraining from adultery can be stealing, or not stealing can be committing adultery, and so forth. If the first-order precepts are inconsistent, it is not here.

Nor does there seem to be any way in which observing the prohibitions of failure to respect others can be injuring oneself, or in which refraining from injuring oneself can violate any prohibition of failure to respect others. I do not harm myself, in any legitimate sense, by not stealing from somebody else (assuming that the institution of property in my society is morally legitimate); and my refraining from suicide or other self-injury cannot be injuring or breaking faith with anybody else.

However, as was pointed out in 5.1, it is possible, by breaking one moral prohibition, to entangle yourself in a situation in which, whatever you do, you must break another: that is, in which you are perplexed *secundum quid*. Can common morality provide consistent contrary-to-duty prescriptions for such cases?

What it provides depends on the fact that, although wrongness, or moral impermissibility, does not have degrees, impermissible wrongs are more or less grave. The explanation of this is simple. Any violation of the respect owed to human beings as rational is flatly and unconditionally forbidden; but the respect owed to human beings may be violated either more or less gravely. It is absolutely impermissible either to murder or to steal; but although murder is no more a wrong than stealing, it is a graver wrong. There is a parallel in criminal law, in which murder and stealing are equally felonies, but murder is a graver felony than stealing. In general, every wrong action impairs some human good, and the gravity of wrong actions varies with the human goods they impair. Although there is room for dispute in some cases as to whether or not this action is a graver wrong than that (for example, whether theft of one's reputation is worse than theft of one's purse), when they find themselves trapped by their own fault in a choice between wrongs, not only do most moral agents have opinions about whether those wrongs are equally grave, and if they are not, about which is the graver; but also, if they adhere to the same moral tradition, their opinions on these questions largely agree. And, given that wrongs can differ in gravity, it quite obviously follows from the fundamental principle of morality that, when through some misdeed a man is confronted with a choice between wrongs, if one of them is less grave than the others, he is to choose it. This precept is a special application of a more general principle, which I shall refer to as the principle of the least evil, and which was already proverbial in Cicero's time: namely, *minima de malis eligenda*—when you must choose between evils, choose the least.[14] However, as we shall see, the limits of its application have not been well understood.

The operation of this principle in cases of perplexity *secundum quid* is illustrated in the following case from Escobar's *Theologia Moralis,* which Pascal made notorious. A monk may violate the papal prohibition of laying aside his canonical garb "if he has laid it aside for an infamous purpose, such as to pick pockets or to go incognito into haunts of profligacy, meaning shortly after to resume it."[15] Of course Escobar condemned both the picking of pockets and profligacy. His point was that, given that a monk was resolved to do either of those infamous things, since causing scandal would be a graver wrong than laying aside his habit, it would then be impermissible for him not to choose also to commit the lesser wrong of laying aside his habit, rather than the greater one of causing scandal. *Ex hypothesi,* nothing that he does in such a situation can be right *simpliciter.* But no inconsistency is thereby introduced into common morality; for any further perplexity to which his action gives rise will also be a perplexity *secundum quid.*

It appears then, that the prohibitory first-order precepts of common morality, both of duties to oneself and duties to others, are consistent, even when taken together with the application of the principle of the least evil by which contrary-to-duty precepts are derived for cases of perplexity *secundum quid.*

Now it is time to turn to the precepts of the first-order system that command the adoption of policies for promoting human good, whether one's own (1b) or that of others (2b). Precepts of the former kind (1b) all derive from the principle of culture (see 3.2); those of the latter kind (2b) from the principle of beneficence (see 3.3).

The distinction between prohibitory precepts and precepts commanding the promotion of certain ends is not one of logical form, and it is a mistake to describe it as one between negative and affirmative precepts. In terms of permissibility, both are negative; and there are prohibitory precepts expressible in sentences of the same form as those expressing precepts about promoting good ends: for example, "It is impermissible for one man not to go to the help of another in serious distress, when it is in his power," and "It is impermissible for a man not to promote the well-being of others, according to his means." The distinction lies in the content of what it is impermissible not to do. In the case of the prohibitory precepts, it is a certain kind of action; in the case of the precepts for promoting ends, it is the adoption of a certain kind of plan of action. The former exclude certain kinds of action absolutely; but the latter do not. In choosing any coherent plan for promoting the well-being of any set of creatures, I shall be confronted with harsh alternatives. I shall be constrained to omit to do things for their good which otherwise I might, and even to do things which cause harm for the sake of some greater good. And if the duty to promote the well-being of a set of creatures excludes neither omissions to do things for their well-being, nor doing things that cause them harm, it certainly excludes no other kinds of action. Kant's puzzling distinction between perfect and imperfect duties becomes intelligible if it is interpreted as a distinction between duties under prohibitory precepts and duties under precepts commanding the promotion of certain ends. Except for precepts which simply prohibit certain kinds of intervention in a situation, such as the prohibitions of murder and theft, which do not require anybody to do anything, most prohibitory precepts call for some kind of action as opposed to inaction. For example, the prohibition of lying requires a man in speaking to speak truthfully, and the prohibition of breaking a promise, to pay a debt say, requires him to fulfil his promise by paying. Hence, Kant's analysis of a perfect duty as "one which allows no exception in the interests of inclination,"[16] glossed by Paton as meaning that there is no "latitude or 'playroom' for mere inclination" in how it may be carried out,[17] will not do at all. As Chisholm has pointed out, this would entail that no duties are perfect except those that require no action at all.[18] For, since there is no end to the possibility of truly describing any concrete action, every action that satisfies a precept of perfect duty, such as the repayment of a ten-dollar debt, will satisfy innumerable descriptions not required by the precept; and what descriptions of this sort it shall satisfy are wholly up to the agent. Hence there is usually " 'playroom' for inclination" in discharging perfect duties as well as in discharging imperfect ones. Yet there is a difference between them. A perfect duty is simply a duty not to do, or not to omit, an action of a certain kind: not to murder, or to lie, not to omit to pay a debt. By contrast, an imperfect duty is always a duty to promote a certain general end; and since carrying out such a duty does not exclude any specific acts of commission or omission, it cannot be simply a duty not to do, or not to omit, an action of a certain kind.

It should now be plain why the principles of culture and beneficence, from one or the other of which each precept of imperfect duty is derived—each precept, that is, commanding the adoption of some rational plan for promoting human well-being—contain the condition, "by morally permissible actions" (cf. 3.2, 3.3). A fundamental principle which categorically forbids violating the respect owed to human beings as rational must condemn any plan for promoting human well-being by which that respect would be violated. Hence the fundamental principle of morality itself entails that every precept of imperfect duty following from it—every precept ordaining the promotion of human well-being generally—shall contain as a condition that no precept of perfect duty following from it—no prohibitory precept—may be violated. And that is the true sense of the Pauline principle that *evil is not to be done that good may come of it.* The evil that is not to be done is the violation of the prohibitory precepts—the precepts of perfect duty; and the good for which it is not to be done, even though common morality requires that it be promoted, is the well-being of oneself and others as human.

The Pauline principle, therefore, is not an external stipulation, like the serial ordering adopted by contractarian theorists, for getting rid of conflicts between perfect and imperfect duties. It is nothing but a general statement of a condition implicit in every precept of imperfect duty that is validly derivable from the fundamental principle of morality itself. It is structurally necessary. And it manifestly entails that the precepts of imperfect duty—the precepts that flow from the principles of culture and beneficence—cannot be inconsistent with the prohibitory precepts.

Can the precepts of imperfect duty nevertheless be incompatible with one another? There appear to be two hypotheses on which they can: first, that the concept of a rational plan for promoting the well-being of any set of human beings as rational creatures be inconsistent; and second, that the adoption of a rational plan for developing one's own powers be incompatible with adopting one for promoting the well-being of others. The first is true only if, when the promotion of one good for the set of beings in question is incompatible with the promotion of another, the concept of a rational plan neither provides a criterion of choice nor permits one to choose freely. But neither is the case. When, as sometimes happens, the goods between which one must choose are not equal, the concept of a rational plan implies that the one to be chosen will involve the least grave loss: *minima de malis eligenda.* It should be observed that, inasmuch as it can be justified within common morality, the scope of the principle of the least evil is confined to contrary-to-duty precepts and to the formation of rational plans under the precepts of imperfect duty, when there is a choice between unequal goods. When, as is also sometimes the case, the goods between which one must choose are equal, it is equally rational to choose any, and the choice is at the agent's pleasure.

Is it not, however, possible that one's rational plan for developing one's own powers under the principle of culture should be incompatible with promoting the well-being of others as required by the principle of beneficence? Not according to the concept of human well-being presupposed in the fundamental principle of morality, according to which, as was pointed out in 3.3, human well-being is largely a matter of each human being's developing and exercising his own powers, to the best of his ability. That is why the principle of beneficence, but not the principle of culture, contains the qualification, "inasmuch as one can do so without proportionate inconvenience" (cf. 3.3). Fulfilment of the principle of beneficence presupposes fulfilment of the principle of culture. Of course, as has been already remarked, both are conditional upon the prohibitory precepts, among them the precept that you are not to stand idly by when you can protect your innocent neighbor from violence or fraud.

It may be concluded then, that the structure of the first-order precepts of common morality as they have been presented—as determined by the relations between duties to oneself and duties to others, between prohibitory precepts and precepts of promoting human well-being, and between institutional and noninstitutional precepts—is such that any inconsistency in it must spring from the special character of individual precepts, hence from individual specificatory premises, and not from the nature of the system as a whole.

This is a result of some importance, even though it does not exclude the possibility of inconsistencies arising from individual precepts. For so acute a critic as Jonathan Bennett has argued that no system which recognizes the foreseen bad consequences (in the wide sense of "consequences") of an action as a reason for not doing it, can be rational if it also contains prohibitions which must be observed "whatever the consequences." His argument is that, in any given situation, since, "in proportion as 'the consequences of not doing so' give some moral reason for 'doing so'—to that extent the action/consequence distinction lacks moral significance in that situation,"[19] it follows that, with reference to any prohibitory precept of such a system, it is always possible that a situation will arise in which the action/consequence distinction will have no moral significance. And in that case it would be irrational to stick to the precept "whatever the consequences."

The defect in this argument is an assumption not made explicit in it: that in a rational system containing exceptionless prohibitions the

avoidance of foreseen bad consequences is an ultimate consideration, to be weighed against other ultimate considerations. That
assumption is a mistake. For any member of the class of deontologi-
cal systems in which the sole fundamental principle ordains respect
for beings of a certain kind—and I do not think that Bennett would
maintain that members of that class are as such irrational—
demonstrably must contain both a counterpart of the Pauline
principle and unconditional prohibitions of certain kinds of action.

Let S be a deductive moral system, having as its single first
principle that all Ks are to be respected as Ks. Grant that there are
goods proper to Ks which they rationally pursue, and evils proper to
them which they rationally avoid. S must, in that case, contain
precepts enjoining the promotion of those goods and the avoidance
and relief of those evils. However, since those precepts derive from
the first principle—that respect may not be withheld from any K—
they must also embody the restriction that it is impermissible,
whether in promoting those goods or in avoiding or relieving those
evils, to withhold respect from Ks as Ks; or, in other words, to
violate any of the prohibitory precepts in which various kinds of withholding such respect are specified. Such a restriction is plainly a
counterpart of the Pauline principle: it ordains that evil (the
withholding of respect from Ks as Ks) must not be done that good
may come of it. Hence it follows that S must prohibit any action in
which Ks are denied the respect due to them, no matter what the
consequences. For, within S, consequences are morally significant
only as being goods or evils to Ks, and such considerations have been
found insufficient as grounds for violating any of S's prohibitory
precepts.

Analysis of such systems as S therefore shows that the absolute
prohibitions which Bennett deplores in Hebrew-Christian morality
(his name for it is "conservatism") do not arise from "mere
obedience" or "mere muddle"[20] but are inherent in its structure as a
system. Of course, that Bennett was mistaken about this neither
disproves his own consequentialist morality nor confirms the traditional system.

5.3   The Theory of the Double Effect

If the argument of the preceding section is sound, then common
morality as presented in the preceding chapters is consistent in

structure, although possibly it contains incompatible individual precepts. The various kinds of precepts of which it is constructed are such that they are internally related according to simple ordering principles, of which the most important is the Pauline principle that evil is not to be done that good may come of it.

These results, however, depend upon the character of the various kinds of precepts as they are derived from the fundamental principle. They would cease to hold should the character of the precepts be altered in certain ways: for example, should the condition "by morally permissible actions" be omitted from the principles of culture and beneficence. Of course, that condition was not inserted *ad hoc,* in order to eliminate inconsistency, but as unmistakably required by the fundamental principle. However, not all moralists in the Hebrew-Christian tradition formulate the fundamental principle in the Kantian way followed in 2.4. And should it be formulated along the lines favored by Grisez (cf. 2.4), the first-order precepts would so be changed that their structure could not be shown to be consistent along the simple lines followed above.

Most Roman Catholic moral theologians have accepted formulations of the first-order precepts that accord better with Grisez's interpretation of the fundamental principle than with Kant's. As a consequence, in order to secure consistency, they have been led to interpret them according to a theory that yields a far more sophisticated ordering technique than do the Pauline principle and the limited principle of the least evil. This theory was not explicitly stated until the Counter-Reformation;[21] and its correct formulation is still disputed by those who accept the idea underlying it. Most of them follow the version of the nineteenth-century Jesuit J.-P. Gury:

> It is lawful to actuate a morally good or indifferent cause from which will follow two effects, one good and the other evil, if there is a proportionately serious reason, and the ultimate end of the agent is good, and the evil effect is not the means to the good effect.[22]

An uncontroversial illustration is that a physician may permissibly expose himself to infection in treating a patient. The physician's exposure to infection is a human evil, and the patient's recovery is a human good. The action of treating the patient has both these effects; but the bad effect is not the means by which the good one is produced. The physician does not bring about the patient's recovery by exposing himself to infection. On the contrary, he accepts or permits that exposure as an unintended and regretted side-effect of the action by which he intends the good effect. And the intended good effect is a proportionately serious reason for permitting the bad effect.

This example is uncontroversial because causing oneself to be exposed to infection is not in itself an impermissible action. The theory of the double effect becomes controversial when it is applied to cases in which the action of causing the bad effect is held to be impermissible when taken by itself. Aquinas is taken by many commentators to have held that killing a human being, that is, being the agent-cause of his death, is impermissible when taken by itself. [23] If that was Aquinas's view, then what he had to say about self-defence in *Summa Theologiae* II–II, 64, 7 is reasonably interpreted as presupposing the theory of the double effect.

So understood, his argument runs as follows. A man defending himself against an unjust aggressor performs an action in itself lawful; for in itself, self-defence is not only permissible but a duty. This lawful action has two effects: one good, that the man's life is saved; one bad, that the unjust aggressor dies. The reason for "permitting" the aggressor's death is proportionately serious; the ultimate end of the agent is good—his own survival; and the evil effect, the aggressor's death, is not the means to the good effect but rather is an incidental consequence of the means—namely, of incapacitating him for aggression.

The requirement that the evil effect not be the means to the good effect is illustrated by its controversial recent application to the problem of when therapeutic abortion is licit. Since an unborn child is a human being, if killing a human being is impermissible in itself, then killing an unborn child is. Hence performing a craniotomy on a foetus in order to save its mother's life has been held to be impermissible. The movements of the surgeon in carrying out a craniotomy indeed have two effects: a good one—that the mother survives; and a bad one—that the child dies. But the mother's survival is brought about by means of the bad effect: namely, by the removal of the child from her body, a necessary condition of which was crushing or dissecting its head, thereby killing it. Accordingly, the principle of the double effect, as Gury formulated it, does not justify therapeutic abortion by such a method. On the other hand, an operation in which a cancerous womb containing an unborn child is removed, with the consequence that the child dies, has been held to be licit. Here the death of the child is not the means of preserving the mother's life: it dies as a consequence of being removed from the mother's body, because it is not viable; it is not killed to make it possible to remove it. Although widely denounced as inhumane and monstrous by critics whose own humanity is not above suspicion, the distinction does seem to be a reasonable deduction from the principle, as Gury formulated it.

Yet, if the analysis of action developed earlier in this study is sound, Gury's formulation itself must be rejected. In Aquinas's example, a man's action in defending himself in such a way that his unjust aggressor dies is truly describable as the killing of his aggressor. It is a serious error to think that his self-defence is one action and his killing of the aggressor another: they are the same action, differently described. It is an error of the same kind to think that, whereas a craniotomy is a killing of an unborn child, a hysterectomy is not. The surgeon's agency extends to the child's death in both cases, although in the former the causal chain is shorter. Hence if killing a human being is unjust in itself, both in a lethal self-defence and in a hysterectomy the good effect is brought about by impermissible means, namely, the killing of a human being.

Gury's radical error in formulating the principle of the double effect was to take the making of certain bodily movements to be a distinct action from the causing of whatever consequences follow from making them, and the causing of one consequence that follows from them to be a distinct action from the causing of another. On the contrary, as we have seen, an action is identical with the causing of each and every consequence to which the doer's agency in doing it extends. Germain Grisez has accepted this, in a searching study of the problem of justified killing. "[W]hen a human agent through his causality initiates a process in nature," he writes, "all effects expected inevitably to follow belong within the unity of his performance insofar as that unity is a principle of the unity of his action."[24] And he has drawn the inevitable conclusion, that if the good effect of an action can justify doing it despite another evil effect, "whether the good or evil effect is prior in the order of nature is morally irrelevant"; for "all of the events in the indivisible performance of a unitary human act are equally immediate to the agent; none is prior (a means) to another."[25]

The foundation of a correct principle of the double effect, in Grisez's view, is that there are two principles of the unity of action:

the unity of performance, or agency, and the unity of intention.[26] Every human action, as we have seen, is intentional as falling under some description. Now the same action may, under the same or different descriptions, be done with two distinct and nonsubordinated intentions, as when two birds, *A* and *B*, are deliberately killed by the same throwing of the same stone, because *A* is edible and *B* is a nuisance. Grisez contends that "a multiplicity of nonsubordinated intentions always determines a multiplicity of acts, regardless of the unity of performance."[27] So, even though from the point of view of agency, or performance, the killing of *A* and *B* is one and the same action, from the point of view of intention it is two actions, when it is done with the independent intentions of readying *A* for the pot and of putting an end to the nuisance of *B*. By contrast, should the agent's only purpose be to have a bird for the pot, and should the only way in which he can achieve it be to kill *A* with a stone, which would also kill *B*, then Grisez would say that, from the point of view of intention, the only action is the killing of *A*. The death of *B* is an incidental effect, lying outside the scope of the action because outside the agent's intention.

In terms of this analysis, Grisez proposes a principle of the double effect distinct from Gury's, which may be formulated as follows: it is lawful to perform a unitary intentional action which has two effects, one good and one bad, provided that the intention with which it is done is to bring about the good effect, and provided that the good effect is a proportionately serious reason for permitting the bad effect. Whether or not the good effect is a proportionately serious reason is determined according to the principle that evil is to be avoided or prevented wherever possible, except at the cost of an equal or a worse evil.[28] If the nonoccurrence of the good effect would be as great an evil, or a worse evil, than the occurrence of the bad effect, then it is a proportionately serious reason for it. However, even if not killing the bird *A* would be as great an evil, or a greater one, than killing the bird *B*, to kill both *A* and *B* by the same throwing of the same stone would not be justified either if the unitary action of throwing the stone could be "divided," and the killing of *A* without the killing of *B* accomplished by "part" of it (say, by throwing it, but not quite so hard), or if a different action could be performed by which *A* would be killed but not *B* (say, throwing the stone from a different position, so that only *A* was in its path).

Grisez's principle can justify such actions as killing in self-defence, without being exposed to the objections to which Gury's succumbs. Gury's cannot overcome the difficulty that if the force employed in self-defence will not be effective for its purpose unless it inflicts deadly harm on the attacker, then killing the attacker is the means of saving the defender's life; and since killing the attacker is *ex hypothesi* impermissible, it is excluded by Gury's principle. By contrast, Grisez's principle, which presupposes that the saving of the defender's life and the taking of the attacker's are the same unitary action, and that the order in which the saving of the one and the taking of the other occur is morally irrelevant, implies that killing in self-defence is permissible provided that it is necessary and is not, as falling under that description, intentional.

In its implications for problems of abortion, Grisez's principle differs sharply from those customarily drawn from Gury's. Since he holds that the order in which the effects of an action are produced is morally irrelevant, Grisez denies that there is any moral difference between craniotomy and hysterectomy, when both are performed as necessary to save the mother's life. Both are unitary actions in which an unborn child is killed in order that its mother may survive. Even more important, Grisez holds that his principle justifies craniotomy. Provided that only so can the mother's life be saved, and that his intention is solely to save it, and not to kill the child, a surgeon may perform a craniotomy, because saving the mother's life is a proportionately serious reason for causing the child's death. However, there is a catch. "On the same principle," Grisez points out, "one would be equally justified in cutting away the mother to rescue the baby."[29]

This is shocking, not merely to post-Christian notions (which are here irrelevant), but to the Hebrew-Christian tradition itself. And it is important to determine why. The chief reason, I suspect, is that both Judaism and Christianity think of a child as owing a debt of gratitude to its parents, in particular to its mother, for its very life. This would explain why the Jewish sages regarded an unborn child whose difficult birth threatens its mother's life "as one pursuing her and trying to kill her".[30] Of course the baby is utterly inculpable and innocent; but that is not a decisive consideration. A man is entitled to return the fire of a hunter who, thinking him to be a deer, innocently shoots at him, if only so can he save himself; and on the same ground he may kill somebody who strictly speaking is not acting at all, for example a berserk or drugged assailant. The crux is that a mother, to whom her unborn child owes its very life, is not obliged to submit to being killed by labor in childbed; and by-standers are called upon, unless she direct otherwise, to save her life by removing from her body the child that is killing her, treating it as an involuntary pursuer. An analogous case would be shooting to kill an insane child who only so can be prevented from cutting his mother's throat. In all these cases, what matters is not the innocence of the assailant but what is due to the victim. And in any threat to a mother's life arising out of her pregnancy, her status as victim is beyond serious question.

The source of Grisez's difficulties is his conviction that the innate dignity, the pricelessness, of a human being forbids that his life ever be intentionally taken. On the contrary, as I have urged in dis-cussing self-defence and the defence of others (3.3), a man who uses violence upon others forfeits his own immunity to violence to whatever extent may be necessary in order to protect them. Aquinas's remark on this subject seems to go much further: namely, "By sinning a man draws back from the order of reason; and so falls from the [state of] human dignity according to which he is naturally a free being existing for his own sake."[31] This gives some ground for Grisez's protest that the self-degradation of culpable wrongdoing "cannot alter one's human nature or detract from one's inherent dignity as a human person."[32]

Yet, despite his unclear way of putting it, Aquinas's thought seems to be that although man cannot lose the dignity that is his as a rational creature, by violating the order of reason he falls from a state in which his freedom among other free men must be respected, and may without prejudice to his human dignity be subjected to coercion to protect others. This coercion extends to killing him to defend the lives of those he attacks; and both Jewish and Christian tradition has held that it extends to inflicting capital punishment, if civil society has decided that capital punishment is the appropriate penalty for certain heinous crimes. Although there are valid objec-tions to capital punishment (for example, that miscarriages of justice are utterly irremediable and that it degrades the execu-tioners), this line of thought seems to me unexceptionable.

If it is, then the principle of the double effect is superfluous. The traditional difficulties it was invoked to resolve, such as that it is in itself wrong to take human life, vanish as exploded mistakes. And the moral doctrines that can be explained in terms of it are correctly explained on other lines—in particular, by recourse to the Pauline principle.[33]

Finally, the doctrine underlying all forms of the theory of the double effect is that what lies outside the scope of a man's intentions in acting does not belong to his action, and so is not subject to moral judgement. My objection to this is implicit in the analysis of action outlined in 2.2 and 4.1–2. Essentially it is this. The unity of action is, in the terms used by Grisez, entirely a unity of production. A man's actions are events of which he is the agent-cause. All actions, as falling under certain descriptions, are done wittingly and so voluntarily; and whatever a man does voluntarily is subject to moral judgement—it is permissible or impermissible in itself, and he is culpable or inculpable in doing it.

Whatever is done voluntarily is also, under some, at least, of the same descriptions, done intentionally. And the intention with which a man acts is morally important, because many moral judgements of what he does, both first-order and second-order, depend upon it. An action that is, in itself, permissible or even obligatory may be impermissible by virtue of a bad intention. And so, when Aquinas wrote that "moral actions are classified [*recipiunt speciem*] with respect to what is intended,"[34] perhaps he was referring to such formal classifications of them. Certainly he could not consistently have meant that something done voluntarily but outside the scope of intention (*praeter intentionem*), such as killing an unborn child by hysterectomy, would not, as such, be materially licit or illicit—would not, that is, fall under the first-order moral precepts.

5.4 Malthusian Problems

Even if common morality, as presented in the preceding chapters, is consistent in structure, the possibility remains that some of its individual precepts are inconsistent with others. The only way to prove the charge that it contains such individual inconsistencies is to exhibit one; and the only defence is to demolish each alleged inconsistency, case by case.

By far the most familiar charge of inconsistency against traditional Hebrew-Christian morality, and the only one that is plausible, has to do with its doctrine of the family. For, while its principle of parental responsibility presupposes, as was pointed out in 3.6, that it is impermissible voluntarily to become a parent of a child you cannot rear, traditional moralists have been agreed in condemning many of the methods by which a couple can limit the number of children they have. Now it is at least possible to argue that, in some societies at least, unless the forbidden methods of limiting families are resorted to, in some cases individual parents, in others society at large, will not be able to discharge the duty owed to the children who will be born. Such problems are fittingly described as "Malthusian," after T. R. Malthus, whose *Essay on the Principle of Population as it Affects the Future Emprovement of Society* (1st ed., 1798) first persuasively presented the hypothesis that population always tends to outrun the growth of production.

Since the precepts of a moral system are inconsistent on a question only if they give rise to perplexity *simpliciter* with regard to it, in considering whether traditional Hebrew-Christian morality is inconsistent on Malthusian problems, attention must be confined to situations that can occur even though all its precepts have been observed. Hence only problems of overpopulation that could arise in a society in which the great majority of births occur in monogamous families are to be considered.

The precepts of traditional morality that bear upon Malthusian problems fall into two groups.

On one side, parents are held to have the duty of feeding, clothing, sheltering, and educating their children, and the right to noninterference in their doing so. Should either parent die or be incapacitated, the relatives of the bereaved children, and if they cannot or will not, society at large, must share or undertake the responsibility. In simpler times, any healthy laborer and his wife were supposed to be able to feed and clothe the children that would naturally be born to them, and to bring them up to be laborers or laborers' wives. That the supposition did not necessarily correspond to reality appears in many accounts of nineteenth-century England, such as this from Richard Jefferies' *Toilers of the Field*:

> He minded when that sharp old Miss — was always coming round
> with tracts and blankets, like taking some straw to a lot of pigs,
> and lecturing his missis about economy. What a fuss she made,
> and scolded his wife as if she were a thief for having her
> fifteenth boy! His missis turned on her at last and said: "Lor miss,
> that's all the pleasure me an' my old man got." [35]

This anecdote places in an unlovely light the presupposition of the Hebrew-Christian precept of parental responsibility, that it is impermissible voluntarily to become a parent of a child you cannot rear. For the indomitable laborer's wife also expresses a position sanctioned by Hebrew-Christian morality, which from the beginning has looked askance at any requirement of prolonged continence in marriage. Hence, without recent contraceptive techniques, in any society in which most people are healthy and marry young, a normal Jewish or Christian married life ensures that most families will be large. And so inevitably, by Malthusian calculations, a time will come of the kind deplored by Jefferies' intrusive bringer of tracts and blankets, when many parents will not be able adequately to bring up those children, and the population of the society will outrun its natural resources.

Yet Hebrew-Christian morality condemns the most common practice by which preindustrial societies have limited their populations, namely, infanticide. Sterilization is also rejected, as violating the precept forbidding nontherapeutic mutilation. And, although not expressly prohibited, the method described in the following grim passage from A. J. P. Taylor's *English History: 1914-1945* is undoubtedly contrary to the sexual ideal of both Jewish and Christian marriage:

> in the eighteen-eighties, when the decline in the birthrate first appears statistically, the middle class, who were the first to limit their families, simply abstained from sexual intercourse. [36]

Two methods of limiting families have nevertheless been proposed as satisfying the requirements of common morality. One is to abstain from intercourse during those days in the menstrual cycle in which the wife is fertile; the other is to make the act of intercourse infertile by physical devices such as the sheath or diaphragm, or by pharmacological treatments rendering either husband or wife temporarily infertile.

The development of effective methods of both kinds in the past fifty years has posed a new set of problems for moralists. At first contraceptive intercourse was condemned as perverse, and, as Taylor records, its advocates "were still being sent to prison shortly before the first World war." [37] Jewish moralists seem to have found least difficulty in drawing the necessary distinctions, but Protestant opinion was not far behind. In Protestantism, lay opinion makes itself felt more promptly and directly than in Roman Catholicism; and Protestant parents of modest means not only accepted it as a duty to bring their children up in a way that was not possible if they had many, but also failed to see anything wrong with the new contraceptive methods. In the Roman Catholic church, however, all forms of contraception remain condemned, an encyclical issued by

Pope Paul VI in 1968, *Humanae Vitae,* being the present authoritative statement. Yet even among Roman Catholics the force of the argument in *Humanae Vitae* has widely been found obscure. There is undoubtedly a genuine distinction between the approved "rhythm" method of bringing it about that intercourse only takes place when the wife is infertile, and the condemned contraceptive method of having intercourse only when it has been brought about by one of a variety of devices, that she, her husband, or the act is infertile. The two methods are not on a par.[38] But what is wrong with the second is not clear. In a useful article, Anscombe has argued that intercourse deliberately made infertile is an act impermissible in kind, only distinguishable from such forbidden acts as copulation *in vase indebito* in being a different pattern of bodily behavior.[39] Yet intercourse within marriage which is normal in every way, except for having been artifically made what most intercourse is naturally, may reasonably be held to have an erotic significance quite different from that of deviant sexual acts. If it does, and if (as has been maintained in 3.6) the wrongness of deviant sexual acts derives from their significance and not from their merely physical character, a demonstration of their wrongness would be unlikely to apply also to contraceptive intercourse. And if that is so, it will be difficult to find any premise from which the impermissibility of contraception can be derived that anybody would take for a principle of common morality apart from his position on the issue in dispute.

Granting the legitimacy of contraception, any society which can produce contraceptive devices or medicines cheaply, and which can teach its members to use them, can solve Malthusian problems. But what of societies lacking those productive or educational capabilities?

The most common answer, the logical adequacy of which is undeniable, invokes the Pauline principle. The duties of bringing up one's children well, and of promoting a reasonable balance between population and terrestrial resources, are duties of beneficence, and contain the qualification "by all lawful means in one's power." The duties not to commit abortion or infanticide, and not to mutilate oneself by sterilization, are all absolute prohibitions. Hence it is not inconsistent with the duty to bring up one's children adequately, or to contribute to the limitation of the population, to refuse to adopt unlawful means of doing so. Evil is not to be done that good may come of it.

Although this argument is logically adequate, its premises are disputable. To begin with, is it merely a duty of beneficence to bring one's children up adequately? Is it not rather an absolute obligation, a perfect duty in Kant's sense, arising from the impermissibility of procreating any child who cannot be so brought up? If it is, and if every self-supporting couple is entitled to marry, and to have a normal sexual relationship in marriage, are there not possible situations in which perplexity *simpliciter* would arise?

It appears so; but, on closer scrutiny, the appearance begins to dissolve. Despite Malthus, human population generally did not outrun natural resources until technology had become advanced, and it did so partly because of it. Like the Victorian predicament described by Jefferies, the disastrous overpopulation that afflicts modern societies like India and Bangladesh seems to have originated in avoidable failures of understanding and will. And it is doubtful whether, in any environment in which a race of rational animals could naturally evolve, the societies formed by members of that race could not prevent overpopulation except by killing the innocent or invading morally legitimate forms of the family. In sum: it has not been shown that, if contraception is permissible, the traditional prohibitions of abortion, infanticide, and sterilization on the one side, and of invading legitimate forms of the family on the other, would give rise to perplexity *simpliciter* in any conceivable society of rational animals. Nor, if it were to be demonstrated that such a society is possible, would it follow that traditional common morality is inconsistent in principle. It is far more likely that the demonstration would disclose some flaw in the specificatory premises by which the traditional doctrine of the family is derived, and indicate how it may be corrected.

Finally, it should be mentioned that a further possible solution of Malthusian problems would be effected if the recent revival of the pagan doctrine that abortion is permissible could be reconciled with common morality. Two distinct lines of argument have been offered.

The first is that procuring an abortion does not, as was traditionally believed, violate the rights of a human child. This is sometimes asserted on the ground that a foetus is not a human being at all. But that is forced. It would be superfluous to rehearse the argument, neatly summed up in a brilliant if occasionally perverse paper by Roger Wertheimer, for the conclusion that "fertilization ...[is] a non-arbitrary point marking the inception of a particular object, a human being." [40] It is difficult, in view of modern scientific biology, to maintain that, although a newborn child, or a twenty-weeks-old unborn one, is a human being, a zygote is not.

Yet it is tautological to assert that the relations between a nonviable foetus and the world are different from those of a viable one or of a newborn child: namely, that the nonviable foetus can only survive in its mother's womb. And it has been argued that it has no absolute right to be there; and that the mother, under certain circumstances, has the right to have her womb evacuated. Judith Jarvis Thomson has put the matter thus:

> If a set of parents ... have taken all reasonable precautions against having a child, they do not simply by virtue of their biological relationship to the child who comes into existence have a special responsibility for it. They may wish to assume responsibility for it, or they may not wish to. And ... if assuming responsibility for it would require large sacrifices, then they may refuse. [41]

As she recognizes, it may be objected that the parents of an unborn child brought into existence, although unintentionally, by their joint voluntary action, stand to it in a relation utterly different from that in which they would stand to a child left on their doorstep, or from that in which either would stand to another human being whose bloodstream had, without permission, been surgically connected with either of theirs, and who would die if the connection were broken.

That what matters here is not "simply ... their biological relationship" is shown by the related case of a woman who has conceived as a result of rape. Here the unborn child has not been brought into existence by any voluntary action of hers. And so, in my opinion, for her to refuse to have it in her womb would not fail to respect it as a rational creature. Although the child is formally innocent, it is an involuntary intruder whom the mother may have removed from her body, even should that cause its death, without violating the prohibition of causing the death of the materially innocent (cf. 3.3). Of course, she would have no right to object to its being reared in an artificial womb, if that were possible, as presumably one day it will be. And it would be a supererogatory act of great nobility for her to choose to give birth to it, out of reverence for its innocent humanity.

Accordingly, as Mary Anne Warren has acknowledged in a strong and original defence of abortion, if a foetus is human, and if moral duties are owed to human beings as such, then Thomson's argument "can provide a clear and persuasive defence of a woman's right to obtain an abortion only with respect to those cases in which the woman is in no way responsible for her pregnancy." [42] If the absolute right of a pregnant woman to procure an abortion is to be sustained, it must be on the ground that a human being is not, as such, owed moral duties. That is the foundation of the second line of argument for the permissibility of abortion.

In Warren's version, that line is as follows. [43] Only "full-fledged members of the moral community" have moral rights. A being becomes such a full-fledged member by virtue of being a person, not by virtue of being a member of the species *homo sapiens*, or of any other species of rational animal. The characteristics that make for personhood are: consciousness, developed reason, self-motivated activity, the power to communicate messages of an indefinite variety of types, and self-awareness. Hence "highly-advanced, self-aware robots or computers, should such be developed," would be persons, as would "intelligent inhabitants of other worlds." Unborn human children, human infants, and senile human dotards, would not— nor would their counterparts among nonterrestrial rational animals.

This argument implies that moral rights are acquired and lost according as one comes to be capable of certain sorts of mental activity, or ceases to be. To be a person, in Warren's sense, is not the nature of any being, but a stage through which some beings pass. And the concept of that stage varies with those who conceive it, despite Warren's belief that it "is very nearly universal (to people)" [44]—that is, to persons. Michael Tooley, her ally in maintaining that moral rights go with personhood and not with membership of a rational species, let the cat out of the bag when he defined a person as a being having "a (serious) moral right to life." [45] Tooley himself would grant this right to any organism that possesses the concept of a self as a continuing subject of experiences and other mental states, and that believes itself to be such a continuing entity. [46] Hence his persons are not identical with Warren's. But that is the nature of our contemporary concept of personhood: it is a do-it-yourself kit for constructing a "moral community" to your own taste.

Yet within the concepts of traditional morality, could not the core of positions like Warren's and Tooley's be preserved without recourse to the factitious concept of personhood? A being whose actions are subject to moral judgement must be a full rational agent;

and is not full rational agency a stage through which rational animals pass? Why then, should not traditional morality be revised by recognizing only beings in a state of full rational agency as proper objects of moral duties, and possessors of moral rights? Although it has been asserted that the dispute between those who take moral rights to go with a state ("personhood," or full moral agency, or what you will), and those who take them to go with membership of a rational species, probably cannot be settled objectively,[47] there nevertheless seems to be an objective ground for settling it. Duties owed to any being arise out of the respect that is owed to it. Let it, then, be provisionally conceded that, in the first instance, respect is recognized as owed to beings by virtue of a state they are in: say, that of rational agency. If there are beings who reach that state by a process of development natural to normal members of their species, given normal nurture, must not respect logically be accorded to them, whether they have yet reached that state or not? The principle underlying this reasoning is: if respect is owed to beings because they are in a certain state, it is owed to whatever, by its very nature, develops into that state. To reject this principle would be arbitrary, if indeed it would be intelligible. What could be made of somebody who professed to rate the state of rational agency as of supreme value, but who regarded as expendable any rational creature whose powers were as yet undeveloped?

Since it would be arbitrary to accord the respect that generates moral duties to beings in a state of developed rationality, while refusing it to beings who naturally develop into that state, there is a fundamental moral difference between a member of the species *homo sapiens*, or of any other species of rational animal there may be in the universe, and a cat or a sparrow.[48] "Ye are of more value than many sparrows" even when your natural development is at the foetal stage.

Abortion is therefore not a possible solution of Malthusian problems within common morality.[49]

6 Consequentialism

6.1 Cases of Necessity

Our survey of the internal problems of common morality, as it is conceived in the Hebrew-Christian tradition, has shown that it is almost certainly consistent as a system, although some received precepts may be inconsistent with one another, and need to be revised. Of course, consistency is no more than a necessary condition of truth. Besides the internal problem of consistency, common morality is confronted with the external problem of the hard cases to which it gives rise. Yet up to a point, hard cases confirm it. On any serious view, tragedy is part of human life; and morality goes hand in hand with tragedy.

Admittedly, a sense of proportion is necessary. Concerning the Torah of Moses, Maimonides wrote:

> Should an idolater arise and coerce an Israelite to violate any one of the commandments mentioned in the Torah under threat that otherwise he would put him to death, the Israelite is to commit the transgression rather than suffer death; for concerning the commandments it is said, "which, if a man do them, he shall live by them" (*Leviticus*, 18:5): "*Live* by them," and not die by them.[1]

However, this permission had two kinds of exception. First, it did not apply to the prohibitions of idolatry, inchastity, or murder. Second, the idolater's purpose must be personal advantage, and not to bring about a violation of the Law for its own sake. If his purpose is to abolish the Jewish religion or any of its precepts, "it is the

Israelite's duty to suffer death and not violate any one," even of the lesser commandments.[2]

Similar exceptions are implicit in common morality. Respect for human beings as rational creatures does not require a man, under credible threat of being killed if he disobeys a command to take something that does not belong to him, to refuse to obey that command; but it does require him to refuse to rape, mutilate, or murder anybody. Indeed, in picking up and removing what does not belong to you, if you are under threat of death or serious injury, you do not steal; for you, as distinct from whoever coerces you, do not appropriate what is not yours. As a rough generalization, you may, under coercion, be an involuntary accomplice (in the colloquial sense of "involuntary") to a wrong, provided that your action does not irreparably violate what is due to some human being as such.

Even allowing for these implicit exceptions, two external objections to common morality are made. The first is that observing it would sometimes lead to irreparable disaster for the individual who observes it. In such "cases of necessity," it is argued, it is reasonable to break any moral precept whatever. The second is that public men, in gaining, keeping, and exercising public authority, must sometimes break the moral law in the common interest. Any member of a civil society may conceivably have a public responsibility thrust upon him; and if he refuses to dirty his hands in the common interest when he has such a responsibility, he falls short in doing his duty as a member of that society.

Should either of these objections be conceded to be valid, then it would follow that common morality, as conceived in the Hebrew-Christian tradition, is not what it claims to be: is not, that is, a law binding upon every human being as a rational creature. It may possibly be binding under certain conditions, but not unconditionally. And what, if any, the conditions are under which it is binding, and what is binding absolutely or unconditionally, may be discovered by investigating what is binding when it breaks down. Since, *ex hypothesi*, it will have broken down because of certain consequences which follow from observing its precepts, what will be binding absolutely will be determined by those consequences. This new absolute system will therefore be, in Anscombe's term, "consequentialist."[3] Unfortunately, consequentialist systems turn out to be, not one, but legion.

But does common morality break down when confronted with

alleged cases of necessity, or with what has been called "the problem of dirty hands"?

A classic budget of cases of necessity, first investigated by the Stoics, is introduced by reflection on what it is permissible to do to a shipwrecked man, neither harming nor threatening to harm anybody, who is keeping himself afloat by clinging to a plank. Even if he has no hope of rescue, it would clearly be murder for somebody clinging to another plank to dislodge him. But would it be murder, would it even be culpable, for somebody without anything to support him to try to wrest away the plank? When ships are wrecked, the survivors often struggle over the possession of flotsam that may support one or two, but not more. Is it reasonable to denounce so wholly natural an action as murder?

The following variations on this theme, preserved by Cicero from a lost work by the Stoic Hecato of Rhodes, were to become familiar topics in Christian casuistry.

> "Suppose that a man who has clung to a plank from a wrecked ship is a fool, shall a sage wrest it away, if he can?" [Kirk glosses "a fool" as "to the Stoic, as to the Jewish moralist, . . . always a moral degenerate"; and "a sage" as "the man of real moral value to the community."]
> [Hecato] denies it, as being wrongful [iniuriam].
> "Well, shall the owner of the ship not repossess his own property?"
> "Not in the least, any more than he may decide, at sea, to throw a passenger overboard, on the ground that [the ship] is his. For until they have reached [the port] for which the ship was chartered, the passengers rather than the owner have the right to use it."
> "Well, if there is one plank, and two shipwrecked men, both sages, may each seize it for himself, or should each yield to the other?"
> "One should yield, but to the one whose life is more valuable, either in itself, or for the sake of the general good [rei publicae]."
> "But what if in those respects the value of each is equal?"
> "Then there will be no struggle, but one will yield to the other as though he had lost a draw or a tossup."[4]

In his opinion about how two sages ought to conduct themselves in such a situation—Nullum erit certamen—Hecato in part anticipated the Jewish and Christian view: everybody ought to do what he can to survive; but he ought also to be prepared to die if he must, and he ought not to buy his life at the price of another's.

Nevertheless, the implications of common morality for such questions are not exhausted by this first-order doctrine. Materially, it is wrong for a shipwrecked man to save his own life by dislodging somebody else from a plank and fending him off, so that he drowns. Formally, how culpable is such an action? Although the other's death is not intended, the agent did act voluntarily. Yet the blame falling to him on that account is generally allowed, in the Hebrew-Christian tradition, to be mitigated by the circumstance that he acted in fear of immediate death. Whewell explained why.

[S]uch a fear, in most persons, [he wrote] produces a paroxysm and agony of terrour and trouble which subvert the usual balance of mind, and the usual course of thought and action. What is done under such circumstances, may be considered as an exception to the common condition of the man's being. [5]

Even though the fear of immediate death probably would not deprive a man of the power to act voluntarily, actions performed in a state of such fear are apt to be uncharacteristic and ill-considered, especially if the danger is sudden and unexpected, or the manner of the impending death horrible. Yet what has been said earlier about fear as diminishing the voluntariness of an action applies here. Although fear exculpates only if it deprives the agent of the power to act voluntarily, it always, according to its nature and degree, diminishes responsibility.

That the danger of imminent death, and the extreme fear arising from it, may mitigate blame but cannot exculpate, was forcibly explained by a Victorian chief justice, Lord Coleridge, in the celebrated case of *R. v. Dudley and Stephens.*[6] His judgement has some claim to be considered a classic expression of the position of common morality.

A jury had rendered a special verdict, finding the facts of the case to be substantially as follows, but referring them to the High Court for a ruling as to the law.

The prisoners, able-bodied English seamen, and the deceased, an English boy between seventeen and eighteen years of age, the crew of an English yacht, were cast away in a storm on the high seas sixteen hundred miles from land, and were compelled to put into an open boat. The food they took with them was all consumed in twelve days, and having been for eight days without food, and for six days without water, the prisoners killed the boy. The boy when killed was lying at the bottom of the boat quite helpless and weak, and unable to make any resistance, and did not assent to his being killed. The prisoners and another man who was with them, fed upon the body and blood of the boy for four days, when they were picked up by a passing vessel. The verdict went on thus: 'That if the men had not fed upon the body of the boy, they probably would not have survived to be so picked up and rescued . . . ; that the boy, being in a much weaker condition, was likely to have died before them; . . . that, under the circumstances, there appeared to the prisoners every probability that unless they then fed, or very soon fed, upon the boy or one of themselves, they would die of starvation; that there was no appreciable chance of saving life except by killing someone for the others to eat; that, assuming any necessity to kill anybody, there was no greater necessity for killing the boy than any of the other three men.'[7]

The submission of the defence was that various authorities, in their definitions of murder, imply that, in order to save your life, it is not unlawful to take the life of another, even though that other neither attacks nor threatens your life, nor is guilty of any other wrongful action.

This contention appeared to the court, "new and strange";[8] and, upon consideration, they utterly rejected it.

[I]t is admitted [Lord Coleridge wrote] that the deliberate killing of this unoffending and unresisting boy was clearly murder, unless the killing can be justified by some well-recognised excuse admitted by the law. It is further admitted that there was in this case no such excuse, unless the killing was justified by what has been called necessity. But the temptation to the act which existed here was not what the law has ever called necessity. Nor is this to be regretted.[9]

In law, that is, in the English Common Law, the necessity that justifies killing is the exculpating necessity of defending oneself or others from physical violence. When it is necessary to do so in order to save one's own life, the temptation to kill another, who commits no offence, may be almost impossible to overcome; but, "if the temptation to murder in this case were to be held by law an absolute defence of it," there would be "an absolute divorce of law from morality," fatal in its consequences.[10]

Yet the court recognized that simply to have declared what the law is on the question would have been monstrous. After alluding to the Sovereign's prerogative of mercy, Lord Coleridge continued as follows.

It must not be supposed that, in refusing to admit temptation to be an excuse for crime, it is to be forgotten how terrible the temptation was, how awful the suffering, how hard in such trials to keep the judgment straight and the conduct pure. We are often compelled to set up standards we cannot reach ourselves, and to lay down rules which we could not ourselves satisfy. But a man has no right to declare temptation to be an excuse, though he might himself have yielded to it, nor allow compassion for the criminal to change or weaken in any manner the legal definition of the crime.[11]

Murder had been done, but in such circumstances that the normal punishment for murder would have been altogether unjust and inappropriate. The final note in the report of the case reads, "The prisoners were afterwards respited and their sentence commuted to one of six months' imprisonment without hard labour."[12]

Alike in its definition of the material precept and in its appraisal of culpability, Lord Coleridge's judgement is a model of how cases of necessity are treated according to common morality. It is therefore of some interest that adversaries of common morality have for the most part preferred to argue from other cases, usually imaginary ones.

In recent discussions, variations upon the following imaginary case have won a good deal of attention.[13] A rockfall occurs, catching the first of a group of potholers who are making their way out of a cave, in which water is rising rapidly. The man caught in the rocks is not seriously injured and may expect to be rescued in a day or two by search parties. Those behind him, however, will be drowned in a few hours by the rising water unless they make a passage through the fallen rocks. They can do so, but only by blasting the rocks away with the explosives they have with them, which will cause the death of the man caught in the rocks.

Of this case, Kai Nielsen has written as follows.

If there really is no other way of unsticking our . . . man, and if plainly, without blasting him out, everyone in the cave will drown, then, innocent or not, he should be blasted out. This . . . does not reveal a callousness toward life, for the people involved are caught in a desperate situation in which, if such extreme action is not taken, many lives will be lost and far greater misery will obtain. . . . Surely we must choose between evils here, but is there anything more reasonable, more morally appropriate, than choosing the lesser evil when doing or allowing some evil cannot be avoided?[14]

Nielsen's argument is twofold: first, that since it is evident that in this case the stuck potholer ought to be blasted out, and since that is incompatible with the traditional moral doctrine that no (materially) innocent person may be killed under any circumstances, the traditional doctrine must be repudiated; and second, that the true moral doctrine is plain from the case, namely, that whenever a certain number of human lives can be saved, but only by taking a smaller number of such lives, the lesser evil is to be chosen and the smaller number taken.

The second part of this argument is unpersuasive, because the moral doctrine advanced is far stronger than the case requires. For example, it sanctions the murder of the ship's boy by Dudley and Stephens, although that would horrify many who would blast out the stuck potholer. And weaker doctrines are to hand that do not have such implications. For example, on Grisez's theory of the double effect, the crucial considerations would be that the blasting away of the obstructing rocks and the killing of the man caught in them is a unitary act, and that, since the sole intention of that act would be to save life, the unintended evil of killing somebody can be disregarded, as being a consequence outside the scope of the agents' intention, for which there is a proportionately serious reason. The action of Dudley and Stephens cannot be justified in this way; for killing the boy was a necessary part of what they intended, and not outside its scope.

However, Grisez's theory of the double effect having been rejected, the system of common morality we have developed cannot be reconciled by means of it to the blasting out of Nielsen's stuck potholer. Can it be reconciled to it by any means at all?

I think it can. Human beings are not morally forbidden to risk their lives on suitably serious enterprises (cf. 3.2), of which it is not unthinkable that potholing is one. And, although it is not beyond dispute, it does not appear to be impermissible for a group of human beings embarking on such an enterprise to agree that, if in the course of it, through nobody's fault, they should be confronted with a choice between either allowing certain of their number to be killed, or doing something that would, against everybody's will, cause the deaths of fewer of their number, the latter should be chosen. In so agreeing, each member of the group would act in his own probable interest. And so, if the situation contemplated came about, and the agreement were put into effect, it would not be a case of one subgroup, because it was larger, sacrificing the lives of another that

was smaller. An agreement of the kind described would have force
even if it was tacit: that is, even if, without saying so, all members of
the group take it as accepted by all that they should conduct
themselves in accordance with it. And perhaps it would have force
even if it were virtual: that is, even if all members of the group, were
they to think about it, would agree that everybody in the group
would think that so to conduct themselves was the only rational
course. If this is correct, then in any group of potholers in which
such an agreement is in force, actually or virtually, it is permissible,
in the circumstances of Nielsen's example, to blast out one of their
number who is stuck. And with most such groups, such agreements
will be in force.

Is the intuitive plausibility of Nielsen's verdict in cases like that of
the potholers to be explained in this way? Evidence that it is may be
found in the fact that, in relevantly similar cases in which the
possibility is excluded of even a virtual agreement that the fewer are
to die, verdicts like his are not plausible at all. Imagine the following
situation. A sizable group of people are trapped in an excavation by
the collapse of the one passage leading out of it. However, there is a
shaft for a periscope, which they can ascend by ladder to within six
feet of the earth's surface. At this point the periscope goes through
to the surface in an airtight steel pipe. Water is rising in the
excavation, and they will all be drowned before they are rescued,
unless they can rapidly break through the six feet of earth between
the top of the periscope shaft and the surface. They can do so only by
blasting it with explosives left in the excavation. However, if they do,
as they can see through the periscope, they will blow up a small party
of picnickers, who are lunching by the periscope's "eye." Signals
through the periscope are not understood, and its shaft is too
strongly built to be dismantled in time for them to call through its
pipe to give warning.

Whether, in this case, Nielsen would reaffirm his unrestricted
principle that the lesser evil is to be chosen, because otherwise
"many lives will be lost, and far greater misery will obtain,"[15] I do
not know. However, many who would sanction the blasting out of
the stuck potholer would intuitively condemn the blowing up of the
innocent picnickers as murder, however great the temptation to
commit it. And if in both cases the many should choose to die, I
suspect that the released potholer would, perhaps with irrational
guilt, think himself the beneficiary of an act of supererogation, but
that the spared picnickers would not.

Although moral intuition is an unreliable and corruptible guide, the doctrine of the legitimacy of consent to possible sacrifice in a common enterprise supplies a ground for the intuitive difference between the two cases—a ground consistent with common morality. By contrast, Nielsen's unrestricted principle of the least evil implies that there is no significant difference between them, or between both and the case of Dudley and Stephens. But that is not made explicit in his discussion.

Every moral system gives rise to hard cases, in which those who accept it must, contrary to their desire, cause harm or permit it. And to the best of my knowledge, no alleged case of necessity among small groups of individuals which has ever been shown to arise in common morality is more than a hard one: none of them compels us to abandon common morality for some alternative like Nielsen's, or to add to it "some form of 'disastrous consequences' clause, allowing prima facie obligations to be overridden when the consequences of keeping them are sufficiently bad."[16] Traditional moralists recognize that there are cases in which the consequences of abiding by common morality will be terrible, and in which almost anybody would succumb to temptation. But they maintain that such consequences as that more die rather than fewer, although tragic, are morally acceptable. Lord Coleridge did not venture to say that, in the place of Dudley and Stephens, he would have acted better than they did; but he thought he had no choice but to say that there was a better way of acting.

6.2   The Problem of Dirty Hands

Cases in which the choice of evils is between the destruction of a whole community, or grave injury to it, and the death or grave injury of one of its members, are on a different footing from cases in which the choice is between the death or suffering of a larger or of a smaller number of individuals. The welfare of a genuine community is a good common to all its members, and most of them will acknowledge that they ought to be prepared, at need, to make sacrifices for it. Yet although there is a distinction between the two kinds of case, it must not be assumed that the sacrifice of an individual for the good of the community is justified; and that if common morality forbids it, then common morality must be superseded. Although the example may be suspect as Christian, one is given pause by the recollection that the high-minded and noble-sounding principle "It is expedient that one man should die for the people," was advanced by the high priest Caiaphas to justify the judicial murder of Jesus.[17] We may begin by disposing of a class of cases with which a number of moral philosophers have recently occupied themselves, apparently in the hope of breaking down the deep and still prevalent conviction that there are some things a man absolutely must not do. All members of the class have a common form: a very powerful person or society (usually, a wicked dictator) threatens to bring a calamity upon a whole community (usually, its destruction by nuclear bombardment) unless it will do something abominable by the standards of common morality (say, to procure the judicial murder of an innocent man).

Such cases of threats to a whole community must be distinguished from imaginary cases in which the devilish tyrant threatens, say to torture all a man's children to death unless the man himself personally tortures one of them to death. These cease to be very persuasive when one perceives their underlying theme—that anybody sufficiently powerful "who wants us to do something we think wrong has only to threaten that otherwise he will do something we think worse."[18] And besides, even from a consequentialist point of view, complying with such threats is not prudent. On the one hand, if you refuse, the tyrant may relent; on the other hand, you cannot rely on him to keep his word even if you comply with his threat—the inductive evidence of previous cases would not be a safe ground for prediction.

In cases of threats to a whole community, not only are the threats more terrible, they are also as a rule rational. In consequence, pertinent nonimaginary examples can be given. During and after the Roman persecutions which followed the Jewish revolts in A.D. 66–70 and 132–135, the Jewish rabbis were confronted with problems of demands made, both by an irresistible government and by hostile gangs of bandits, upon communities and groups of a people disarmed and helpless. It was accepted as Halachah, or binding rabbinic law, that when a company of Jews was threatened with death unless they surrendered one of their number, "though they all be killed, they shall not surrender a single soul from Israel."[19] The word "surrender" (*masar*) is here used in its usual pejorative sense, which implies treachery, by contrast with the neutral "give up" (*yehabh*) and "give" (*nathan*).[20] There are cases in which the giving up of a man by a community would not be "surrendering" him, and it fell to the rabbis to define the difference.

Just as there are Christians who do not discriminate between any voluntary homicide and murder, so there were rabbis who maintained that to give up anybody under any circumstance, was to "surrender" him; but the received opinion was that there are distinctions, and that they differ according as the demand is to hand over a man to be killed, or a woman for defilement.

In the former case, the accepted rule was as follows.

> If a company of Jews ... is threatened by heathens who say, "Give us one of you that we may kill him, otherwise we shall kill you all," they must rather all be killed. However, if the demand is for a named individual, like Sheba son of Bichri, then, in order to avoid wholesale slaughter, he should be surrendered. [21]

The rationale of this ruling, as Daube explains it, was this. A demand for a named individual would normally be made in the name of some institution claiming civil authority, because the individual demanded was, rightly or wrongly, held to have transgressed its laws, or the commands of its officials, in some way deemed capital. In such cases the man would often be quite innocent by Jewish law. But, since presumably his relations with the authority he offended were voluntary, he could not expect a whole company to die rather than give him up. Even in such a case, however, one rabbi, Resh Laquish, held that the company should not give anybody up unless it had satisfied itself that, from the point of view of the authority making it, the demand was justified. [22] And nobody denied that a demand for an unnamed man could only be made out of cruelty or hatred for Jews as such, and was never to be complied with.

The rule for treating a demand to hand over a woman for defilement was different. First, it is limited to companies consisting only of women, presumably for the reason Daube gives: "where men are present, Oriental men, there is no need to lay down that not one woman may be handed over." [23] And second, there is no exception for a named woman; for that a particular woman was wanted for purposes of defilement could not possibly imply any special responsibility on her part. However, two exceptions are allowed: a company of Jewish women, to whom such a demand is made, may hand over one "already unclean" or a slave, that is, a harlot or one already presumably used for concubinage. [24]

These rulings in rabbinic law, although they are disputable and were disputed, show far better than any moralist known to me has done how common morality would deal with the same questions. As Daube writes of one set of such rulings, and might have written of nearly all, the rabbi who made them (in this case Judah ben Ilai) implied no abdication of ethical standards. Fervently desirous of preventing the abolition of Palestinian Jewry, he did draw the line where reprieve would be bought at the price of moral cohesion and self-respect.[25]

This comment anticipates the reply that must be made, from the point of view of common morality, against the external objection that it is irrational to stick to common morality if it brings about the destruction of one's community.

Common morality is outraged by the consequentialist position that, as long as human beings can remain alive, the lesser of two evils is always to be chosen. Its defenders maintain, on the contrary, that there are minimum conditions for a life worthy of a human being, and that nobody may purchase anything—not even the lives of a whole community—by sacrificing those conditions. A community that surrenders its members at the whims of tyrants ceases to be anything properly called by that name; and individuals willing to accept benefits at the price of crimes committed upon other individuals degrade their humanity. Common morality allows a certain room for compliance with tyrannical external force, when resistance has become impossible; but there is a line that must be drawn beyond which compliance is excluded, and the example of rabbinic teaching is a guide in drawing it.

Contemporary consequentialists have gone far beyond licensing such actions as betrayal and murder by communities desperate to preserve a remnant in face of irresistible external threats. Impressed by Machiavellian arguments that a state may flourish more under rulers who do not regard themselves as bound by common morality than under rulers who do, they have drawn the Machiavellian conclusion that it is a ruler's duty as a ruler to disregard morality when it collides with *raison d'Etat*. On this view, a good ruler is not a man of what Kant called *gute Wille* but one of what Machiavelli called *virtù*, that is, of "vitality, or energy and courage without regard for their objects, energy and courage both for good and for evil."[26] And every successful ruler whose success was not an accident will have the same confession to make as Hoerderer, the Communist leader in Sartre's *Les Mains sales:*

I have dirty hands right up to the elbows. I've plunged them in filth and blood. Do you think you can govern innocently?[27]

If this is so, then common morality is not for humanity's true representatives, the leaders who, by holding themselves above the petty scruples of the led, make possible a better life for them. The superiority of political leaders to ordinary moral scruples has been depicted romantically. Michael Walzer, for example, has recently revived Max Weber's portrait of the successful politician as a tragic hero, in whom the genius of politics lives in discord with the god of love; and who, when that discord breaks out in irreconcilable conflict, chooses to save the public rather than his own soul.[28] It is true that he wistfully adds that it would be a good idea if successful politicians were to be called upon to end their careers with a public penance, in the same way as Camus's anarchist assassins willingly submit to their executioners. But if Weber's portrait is a true one, to exact such a penance would be hypocritical. If citizens are unwilling to forgo what can only be obtained by actions they are unwilling to do themselves, they are not entitled to exact penance from anybody they appoint to do them on their behalf.

Hence R. B. Brandt and R. M. Hare have argued irresistibly against Walzer that, if no consideration outweighs the ends of good government, and if the ends of good government can be accomplished only by sometimes traversing the precepts of common morality, then whatever validity common morality has, it has conditionally, within the scope of a more embracing consequentialist system.[29] If they are right, successful politicians are not tragic heroes, but simply good intelligent men making hard decisions, as good intelligent men sometimes must. The notion that they are sinning on our behalf must be rejected, as proceeding from an uncritical and primitive conception of morality.

Before succumbing to the arguments of Brandt and Hare, it is well to scrutinize the Machiavellian assumption on which they rest: that in politics nobody succeeds except by getting his hands dirty. This is not the truism that politicians are men, not angels, which no moral theory has ever denied. It is rather the proposition that the political goods that matter, liberty, prosperity, and peace, can only be procured by courses of action which involve grave violations of common morality, if not in the use of power, then in its acquisition. Although this bit of cynicism sometimes passes as popular wisdom, it is not seriously defensible.

Certainly no such conclusion follows from Hegel's valid observation that the major progressive movements of history are seldom foreseen by progressives as they in fact come about, and that they are as often traceable to wicked or imprudent actions as to good or prudent ones, and to motives that are anything but progressive. It is a fallacy to infer, because a wicked action was necessary to a politically good result, that it could have been part of a rationally justifiable political program.

Hegel went on to maintain that not only are "the miseries that have overwhelmed the noblest of nations and polities, and the finest exemplars of private virtue, . . . a fatality which no intervention could alter," but also that "the vast congeries of volitions, interests, and activities" which bring those miseries about are "the instruments and means of the World-Spirit for attaining its object."[30] Both positions depend upon a vulgar illusion. Hegel's eyes, like those of most historians, were drawn to the events that have led up to the great periods in the culture of the past, and especially to the period he considered the greatest known to him—his own present. But since he simply dismissed the possibility that things could have happened otherwise, he gratuitously denied what common morality presupposes, that no great political and cultural goods yet brought into existence could not have been brought into existence in other ways. That good has come about through crime does not show that it could only have come about through crime. Furthermore, by approaching the crimes and follies of history through the goods to which they give rise, he averted his attention from the evils to which they also give rise. It need not be disputed that a number of political goods were conferred on Europe by Napoleon; but history is largely silent about the long-term miseries directly produced by his aggressive wars, and yet more silent about the connection between his career and the fatal forms taken by the militarization of Europe in the following century and a half. No philosophy of history has produced any evidence worth the name either that, in the long run, any great political good could only have come about through barbarous or oppressive means, or that the barbarous and oppressive actions without which some political goods would not have come about have not also brought about compensating evils.

To be fair, Walzer does not offer historical justifications of the great historical crimes: aggressive wars, religious persecution, slavery, despotism, economic oppression. His chosen examples are lesser, more personal misdeeds, of kinds which occur in ordinary "bourgeois-liberal" politics. He does not pretend that any great political good has ever been attained by the methods of Stalin, or Napoleon, or Robert Clive, but he cannot rid himself of the Machiavellian conviction that common morality incapacitates ordinary politicians in constitutional states for acting effectively when confronted with unscrupulousness or criminal violence. The weakness of his case sufficiently appears from his two chief examples. The first is of a reforming politician, who would govern effectively and well if elected to office, but who cannot be elected "unless he makes a deal with a dishonest ward boss, involving the granting of contracts over the next four years." [31] Walzer agrees that effective reformers must sometimes make such deals, but maintains that they dirty their hands in doing so. Common morality, I think, is subtler.

A case of judicial bribery examined by Richard Baxter is a close parallel to Walzer's. In a state in which public officials regularly demand bribes, may a man bribe court officials to do him justice, or to keep them from doing him injustice?

> You may not in case your cause be bad, give any thing to procure injustice against another; no nor speak a word for it nor desire it: this I take as presupposed. You may not give money to procure justice, when the law of the land forbiddeth it, and when it will do more hurt accidentally to others than good to you; when it will harden men in the sin of bribery, and cause them to expect the like from others. But except it be when some such accidental greater hurt doth make it evil, it is as lawful as to hire a thief not to kill me; when you cannot have your right by other means, you may part with a smaller matter for a greater. [32]

The principle underlying Baxter's ruling resembles that by which self-defence is allowed. Even in a society in which corruption is normal and lawful, it is wrong to initiate the corruption of others or to harden them in it; but it is not wrong to defend yourself by means of corruption against corruption already initiated by others.

There is much that a reforming politician in the situation Walzer describes may not do without dirtying his hands. He may not initiate the corruption of a previously honest ward boss. He may not promise to secure him a contract unless he can do so lawfully; and he may not make other wrong or unlawful promises, for example, to arrange to have work contracted for inadequately inspected. Moreover, the harm done in granting the contract—presumably that the public will pay more than it would with another contractor—must be outweighed by good gained by means of it. Yet Carl Sandburg has recorded that it was by "patronage gifts that would have raised a high and noisy scandal if known by the opposition" that Abraham Lincoln procured the passage through the House of Representatives of the constitutional amendment abolishing slavery.[33] And Sandburg, like Baxter, and like most ordinary decent men, would rightly have been taken aback at the suggestion that by doing so Lincoln violated common morality.

Walzer's second example is that of an honest politician who has seized power in an imperialist country during a disastrous colonial war, with a pledge to decolonize. In going to the colony to treat with the rebels, he finds that terrorists have hidden bombs in a number of apartment buildings in the capital, which are set to be detonated within a day. Shall he order the torture of a captured terrorist, to find where the bombs are, or shall he permit many people to be killed by their explosion?

Walzer appears to think it the politician's political duty to have the terrorist tortured, even though torture is always and in all circumstances abominable.[34] Yet as he has described the situation, it is far from evident that torture would even be expedient. Could not the buildings be evacuated and searched?

Let it be the case that they cannot. Let it also be the case that the information by which alone the explosions can be prevented is in fact locked in the bosom of a certain terrorist. Would it even then be expedient to torture him? The answer, I think, turns on whether he is known to possess the information—known, not suspected. I assume that Walzer would agree that, given civilized political aims, it is not expedient to sanction torture in order to extract information from those not known to possess it.

An additional circumstance should not be forgotten: namely, what the law of the land is. Although this study allows no scope for entering into political questions, I assume that no legal system can permit the use of torture for any purpose and also secure to those who live under it that immunity from arbitrary mistreatment that is necessary to civilized life. And if a law forbidding the use of torture is in force, it is doubtful whether any officer of state may expediently break it, even in a case such as that described. However, by stipulating that his politician has assumed power in a disastrous colonial war, and is acting in the colony, Walzer entitles us to presume that, in the case under consideration, laws safeguarding personal liberties have been suspended. Correspondingly, rebels and revolutionaries whose cause is just would not be bound by the laws of the society against which they were fighting. Given that the political ends of the politician under consideration are civilized and that he keeps all of them in mind, even in situations of the kind described there can be few sets of circumstances in which he could reasonably conclude that to torture the captured terrorist would be politically expedient. Yet it cannot be denied that there are some such sets of circumstances. Suppose that such a set was to occur, is Walzer's assumption correct that to torture the prisoner would be morally impermissible?

Walzer's reason is curious: namely, that even those responsible for terrorist campaigns do not deserve to be tortured. In itself, his point is a good one. Torture is impermissible as punishment; for it degrades the person tortured, and to degrade a culprit violates the respect due to him as a rational creature. But, since the problem in our example is not one of punishment, the desert of the prisoner is irrelevant. The politician in question wants to know whether it violates the conditional immunity from violence owed to every rational creature, to wring by torture from a prisoner known to be withholding it, and from whom it can be obtained in no other way, information necessary for saving the lives and limbs of many innocent people. He is resolved to obey the precept, *Thou shalt not stand idly by the blood of thy neighbor;* and his question is whether, in the case before him, that precept sanctions the use of torture.

The answer must turn on whether or not the prisoner satisfies the conditions for immunity to violence. And unless positive law prohibits it (and in the case described it does not) it is hard to discern how the terrorist in question could be supposed to satisfy them. For one condition of immunity to violence is that one not be participating in an attempt on the lives or the bodily security of other innocent persons; and the terrorist *ex hypothesi* is so participating: he is, at the very least, deliberately allowing innocent persons to be killed and mutilated by withholding his knowledge; and if he had a hand in placing the bombs, he is allowing the consummation of murders and mutilations he himself has set in train. Until the nineteenth century, positive law and moral opinion joined in permitting torture in such a case. In the past century and a half, torture has come to be prohibited by law in all civilized countries; and rightly, because it has been found practically impossible, while allowing it at all, to confine its use to the very few cases in which it would be morally permissible. But we must not confound the moral prohibitions deriving from a good positive law with prohibitions of common morality per se. And so the problem of dirty hands dissolves. It arises from a twofold sentimentalization: of politics, imagining it as an arena in which moral heroes take hard (that is, immoral) decisions for the good of us all; and of common morality, ignoring the conditions it places on the immunities it proclaims.

6.3   Consequentialist Theories

Even though unprejudiced investigation discloses that Hebrew-Christian common morality does not lack defensible ways of treating cases, not only of necessity but also of institutional corruption and of grave public danger, the tragic choices it sometimes calls for remain disquieting. Perhaps traditional morality is so constructed that observing it will not lead to disaster, but is it not rational to look for something better? Any acceptable moral system exalts benevolence. Of course, false conceptions must be corrected, in which bene-volence is confounded with willingness to barter fundamental human goods for mere animal survival. But, those corrections made, is not the way open for a traditional morality of benevolence, the principle of which would be that human good—genuine and not merely apparent human good—is to be maximized?

In terms of the theory of action presupposed in our investigation of traditional morality, a theory of morality founded on benevolence would distinguish a right action from a wrong one solely on the ground that its consequences, in the extended sense in which not all consequences are causal (cf. 2.2), are better than the consequences of any alternative action open to its agent. With respect to the properties directly mentioned in their minimal or basic descriptions, such goodness or badness as actions possess is insignificant. Vir-tually all the good or evil produced by human beings is to be found, not in their actions in themselves, but in the consequences of their actions. Hence a truly rational system of morality, so it may be argued, must begin with the principle that actions are right if and only if their consequences are better than those of any other actions that could be done instead.

I shall speak of all moral theories deriving from this principle as "consequentialist." The word was introduced into technical philo-sophical English by G. E. M. Anscombe, in a paper which for many of us remains a landmark.[35] There, she applied it to any theory according to which it is right to violate any rule or precept, as long as the foreseen consequences of abiding by it are sufficiently horrible.[36] But such a usage is arbitrarily restrictive. The theories that are "consequentialist" according to it constitute only one species of theories according to which actions are judged morally solely according to the nature of their consequences per se, and it seems preferable to use the word "consequentialist" for the genus rather than for the species.

The specific variety of theory which Anscombe called "consequentialist" derives from an assumption which not all consequentialists make: that the only consequences pertinent to calculating the rightness or wrongness of an individual action are its consequences as an individual action. Although *prima facie* plausible, there are two reasons for rejecting this assumption.

First, some of the most important consequences of actions flow from them, not as individual actions in a certain natural environment, but as members of sets of cooperative or group actions. But it is doubtful whether many beneficial cooperative actions would be done at all, if each cooperator were to stand on the principle that he would not act until he had satisfied himself that the others would. If we want cooperation, we had better not all wait to act until we know what others will do.

Second, there are mental acts, such as intending and resolving, which involve continuing dispositions to action. Whether or not such acts are to be classified as actions (cf. 4.1) it is unnecessary to decide: under certain descriptions they are voluntary, but under none can intending be intentional. What matters in the present connection is that they have consequences. And the complex of mental acts of judgement and resolution that constitutes accepting a way of life is of central importance in both the Jewish and the Christian religious traditions. Such acts of acceptance are continuous. Their doers may either persevere in them or not, and whether or not they persevere will show itself in the dispositions to action they exhibit.

Acts of accepting a way of life are important for consequentialist theories because they usually have consequences over and above the consequences of the individual actions to which they commit those who persevere in them. Thus, that you are committed, by your acceptance of a way of life, to doing certain things in certain circumstances, can become known to others and affect their conduct quite apart from your doing those things on any occasion whatever.

Hence it is not unimaginable that the consequences of somebody's accepting a certain way of life, say, the way of life involved in joining Alcoholics Anonymous, may be better than the consequences of accepting some other or none, even though on occasion it commits him to individual actions the consequences of which are worse than those of some other individual action open to him. Even for alcoholics, one drink does not always have bad consequences, and may have good ones.

In such a situation, consequentialists would be true to their own principle if they insisted on weighing the goodness of the consequences of the alcoholic's acceptance of the way of life of Alcoholics Anonymous against the goodness of the consequences of any alternative pattern of individual actions actually open to him, in which some individual actions would have better consequences than some of those in the pattern Alcoholics Anonymous would impose. And if the only alternative patterns of individual action actually open to our alcoholic are those of chronic drunkenness, consequentialists would justifiably conclude that, since the consequences of his accepting Alcoholics Anonymous are better, it is simple consequentialism that it is right that the alcoholic join Alcoholics Anonymous, even though, if he does, his individual actions will sometimes have alternatives with better consequences.

Provided that the consequentialist principle is interpreted liberally, it is customary to assume that coherent and internally stable forms of consequentialism can be developed, which, even though they may be false, can be overthrown only by external objections. And yet, as we shall see, the results of our investigations so far afford reasons for doubting this customary assumption. In all the vast and imposing body of work on consequentialist moral theories, there are many sketches and projects for constructing moral systems. But none has been constructed. As its title proclaims, the greatest of all utilitarian treatises, Sidgwick's *Methods of Ethics,* is a study of three ethical "methods," and an attempt to reconcile them. The only moral system investigated at length in it is that of "jural" intuitionism, of which Sidgwick wrote that "it is my own as much as it is any man's."[37] And examination of the indispensable work of those philosophers who have tried to design an acceptable consequentialist moral system has deepened my suspicion that the supports for such a system are so weak, that on any serious attempt to complete one according to plan, it will collapse under its own weight.

6.4   Utilitarianism

The strength or weakness of the structure of consequentialism may be tested most effectively by exploring its most persuasive and most thoroughly investigated variety: utilitarianism. Utilitarianism is that species of consequentialism in which better consequences are held to be consequences involving more happiness. Accordingly, the principle of utilitarianism is that actions are right if and only if their consequences involve greater happiness than those of any other actions that could be done instead.

From the beginning, utilitarians have quarrelled about the nature of happiness. Bentham understood it hedonistically, as a favorable balance of pleasurable over unpleasurable feeling. John Stuart Mill parted from him on this; and the ultimate tendency of Mill's understanding of happiness is Aristotelian—that it is a favorable balance of human well-being over human ill-being. Health, membership in a flourishing family and in a flourishing civil society, friendship, liberty, and having and making the most of opportunities to engage in pursuits found worth engaging in seem to constitute human well-being; and the want of any of them to be ill-being.

Mill also divided utilitarians upon whether the greatest happiness that is to be promoted is the greatest aggregate happiness ("classical utilitarianism") or the greatest average happiness ("average utilitarianism").[38] If, in a given society, there is slightly more happiness than unhappiness in the lives of most of its members, then a large increase in a population whose average happiness remains constant will enormously increase total happiness. By and large, however, utilitarians have been comparatively unconcerned with increases of that kind: their object has been to increase individual happiness as much as possible, without corresponding decreases; and if a considerable increase in individual happiness can be procured only by preventing an increase in population, even though that would entail forgoing the greatest possible increase in total happiness, they would cheerfully pay that price.

On these two issues, utilitarian sentiment at the present time appears to side with Mill. Accordingly, in what follows, "having consequences involving greater happiness than those of any alternative," or in utilitarian parlance "having greater utility than any alternative," will be taken as meaning "having consequences involving greater *average* happiness than those of any alternative," and 'happiness' will be understood eudaemonistically, not hedonistically.

Perhaps the most radical of the questions that have divided utilitarians has to do with the place of rules in their theory. In Mill, it shows itself not as an issue, but as an ambiguity. On a straight-forward reading, his position in all his writings on morality is that now usually known as "act utilitarianism": namely, that it is the moral duty of every human being so to act that to none of his individual actions is there a possible alternative with greater utility; in other words, that everybody ought so to act that each of his actions will "maximize utility" or be "optimific." On the other hand, his frequent acknowledgement that human beings recognize actions as right or wrong in large measure as they accord or do not accord with moral precepts they accept, and the interest he shared with Bentham and other early utilitarians in reforming not only positive law but also received moral rules, has prompted more than one reader to take his real position to be: (1) that individual actions are right or wrong according as they are commanded or forbidden by correct moral rules; and (2) that a moral rule is correct if and only if its adoption by everybody would be of greater utility than the adoption of any alternative, or of none.[39] This general position, which as we shall see has many specific forms, is now usually known as "rule utilitarianism."

Maurice Mandelbaum has established that Mill's considered view of moral rules was act utilitarian,[40] and that it is decisively summed up in a passage from *A System of Logic* (VI, 12, 3):

> By a wise practitioner, . . . rules of conduct will only be con-sidered as provisional. . . . [T]hey point out the manner in which it will be least perilous to act, where time or means do not exist for analysing the actual circumstances of the case. . . . But they do not at all supersede the propriety of going through (when circumstances permit) the scientific process requisite for framing a rule from the data of the particular case before us.

As Mandelbaum has put it, all that such provisional rules can offer is "rule of thumb guidance."[41]

Yet, as J. D. Mabbott has pointed out, Mill nevertheless incon-sistently asserted that there are kinds of case in which it is for the general good that everybody observe set rules, even though that observance will not in all cases be optimific.[42] For example,

> In the case of abstinences [Mill wrote] . . . *though the conse-quences in the particular case might be beneficial*—it would be unworthy of an intelligent agent not to be consciously aware that the action is of a class which, if practised generally, would be

generally injurious, and that this is the ground of the obligation to abstain from it.[43] [Emphasis mine.]

Mandelbaum has acknowledged this, although he has pointed out that Mill allowed for the abrogation even of such rules in cases "of a very peculiar and extreme nature."[44]

Since, at the present time, act utilitarianism and rule utilitarianism are each strenuously advocated, it is necessary to consider them in turn.

The utilitarian case for act utilitarianism is straightforward, and has been lucidly argued by J. J. C. Smart.[45] It is undisputed that the utilitarian principle requires everybody, as far as he can, to maximize utility. But every form of rule utilitarianism that is not extensionally equivalent to act utilitarianism ordains that, in certain kinds of situation, actions are to be done in conformity with set rules, even though in some cases alternative actions, taken by themselves, would have more utility. That, Smart objects, is inconsistent rule worship. Since the rule utilitarian professes to be concerned solely with maximizing utility, "why ... should he advocate abiding by a rule when he knows that it will not in the present case be most beneficial to abide by it?"[46]

The earliest objection to such views was that the knowledge they presuppose cannot in fact be obtained; that in no case can it be validly calculated whether or not a given action will maximize human happiness. Adam Sedgwick urged against Bentham that "man has not foreknowledge to trace the consequences of a single action of his own; and hence ... utility ... is, as a test of right and wrong, unfitted to his understanding, and therefore worthless in its application."[47] However, the implications of this formidable objection ramify so far—if sound, it will have grave consequences, if not fatal ones, for every form of consequentialism—that it is convenient to reserve examination of it for the following section (6.5). Nor will this postponement distort our examination of historical utilitarian theories; for in them, as in Mill's rejoinder to it, Sedgwick's objection is met by evasion rather than by argument.[48]

The problems confronting them which act utilitarians themselves judge to be the most formidable are: first, how to determine the utility of a possible action, when it depends upon how others act; and second, how to allow for consequences which are pertinent to the utility of actions but which are not consequences of those actions themselves.

The problem of determining the utility of a possible action, when it is affected by how others act, is exhibited in the following conundrum. In a democracy, that a substantial majority of the eligible voters vote in national elections is of much greater utility than that they not. But to nearly everybody, it is irksome to vote. And so it appears that, for any individual voter, there will be an alternative to voting which has greater utility. For whether he votes or not will make no difference either to the result of the election or to whether or not a substantial majority of the eligible voters vote. Hence there are two possible situations to be considered: that in which a substantial majority of the citizens will vote, and that in which they will not. In the former, the utility of his not voting will be greater, because voting would be irksome, and the utility to which it would contribute will be produced nevertheless. In the latter, the utility of his not voting will also be greater, because voting would be irksome, and the utility to which it would contribute if others voted will not be produced anyway.

Act utilitarianism, in short, seems to imply that, for any proposed cooperative action, there are two kinds of exempting conditions. When the utility of cooperation will be attained even if a given cooperative action by an individual is not performed, then, if apart from the benefits of cooperation, some alternative to that action will have higher utility, utility is maximized by doing that alternative. Hence Lyons has called exempting conditions of this kind "maximizing." On the other hand, when the utility of cooperation will not be attained even though a given cooperative action by an individual is performed, then if, apart from the benefits of cooperation, some alternative to that action will have higher utility, disutility is minimized by not adding to the disutility of the other abortive cooperative actions. Lyons has called exempting conditions of this kind "minimizing."[49]

In most cases when, ignorant of how his fellows will act, an agent must decide whether or not to participate in a beneficial cooperative action, even though his participating action, taken by itself, would not be beneficial, no calculation within the limits of act utilitarianism can furnish a rational ground for his participation. For in most cases it will be evident that either maximizing or minimizing exempting conditions obtain, although it may not be evident which.

That is why the grounds that are generally accepted for independent participation in socially necessary cooperative actions are not, in flourishing societies, act utilitarian. Eligible voters in a healthy democracy vote in national elections, not for reasons of utility, but because they believe that it is their privilege and duty to do so. It is true that if as a group they did not vote, democracy would perish, and that would harm them individually. But that consideration at best furnishes a rational ground for their accepting a rule that eligible voters should vote irrespective of any maximizing exempting condition. And that, of course, would violate act utilitarianism.

A more general difficulty emerges when cooperative actions in economic life are considered: for example, productive ones, whether the individual participating actions are done simultaneously or successively. Disregarding cases in which the unfinished product has value other than as raw material, individual participating productive actions (except the last one) have negative utility unless the others are done. For example, the work that goes into constructing the steel frame of a building is wasted unless the building is completed. But the consideration that the production of a building is beneficial, and that it will not be produced unless a large number of cooperative productive actions are done, does not by itself constitute a utilitarian ground why any individual should do any of those actions. The difficulty is not that it is impracticable for him to calculate what productive actions open to him would have the greatest utility but that the calculation itself has no definite solution. For whether or not a possible productive action is to be done, according to act utilitarianism, depends on its utility. But the utility of most possible productive actions in turn depends upon what other actions are being done and will be done. And so, when *all* individual participating productive actions are considered merely possible, most of them have no definite utility at all. That the actions themselves have exchange value depends on the willingness of entrepreneurs to pay for them, in the expectation that they can arrange to have done whatever others may be necessary to complete the product. That is why entrepreneurs are useful.

The benefits of cooperative actions like voting, which, as has been remarked, most democracies ensure by teaching appropriate moral rules, suggest a second kind of difficulty, which most act utilitarians also confess to be serious. There seem to be rules the general acceptance of which in a society has a utility ("acceptance utility") that is not exhausted by the aggregate utilities of actions done in that society in conformity with it (by its "conformance utility"). [50] It may be conceded that the general acceptance of a rule in a society has utility only by way of the actions to which it gives rise; but it will give rise to many actions besides those that conform with it.[51] The general acceptance of a rule in a society is a matter of complex dispositions in a large proportion of its members. Social anthropologists have found it necessary to explain in different ways why various rules are generally accepted in various societies. However, in no open society can a system of moral rules be generally accepted unless at least a substantial body of its opinion-makers have accepted it by conscious acts, after becoming aware of alternatives and rejecting them. These acts of acceptance by opinion-makers have always been of particular concern to utilitarian moralists.

The difference is reasonably plain between general conformance to a rule by a society and general acceptance. General conformance is general observance of the rule, for some reason or other—it may be out of fear. General acceptance is general observance because the rule is, reflectively or otherwise, generally taken to be binding. The members of a society who, out of fear, conform with a rule they repudiate, will exhibit dispositions to behavior very different from those who conform out of acceptance; and a society in which general conformance with a rule proceeds from general acceptance will be very different from one in which it proceeds from anything else.

The acceptance utility of a code of rules in a given society will therefore be the sum of: (1) the utilities of actions done in conformance with it, and (2) the utilities of actions, other than those of conformance, which result from its general acceptance. The acceptance utility of a code will be the maximum for a society, if and only if no alternative code, which by some socially possible change could become generally accepted in it, has equal or greater acceptance utility.[52]

That there is such a thing as acceptance utility entails that the spirit of utilitarianism may be consistent with forms of it other than act utilitarianism. For should some moral code other than act utilitarianism be of maximum acceptance utility in a given society, nobody inspired by the utilitarian spirit could do other than wish for its general acceptance in that society.

Yet no consideration so far presented shows that act utilitarianism does not have maximum acceptance utility in any given society. True, it cannot account for duties of cooperation; but other benefits of its acceptance, obtainable in no other system, may more than compensate for that loss. True, benefits may accrue to a society from its general acceptance of rules, conformance with which, in itself, has often little or no utility; but the disutilities resulting from these departures from act utilitarianism may outweigh those benefits. With respect to no society is it a closed question what moral code (whether act utilitarianism or another) possesses maximum acceptance utility.

And, even if that question were closed, others would remain about what moral position any individual utilitarian ought to accept. For the fact that a moral code would have maximum acceptance utility in a given society does not entail that any individual would maximize utility by adopting it. Let us see why this is so.[53]

Anybody trying to decide how, according to the principles of utilitarianism, he should live, must begin by answering three questions: whether or not the moral code generally accepted in his society has maximum acceptance utility; whether or not in his society act utilitarianism has maximum acceptance utility; and whether or not act utilitarianism is generally accepted in his society. Of the possible situations which, depending on his answers, he will take to be his, the following five seem to be of particular interest. With regard to each, I have ventured to set down what I take to be the way of life required by utilitarianism.

Situation (1a): *the code generally accepted in his society has maximum acceptance utility, and is act utilitarianism.* In this case, any utilitarian must accept act utilitarianism.

Situation (1b): *the code generally accepted in his society has maximum acceptance utility, and is not act utilitarianism.* In this case, a utilitarian must support the generally accepted code; but, if there are individual cases in which, without compromising his support for the accepted code, he could beneficially violate it, he should act upon a maximizing condition and violate it.

Situation (2a): *the code generally accepted in his society is act utilitarianism, and does not have maximum acceptance utility.* In this case, a utilitarian must work, as effectively as he can, for the acceptance of whichever code would have maximum acceptance utility. Subject to that overriding purpose, which might in some respects require him to act on the ideal code, he should conform with act utilitarianism.

Situation (2b): *the code generally accepted in his society does not have maximum acceptance utility, and act utilitarianism does.* This is the situation in which act utilitarians like Smart believe they are. Here, as in situation (2a), a utilitarian must work for the acceptance of the code having maximum acceptance utility, in this case act utilitarianism, and he may be required in some cases to act on it. However, he will only live by it in a measure as the disutility of his doing so, in a climate of misunderstanding and disapproval, is not too great.

Situation (2c): *the code generally accepted in his society, which is not act utilitarianism, does not have maximum acceptance utility, and neither does act utilitarianism.* This case combines features of (1b) and (2a). As in (2a), a utilitarian must work for the general acceptance of a code that is not act utilitarianism. However, he will act on the ideal code only as doing so will promote its acceptance, and not when the disutility of doing so is too great. And, although the generally accepted code he will fall back on will not be act utilitarianism, he should, as in (1b), act upon the maximizing condition of violating either code whenever it would be beneficial to do so and would not compromise his promotion of the ideal code.

If my submissions as to what ways of life utilitarianism requires in these situations are accurate (those have been passed over in which no code is generally accepted, or in which none has maximum acceptance utility), then in only one of them, namely (1a), does it require anybody both to support and to live by act utilitarianism. And in only one other, namely (1b), does it require anybody to support and live by an ideal utilitarian code other than act utilitarianism—and then only if that code leaves no room for supplementation by a maximizing exempting condition. Hence if most utilitarians are right in thinking that, of the five possible situations considered, the only ones ever to have been actual are (2b) or (2c), then there may well never have been an actual situation in which utilitarianism has required anybody to live either by act utilitarianism *or by any ideal utilitarian code.*

6.5   The Factor of Ignorance

Ever since Sidgwick, with characteristic intellectual honesty, distinguished between what it is beneficial to praise and what it is beneficial to do, it has been an open secret that, depending on circumstances, utilitarianism can justify supporting almost any practicable moral code. Smart, with equally characteristic candor, has confessed that circumstances are conceivable in which utilitarianism would demand support for "a form of magical taboo ethics."[54]

Even when utilitarianism was naively conceived as pure act utilitarianism, according to which the rightness or wrongness of an individual action is determined solely by its consequences as an individual action, Sedgwick's objection was formidable: "man has not the foreknowledge to trace the consequences of a single action of his own."[55] But the force of his objection must not be exaggerated. Smart has pointed out that act utilitarianism requires, not a summation of all the happiness and unhappiness that results from each alternative course of action, but only a comparison of the total consequences of each. "All we have to do," he remarks, "is to envisage two or more total situations, and say which we prefer. A purely ordinal, not a quantitative, judgement is all we require."[56] And we can reach such ordinal judgements without summation, because the consequences of alternative courses of action will to a considerable extent be the same: all we need to do is to compare the differences.

Even so, I think that Sedgwick would have contended that the calculations needed for such ordinal judgements would be impossible. And Smart does not seriously dispute this. "[U]ntil we have an adequate theory of objective probability," he concedes, "utilitarianism is not on a secure basis"—adding, to cheer himself up, "Nor, for that matter, is ordinary prudence."[57] This revives Mill's rejoinder to Sedgwick.

> Some of the consequences of an action are accidental [Mill wrote]; others are its natural result, according to the known laws of the universe. The former, for the most part, cannot be foreseen; but the whole course of human life is founded upon the fact that the latter can. In what reliance do we ply our several trades—in what reliance do we buy or sell, eat or drink ... except on our foresight of the consequences of those actions.[58]

This doubly misses the point. Human beings ply their trades, buy and sell, eat and drink, and exhibit ordinary prudence with respect to limited definite ends—particular pleasures, nourishment, honest profit, the best possible return for an outlay. None of these calls for an ordinal judgement of the *total* consequences of alternatives; and it is bewildering that philosophers as acute as Mill and Smart should imagine otherwise.

As for Mill's distinction between accidental and natural consequences, the wide sense of "consequence" employed by utilitarians covers both. And there is no reason to doubt that sometimes the equivalent of a kingdom may be lost, as in the nursery rhyme, "for want of a horseshoe nail." To illustrate utilitarian calculations, it is necessary to go to science fiction; and one of the few examples I have encountered even there is in Isaac Asimov's tale of time travel, *The End of Eternity*, in which time travellers, armed with full information of the actual course of history, and with computing techniques for calculating objective probabilities, look for "minimum necessary changes" by which great calamities can be eliminated from history. It is a great coup for a technician in the story to point out that, in order to eliminate a major evil (mass drug addiction at a certain period) without compensating ill-effects, the minimum change necessary is that a container be displaced from one shelf to another, and not, as a rival had calculated, that a space vessel be caused to malfunction, killing a dozen men.[59] That by no technique now known could such a calculation be made, even granted knowledge of the actual future, is itself a serious objection to act utilitarianism. But another implication may be more embarrassing. For the example from Asimov shows that, according to act utilitarianism, a commonplace dutiful action, such as putting a container on its correct shelf, may be a far graver wrong than a multiple murder, because its consequences involve far more unhappiness.

Smart has replied to such cases (unfortunately he discusses the horseshoe-nail case, where the blacksmith was negligent, and not one like Asimov's, in which an innocent action has bad consequences) that it is not inconsistent for a utilitarian to refuse to blame the agent, or to blame him very much, even though it is recognized "that his action was *in fact* very wrong."[60] But there are other faults than inconsistency. By making the word "wrong" synonymous with "having worse consequences than some possible alternative," Smart's reply seems to evacuate it of moral significance. That actions can be such that, by some unforeseeable chain of accidents, great calamities would be averted were they not done, is on the face of it irrelevant to the question whether or not they are permissible.

Although this last difficulty is avoided by most utilitarian moral codes based on acceptance utility, the problem of calculation remains. Whewell urged against rule utilitarianism an objection parallel to Sedgwick's against act utilitarianism. He rejected out of hand any "system which deduces *all* its Moral Rules from the Principle of increasing human happiness, and from that *alone*" on the ground that we do not think that we *can* determine in all cases what [i.e. the acceptance of what moral rule] does increase human happiness. The calculation is too vast, vague and complex.[61]

Whewell did not deny that in some cases it can be shown that the general acceptance of a rule maximizes human happiness. But rule utilitarianism cannot be content with that; for, according to it, whether or not a given complete moral code ought to be generally accepted depends on whether its general acceptance would increase human happiness more than the general acceptance of any other. And, since it asserts that we can determine whether or not a given moral code ought to be generally accepted, it is committed also to asserting what Whewell denied: that in *all* cases, we can determine whether the general acceptance of a specific moral rule would maximize human happiness.

What reply can a rule utilitarian make to Whewell? The one Mill actually made was an *ignoratio elenchi.* He began by quoting, from Whewell's lectures on the *History of Moral Philosophy in England,* a passage in which, after arguing that it is impossible to prove, on rule utilitarian principles, that "mendacious flattery and illegitimate sensuality" are "vicious and immoral," Whewell concluded:

And the like is true of other vices [not, "*all* other vices"]; and on this ground, the construction of a scheme of morality on Mr. Bentham's plan is plainly impossible.[62]

To this, Mill proceeded to reply that it can be shown that the rule against murder is one the general acceptance of which maximizes happiness (he does not show it, but reasonably judges that Whewell would not dispute it), and that, by drawing "an illustration" from flattering lies, "Whewell [gave] to the side he advocates a colour of rigid adherence to principle, which the fact does not bear out."[63] We rub our eyes. What has this to do with Whewell's argument? It was, of course, open to Mill to agree that the rules against mendacious flattery and illegitimate sensuality cannot be justified on utilitarian grounds, and to conclude, "So much the worse for them—they ought not to be generally accepted as moral rules." But he did not. Instead, although he remained silent about illegitimate sensuality, about flattery he ventured the curious opinion that it "should be only permitted to those who can flatter without lying"—that is, to the sensitive and quick-witted; but he did not attempt a utilitarian justification of it.[64]

Nor does the enormous mass of utilitarian publication provide what Mill withheld. There are utilitarian justifications of specific rules; but the most successful resemble R. B. Brandt's admirable demonstration, in a recent discussion of the rules of war, that with respect to the limited kinds of consequence that affect them as belligerents there are various rules about the humane treatment of prisoners, abstention from employing certain weapons, and the immunities of enemy civilians in occupied territory, by accepting which all belligerents may expect to gain more than they lose.[65] Yet neither demonstrations of the utility of certain highly specific rules to parties with definite and limited interests, nor utilitarian arguments for the general acceptance of vaguely specified rules, without any examination of exceptions, are what Whewell demanded and what utilitarians profess to be able to supply: namely, the construction of a complete scheme of morality on the utilitarian principle. And if Whewell's objection is to be met even in part, without constructing such a system, it must be by examining representative difficult cases, not easy ones.

Utilitarians sometimes attempt to show that the calculations their theory calls for are neither as complex nor as difficult as their critics make out. Yet what ought to astonish readers of their work is neither the complexity nor the difficulty of utilitarian calculations, but their absence. Consider a case, credited by Smart to H. J. McCloskey, which is frequently discussed: "The sheriff of a small town can prevent serious riots (in which hundreds of people will be killed) only by 'framing' and executing (as a scapegoat) an innocent man."[66] The issue, from the point of view of rule utilitarianism, is whether cases in which rioting and the deaths of many will be the consequences of failing to arrest, convict, and execute somebody for a notorious crime are, on utilitarian principles, exceptions to the rule that law enforcement authorities may not corrupt the processes of justice, and especially not when they commit murder by doing so. Here, as Mill pointed out,

> The essential is, that the exception should be itself a general rule; so that, being of definite extent, and not leaving the expediencies to the partial judgement of the agent in the individual case, it may not shake the stability of the wider rule in the cases to which the reason of the exception does not extend.[67]

The rule allowing the exception here would of course be moral, not legal.

It was once my opinion that the consequences of the general

acceptance of such an exception would plainly involve less unhappiness than the consequences of its general rejection. For the case would necessarily be rare; it need never be known that the victim was framed; and (as the Dreyfus case showed), many people are comforted rather than appalled by the thought that their officials act on Caiaphas's principle, "it is expedient that one man should die for the people."

Kai Nielsen's opposed opinion about the consequences of allowing such an exception finally opened my eyes:

> knowledge that the man was framed, that the law had prostituted itself, would, surely [he argued] eventually leak out. This would encourage mob action in other circumstances, would lead to an increased scepticism about the incorruptibility or even the reliability of the judicial process, and would set a dangerous precedent.[68]

I was inclined to stick to my opinion, and began a rejoinder. But in the course of doing so, our joint performance began to appear comic. Utilitarianism prides itself upon being a scientific system, in which questions of right and wrong have scientifically ascertainable answers. Yet we were debating, not exchanging scientific results. And then it became plain that there are no pertinent scientific results. On this debated issue, no utilitarian calculations are available, mistaken or otherwise: there is nothing but advocacy.

A new light was thrown by this on a contention of Henry Sidgwick's which had puzzled me, that disputes in ordinary morality, which the method of jural intuitionism fails to resolve, are "very commonly determined by utilitarian reasonings, implicit or explicit."[69] It has already (1.3) been argued that Sidgwick's charge that jural intuitionism is helpless when confronted with casuistical problems was as superficial as it was unjust; his unnamed adversary, Whewell, had successfully employed that very method in resolving some of the problems Sidgwick himself offered as examples. But what matters now is that the "utilitarian reasonings" by which Sidgwick himself determined such questions rested on nothing more solid than his personal impressions.

Here is an example. Should it be generally accepted as a moral rule that contracts are valid if one party has performed his part, even when they were only made because that party employed duress? For example, is a contract to a bandit to pay a ransom upon release to be kept after release? Sidgwick's utilitarian reasoning was as follows.

It is obvious ... that it is a disadvantage to the community that men should be able to rely on the performance of promises procured by ... unlawful force, so far as encouragement is thereby given to the use of ... force for this end.[70]

Is this "reasoning," obviously valid as far as it goes, any more final than the following from Whewell, which probably was not written tongue in cheek?

Is it probable that the banditti will give up their practice, simply because their captives, liberated on such promises, do not perform them? ... Do we not, in making and adhering to such contracts, prevent their adding murder to robbery? ... [Until banditry is suppressed] may it not tend to preserve from extreme cruelties, those who fall into the hands of the robbers, that they should have some confidence in the payment of the ransom agreed upon? Even on the balance of probable advantage, it would seem that such a promise is to be kept.[71]

Whether, in early nineteenth-century Italy, the consequences of generally accepting Sidgwick's rule would be more beneficial than those of generally accepting Whewell's, they had no scientific way of determining. Nor have we. And so we cannot form a rational opinion about which of the two rules belongs in the system of morality which, in that society, has maximum acceptance utility. Nor can we rationally decide similar questions about numerous other possible rules. Hence Whewell's objection was sound: it is impossible to construct a scheme of ideal morality on utilitarian principles. A fortiori, it is impossible to determine what moral rules individuals should live by, after they have ascertained the relation of the ideal system to the one generally accepted in their own society.

That the calculations which utilitarianism calls for cannot be made was pointed out, as we have seen, more than a century ago: by Adam Sedgwick for act utilitarianism, and by Whewell for rule utilitarianism. And perhaps the most puzzling thing about discussions of the subject at the present time is that what they pointed out is not commonplace. G. E. Moore, it is true, accepted Sedgwick's conclusion about act utilitarianism and made use of it in his consequentialist defence of a strict, largely conservative deontology.[72] But most have chosen to disregard what the practical incalculability of the utilities either of actions or rules may imply, and to occupy themselves with the logically interesting problems that arise in pure utilitarian theory on the assumption that ordinal utilities can be calculated.

Yet something of utilitarianism is apt to remain, even after the dream has vanished of constructing a utilitarian system along the lines shown in the preceding section to be necessary. Critics of utilitarianism like Bernard Williams, and chastened utilitarians like R. M. Hare, even as they embrace moral systems very like the traditional one, tend to think of them as justified by their acceptance utility.[73] And they retain their distrust of any system of rules advanced as absolute.

Whenever a defender of traditional morality protests that there are moral rules which, whatever the consequences, must not be broken, such as the rule prohibiting murder—the killing of the materially innocent—a natural reaction is to confront him with imaginary horror upon imaginary horror, and to inquire whether it would not be permissible, nay right, to commit murder if these horrors would be the consequences of his not committing it. And so it has come to seem natural to accept as much of utilitarianism as this: that no moral system can be philosophically acceptable unless it is supplemented by an escape clause, to the effect that, in all cases of a choice of evils, if one of those evils is so great that incurring it rather than any of the others would be calamitous, and if it can only be avoided by taking a certain action, then that action is to be taken even if it is in breach of a precept of the system.[74]

Our investigation of the hard cases to which traditional common morality gives rise has shown why it rejects such an escape clause as crude and unnecessary. For, in laying down that its precepts are to be observed no matter what the consequences, traditional morality does not imply that they are to be observed, let us say, if the consequences should be the death of everybody on earth. It has been constructed at every point with careful attention to the nature both of human action and of the world in which it takes place. The worst efforts of "situation ethics" to invent situations in which the consequences of abiding by traditional morality would be some world calamity have resulted in nothing but absurd fantasies. In short, the nature of traditional morality is such that observing it cannot, except by unpredictable accidents, have calamitous consequences. However, since observing it can have tragic consequences —consequences that would tempt almost anybody to deviate from it—it commands that, after you have pondered what bad consequences may flow from abiding by it, and made what dispositions you can to avoid them, you are to disregard them. You are to obey, "whatever the consequences." This is sometimes expressed hyperbolically, as in the precept: *Fiat justitia, ruat caelum*. That precept was enunciated in a culture in which it was held to be impossible that the heavens should fall as a consequence of your doing what you ought. Its sufficiently plain sense is that you are to do what you ought, no matter what tragedy may befall. But such a precept can only be taken seriously if it is understood that nothing beyond tragedy will be a consequence of justice.

While it repudiates escape clauses by which its precepts may be violated if the consequences of observing them are "bad enough," traditional moral theory does not concede that the consequences of generally accepting such an escape clause would be better than those of rejecting it. Nor, in refusing this concession, does it rely on general considerations about the incalculability of acceptance utilities. For there are direct objections to the argument for such escape clauses. That argument reduces to this: the only difference between the consequences of the general acceptance of traditional morality, and the consequences of its general acceptance when supplemented by an escape clause, will be that, in cases in which observing it in its unsupplemented form would be a calamity, that calamity would be avoided, together with the good educational consequences of perceiving that fact. And the chief objection to it is that, since nearly everybody's judgement is disturbed by the anticipation of calamity, it is probable that much of what is done on the ground of such escape clauses will be mistaken.

The examples commonly offered in support of escape clauses conceal this fact by imputing to the agents a knowledge they cannot possess. Consider the following, from Bernard Williams's attack on utilitarianism.

> Jim finds himself in the central square of a small South American town. Tied up against the wall are a row of twenty Indians, most terrified, a few defiant, in front of them several armed men in uniform. A heavy man in a sweat-stained khaki shirt turns out to be the captain in charge and, after a good deal of questioning of Jim which establishes that he got there by accident while on a botanical expedition, explains that the Indians are a random group of the inhabitants who, after recent acts of protest against the government, are just about to be killed to remind other possible protesters of the advantages of not protesting. However, since Jim is an honoured visitor from another land, the captain is happy to offer him a guest's privilege of killing one of the Indians himself. If he accepts, then as a special mark of the occa-

sion, the other Indians will be let off. Of course, if Jim refuses, then there is no special occasion, and Pedro here will do what he was about to do when Jim arrived, and kill them all.... The men against the wall, and the other villagers, understand the situation, and are obviously begging him to accept. What should he do?[75]

What is objectionable about this is its implication that the situation described must be one in which the death of twenty Indians will be the consequence of Jim's refusal.

How might somebody in such a situation reasonably appraise it? I submit that he might well reason as follows. "In Latin countries, the office of executioner is not an honored one; so the offer of the 'privilege' of executing a prisoner is probably not in good faith. Moreover, officers in military regimes customarily pretend that anybody they execute is guilty of rebellion or some serious crime: that he is eager to exhibit what he proposes to do as something generally considered atrocious seems to imply that he doesn't expect me to report what happened. Yet what could stop me? Well, the whole thing may be a particularly nasty hoax—the gun he'll give me may be loaded with blanks. Or he may intend to murder me. Or he may think to make me an accomplice: if I should kill one prisoner, he could kill the others with impunity; for my testimony would incriminate myself as well." Were Jim to act upon these reasonable reflections, he would presumably intercede for all the prisoners, flattering the captain as patriotic but humane, while trying to present himself as somebody of credit and integrity; but he would on no account agree to kill anybody.

In a given case, the consequences of acting on this reasoning may be tragic: the heavy man in the sweat-stained shirt may turn out not to be bluffing, and may be deaf to persuasion. But would not general acceptance of the rule that one is to comply with such invitations to murderous complicity be more likely to have bad results than not? Fifty years ago, seeking a case in which a breach of the rule forbidding lying might be permissible (that there might be a permissible breach of the rule forbidding murder seems not to have occurred to him), Bishop Kirk turned up "the well-known instance of the British officer, himself an atheist, who refused to save his life from his Mohammedan captors by abjuring Christianity, lest it should bring the British name into discredit."[76] Juxtaposition of Williams's and Kirk's examples has left me suspecting, perhaps quite wrongly, that even in our time, the acceptance utility of simple Victorian rectitude would be high.

The duty of beneficence in the Hebrew-Christian tradition is not the indiscriminate and unlimited maximizing of good imposed by utilitarianism. It is the duty to do what good one reasonably can, without omitting any perfect duty. The religious ideal of charity goes far beyond it. But beneficence and charity alike have to do only with those consequences of actions that are within human foresight. Nor is that all. Some portion of the evil in the world is a consequence of human wrongdoing and culpable folly; of that portion, at least some does not fall upon the blameless but returns to plague its inventors. Utilitarianism pays little attention to this. The task it lays upon the benevolent is to maximize good; and it will not relieve them of that task even if it may happen largely to consist in rescuing the idle, the headstrong, and the wicked from the ill consequences of their own conduct. Williams has denounced utilitarianism as an attack on human integrity, because it reduces each individual to "a channel between the input of everyone's projects, including his own, and an output of optimific decision."[77] That is perhaps extreme. Nobody's integrity is attacked by requiring him to defer his own projects in order to shield some innocent from violence or fraud. But at bottom it is an unanswerable criticism of the utilitarian concept of benevolence. Genuine benevolence, or willing the well-being of others, is willing that they live a decent human life, and so being prepared to help them in their efforts to do so; it is not an interminable bondage to alleviating the woes brought upon themselves by those who make little or no effort to live well.

If its theory is sound, strict adherence to traditional common morality will never, except by unforeseeable accident, have calamitous consequences, although it may now and then have tragic ones. Yet it does not follow that the general acceptance of any other system in preference to it would have better consequences. It may or may not, depending on circumstances; but, either way, we cannot know. That is why attempting to choose a moral system by its consequences is not only a mistake in moral theory but also futile.[78]

7

The Foundation of Common Morality

7.1 Can Reason Be Practical?

Even if it is internally sound, the system of morality presented in the preceding five chapters can be what it professes to be only if its fundamental principle is true. Yet, since it is fundamental to an independent field of inquiry, that principle cannot be established by deducing it from others yet more ultimate. There is no substantive principle in its field that does not rest upon it: it is the foundation.

Nor, if the objections to intuitionism in 1.3 are well taken, can that principle, or indeed any other, legitimately be advanced as a self-evident intuition, and denied to need rational justification. Like fundamental principles in any independent field of inquiry it must be legitimated: in one way or another, it must be shown that it is intellectually impossible to get on without it. But how?

Like the precepts derived from it, the fundamental principle of morality is a proposition to the effect that reason, if it functioned without error, would prescribe that actions of a certain kind—in this case, those in which not every rational being is respected—are unconditionally not to be done. Such a principle presupposes that reason can be practical: that, when it functions without error, it can prescribe that actions of certain kinds are or are not to be done. Would an investigation of how reason can be practical perhaps throw light on how what purports to be a fundamental principle of practical reason may be rationally justified? Let us see.

Aristotle, in his brief discussion of practical reason, treats it as having to do with how an end, which is laid down by *boulesis*, or wish, is to be achieved.[1] The structure of a "syllogism" in which an operation of practical reason takes shape corresponds to the structure of a piece of reasoning upon which a man of practical wisdom, having that end, might settle upon an intention to act. In Aristotle's examples, which, as W. F. R. Hardie has pointed out, are no more than examples,[2] such syllogisms consist of (1) a major premise, in which something wished for or wished to be avoided is specified, perhaps along with some effective means appropriate to attaining it or avoiding it; and (2) a minor premise or premises, in which more and more specific means are brought under the end specified in the major premise, until a means apt to be acted upon is reached.[3] An example in *de Motu Animalium* is as good as any:

> I need a covering, a coat is a covering: I need a coat. What I need I ought to make, I need a coat: I ought to make a coat. And the conclusion—"I ought to make a coat"—is an action (701a 18-20).

All the premises of such syllogisms are true or false in the same sense as are those of theoretical syllogisms: they say either that something is wished for, whether as needed or beneficial or pleasurable or the like, or that something is a means to what is thus wished for; and that somebody needs something, or will be benefited by it, or will take pleasure in it is treated by Aristotle as being as much a matter of fact as that somebody is starving, or will improve in health if he eats more protein, or enjoys tennis. Yet there is an important respect in which practical syllogisms like that quoted above from *de Motu Animalium* differ from theoretical syllogisms: their conclusions do not follow from their premises apodictically. A cloak is a covering as well as a coat. If I need a covering, and am offered a cloak, then, even though a coat is a covering, I shall not need a coat.

Yet this, as G. E. M. Anscombe has pointed out, does not invalidate the practical force of Aristotle's syllogism.[4] If my end is to have a covering and I can achieve that end by making a coat, that I can also achieve it by making a cloak does not make it any less rational for me to make a coat. I have set myself the practical problem of finding an action I could perform by which to achieve my end of obtaining a covering, and I have solved it. That other solutions would have done equally well is beside the point.

Along with nonapodictic practical syllogisms such as the coat example from *de Motu Animalium*, there are, as Anscombe has pointed out, numerous apodictic practical syllogisms.[5] If all human coverings are coats, or if the human coverings that are best or easiest to make are coats, and if I wish for a covering, or for the sort of covering that is best or easiest to make, then that I ought to get a coat will follow apodictically. Kant had the conclusions of such arguments in mind when he remarked that "there are in fact innumerable principles of action so far as action is thought necessary to achieve some purpose which can be effected by it," and called such principles "imperatives of skill" (*Geschicklichkeit*).[6] Imperatives of skill—that is, practical conclusions about what is to be done as a necessary and effective means to achieving some wished for end—are genuine prescriptions. Some philosophers have nevertheless objected that they are no more than descriptions— necessarily true ones—of how rational creatures act, inasmuch as they are rational. But that confounds prescriptions with their grounds. The following is repeatedly presented by Kant as the ground of imperatives of skill:

Whoever wills an end, inasmuch as he wills rationally, wills also the indispensably necessary means to it, if they are in his power.[7]

This is, as Kant maintained, an analytic proposition: a truth about how rational creatures act, not necessarily in fact, but inasmuch as they choose to act rationally. It is not an imperative: nothing in it can be construed as prescribing that anybody act in one way rather than another.

And yet, Kant contended, this analytic truth implies a prescription. For it can be equivalently reformulated as a proposition about what reason prescribes. A rational creature, inasmuch as he is rational, acts in a certain kind of way rather than any other, if and only if it would be contrary to reason for such a creature to act in any kind of way but that. Hence it cannot be true that whoever wills an end, inasmuch as he wills rationally, wills also the necessary means to it, unless it is also true that reason, functioning without error, would prescribe that a rational creature, given that he wills an end, should also will the means necessary to it. Now from Kant's proposition, reformulated in this way, a prescription of practical reason can be detached, namely:

Whoever wills an end is to will the means necessary to it (if they are in his power).

This is a general formula of what Kant called "hypothetical imperatives."

This general formula, and the innumerable imperatives of skill derivable from it, are hypothetical or conditional in content but not in force. They unconditionally prescribe that, *if* you will a certain end to which certain effective means are necessary and in your power, *then* you are to take those means. Yet their content is conditional, because they do not prescribe that you continue to will whatever end is in question after discovering what means are necessary to attaining it. Should anybody decide, for any reason, that one of his ends is not worth the necessary means to its attainment (and according to common morality, no end is worth immoral means) he may comply with the general formula of hypothetical imperatives by abandoning that end. Imperatives of skill, in short, are unconditionally prescriptive; but what they unconditionally prescribe is a choice—either abandon your end or take such available and effective means as are necessary to achieving it. Only if you refuse to relinquish an end, having ascertained what effective means open to you are necessary for attaining it, do Kantian imperatives of skill prescribe that you follow through, and adopt those means.[8]

Hence the relation of the general formula of hypothetical imperatives to desire is in large measure that of Freud's reality principle to his pleasure principle. One who offends against a hypothetical imperative flouts his own awareness of reality. Characteristically, as Thomas E. Hill, Jr., describes him, he is one "who continues to declare himself for a goal, takes many steps toward it, and half hopes to achieve it even though he systematically refuses to take some means obviously necessary to reach [it]."[9]

Anscombe has argued that the part played by wanting (*orexis*) in the practical syllogism is quite different from that of a premise. "It is," she maintains, "that whatever is described in the proposition that is the starting point of the argument must be wanted in order for the reasoning to lead to any action."[10] This is true of practical deliberation as exemplified in Aristotle's work. For the problem whose solution is sought in it, as we have seen, is to find an action by which the end wished for can be attained. Should the potential agent's deliberations turn towards a means to which he is averse, he would try to think of other means that are acceptable. And should he cease to wish for the end, both deliberation about how to attain it and action towards attaining it would cease.

This is not true of practical reasoning in accordance with the Kantian hypothetical imperative. Such reasoning would begin with an end proposed, presumably as desired or wanted for some reason; it would proceed to establish that a certain course of action is a necessary effective means to that end; and it would conclude by prescribing a choice: either abandon the end proposed or embark upon that course of action. But a decision to abandon the proposed end would be as much an upshot of the imperative as would a decision to embark on that course of action. Hence practical reasoning in terms of that imperative is not merely, as it were, a channel through which wants exert their power. What the conclusion of such reasoning prescribes is not anything wanted or desired at all. It does not, for example, prescribe that you are to do what you most want to do, whether that be to achieve the end proposed, or to abstain from the only effective means of achieving it. It prescribes, no more and no less, that *either* you abandon the end *or* embark upon the course of action necessary for achieving it; and that may be a choice you desperately want to avoid. In requiring you to make it, then, reason is not the slave or even the agent of the passions. It is practical in its own right.

Yet it does not follow that reason gives rise to prescriptions of the kind found in common morality, in which what is prescribed is not hypothetical (in the sense of being conditional upon whether or not those to whom the prescription is addressed hold to a proposed end) but categorical. And, in a timely paper, Philippa Foot has contended that practical reason cannot go beyond hypothetical imperatives. Against moralists like those in the Hebrew-Christian tradition, who maintain that practical reason unconditionally prescribes that no action be done in which every rational creature is not respected, she argues that human beings may or may not wish to comply with that prescription, and that to choose not to is in no way contrary to reason.

> The fact is [she writes] that the man who rejects morality because he can see no reason to obey its rules can be convicted of villainy but not of inconsistency. Nor will his action necessarily be irrational. Irrational actions are those in which a man in some way defeats his own purposes, doing what is calculated to be disadvantageous or to frustrate his ends. Immorality does not *necessarily* involve any such thing.[11]

It must be conceded at once that if what Foot presupposes in these remarks is true, that practical reason can condemn only inconsistency and what she calls irrationality—which seems to reduce to the violation of imperatives of skill—then her position is unassailable.[12] One can reject the fundamental principle of common morality without being either inconsistent or irrational in this sense. Accordingly, the question that must now be asked is whether practical reason imposes any other conditions on action than the avoidance of inconsistency, and of irrationality in the sense of willing ends while not willing the means that are necessary to achieve them. That there are imperatives of skill shows that reason is genuinely practical. But is practical reason confined to imperatives of skill?

7.2   Interlude: Universal Prescribers, Ideal Observers, and Rational Contractors

Most moralists today (some distinguished exceptions will be mentioned later) have despaired of establishing directly that reason prescribes anything categorical. But many nevertheless hope to establish it indirectly, most of them by what R. M. Hare has called a "hypothetical choice" theory of one sort or another. In every hypothetical choice theory, it is assumed that practical reason requires that every rational creature act on principles on which any rational creature would choose to act if subject to certain conditions.[13] The ground of this assumption is that, although the only prescriptions that can be directly inferred from the concept of practical reason itself are to be consistent and to observe the Kantian hypothetical imperatives, it is sufficiently evident that reason also requires the observance of such other prescriptions as would be laid down by any rational creature under certain ideal conditions. And it is held to be possible for us to calculate what those prescriptions would be.

Three such theories are now before the public: Hare's own, which he calls "universal prescriptivism"; the ideal observer theory of Roderick Firth and R. B. Brandt, which, as a matter of history, was the first to be developed; and John Rawls's theory, which Hare has felicitously called the "rational contractor theory." The principal characteristics of the two latter theories appear most distinctly when they are set alongside Hare's.

The foundation of Hare's theory is his analysis of the nature of moral judgements. The theory has two parts.[14] First, all moral judgements are advanced as either being or presupposing universal prescriptions; that is, prescriptions which can be formulated without referring to individual persons or things except by descriptions.

By this requirement, the prescription "Montagues are to raise their hats to all Venetians they meet" is not universal; for it refers implicitly both to the individual person who founded the Montague family and the individual city, Venice. On the other hand, "Thin red-haired men over fifty are to raise their hats to fat men with more than one wart on the nose," is a genuinely universal prescription, although a bizarre one. Second, whether a universal prescription is or is not moral is relative to whoever prescribes it: it forms part of its prescriber's moral code if and only if its prescriber will refuse to consider it overridden by any other universal prescription. Thus the prescriptions of etiquette are universal, but even sticklers for etiquette will consider them overridden by the universal prescription that guests are to be put at their ease.

Unquestionably, many judgements that are moral, in Hare's sense, are incompatible with each other. Not only does one person often consider a universal prescription to be overriding when another does not, but one person often considers a certain individual action to be commanded by an overriding universal prescription when another considers it forbidden. When such moral differences and conflicts occur, is there any rational procedure for resolving them?

Hare proposes the following. As a rough but serviceable generalization, the moral prescriptions over which serious disputes occur are those in the following of which somebody is hurt, although not necessarily physically, and what is disputed is who is to get hurt. Now would it not be contrary to reason for anybody to prescribe something universally and overridingly, and yet be unwilling to prescribe that he be hurt, should he find himself in a situation in which his universal prescription would require it? It would. Hence everybody who prescribes anything universally and overridingly should put to himself seriously, and answer honestly, the question, "Would I, if I were to find myself in any situation in which my own prescription would ordain that I be hurt, nevertheless persist in prescribing it?" And only if he can honestly answer that he would persist can he be held genuinely to prescribe it.

Hare's procedure, or others like it, is familiar in moral reflection in the Hebrew-Christian tradition. But, as Hare recognizes, it is not enough. For there are advocates of barbarous moralities (Hare's well-known example in *Freedom and Reason* is that of Nazi advocates of the extermination of Jewry) who would honestly profess their readiness to prescribe that they should suffer under their own morality should they turn out to fall under one of its barbarous provisions (for example, should they turn out to have a Jewish grandparent). To exclude this possibility, Hare therefore adds a further condition: his procedure will yield acceptable results only if those who follow it are not fanatics. It is not to count that a fanatic would adhere to his barbarous morality even though he were to suffer by it.

The difficulty with Hare's further condition lies in the very concept of a fanatic. At first sight, it is psychological. But, if there is any psychological test by which fanatics can be distinguished from moral heroes and saints, Hare has not made use of it. And so he has had no choice but to fall back on a criterion that is unabashedly moral. In *Freedom and Reason*, he described a fanatic as somebody who makes some ideal of his "override all considerations of people's interests, even . . . [his] own in actual or hypothetical cases."[15] In a subsequent paper, he asked, "What is it . . . which distinguishes the fanatic, and makes him immune to our arguments?" this time using Stalinists for illustration, and answered: the fanatic "is prepared to push . . . [his] ideal to the exclusion of other aims. . . . This means that he puts his ideal . . . above the interests of himself and other people."[16]

This answer is not perfectly clear. For, as Hare has acknowledged, ideals themselves create interests. But his line of thought appears to be that, since in moral disputes there is *ex hypothesi* a conflict of ideals, the ideals on both sides, along with the interests springing from them, can be treated as cancelling each other out. What remains to be considered are those interests, of whoever may be affected by the acceptance of the disputed prescription, that are independent of any ideal. A fanatic, then, is one who is unwilling to abandon an ideal when the sum of such interests of himself and others as exist independently of any ideal would be adversely affected by his clinging to it. The practical effect of this is to set down all nonutilitarians as fanatics.

Our present interest is not how Hare uses his particular hypothetical choice theory in constructing his own moral system, but how far it may be used to support or correct the moral system developed in the preceding chapters. That system may be defended at all points in terms of Hare's theory, I submit, by the simple device of modifying his conception of fanaticism. Let a fanatic be conceived as one who puts his own ideals, not above the *interests* of himself and others, but above what is *due* to them, taken as proceeding from the respect owed to every rational being as such, and the practical effect would be to identify fanatics, not with nonutilitarians, but with those who reject Hebrew-Christian common morality. The conception of fanaticism by recourse to which Hebrew-Christian morality becomes derivable within Hare's system is neither more arbitrary than that which Hare himself employs nor less. Whatever sense "fanaticism" may possess in character analysis in scientific psychology is disregarded by Hare, and may be dismissed as irrelevant. But it is not hard to understand that anybody whose moral convictions are strong, on discovering that those who oppose them are unmoved by his arguments, might ascribe their obduracy to a nonrational cause, and set them down as fanatics. The upshot is that advocates of moral systems which are internally consistent, on finding themselves opposed to one another, may each of them avail himself of the procedures of universal prescriptivism by equipping himself with an appropriate persuasive definition of fanaticism. The nature of the contest that will follow has been authoritatively analysed by C. L. Stevenson, in two well-known chapters of *Ethics and Language*.[17] And, given that the conflict does not arise from differences of opinion about nonmoral facts, Stevenson's conclusion must stand that no decision can be reached by rational methods.[18] If the issue between two opposed consistent moral systems is to be resolved rationally—perhaps by rejecting both—it must be by resources which universal prescriptivism does not supply, true though it is in most of its positive doctrine.

The second hypothetical choice theory that must be considered, the ideal observer theory of Roderick Firth and R. B. Brandt,[19] identifies rational moral principles with those that would be adopted by an ideal observer. But whereas Hare, in laying it down that only nonfanatics could successfully follow his procedure for testing proposed moral principles, persuasively defined fanaticism by reference to attitudes sanctioned by a particular moral system, Firth and Brandt studiously purge their descriptions of the ideal observer of any such reference.

They trace the origin of their theory to Adam Smith's observation that human beings are likely to reach agreement in their attitudes to one another's deeds and sufferings only in a measure as they can imaginatively both enter into the doings and sufferings of others and distance themselves, as spectators, from their own.[20] From this original insight, Adam Smith went on to speculate that, for every action that arouses attitudes of approbation or disapprobation, the only right attitude would be that which such a spectator would take:

that is, a spectator who can both enter into the points of view of others while "distancing" himself from his own. The right resentment for injuries suffered, for example, Smith held to be

the indignation they would call forth in [the breast] of the impartial spectator; which allows no word, no gesture, to escape it beyond what this more equitable sentiment would dictate; which never, even in thought, attempts any greater vengeance, nor desires to inflict any greater punishment, than what every indifferent person would rejoice to see executed.[21]

In his persuasive version of the theory, Brandt endows an ideal observer with three principal characteristics. First, he is fully informed and vividly imaginative. There is nothing he does not know about the nature and circumstances of the actions he observes, and he imagines them vividly and accurately from the points of view of all those in any way affected by them. Second, he is impartial. In imagining the various interests of all who are affected by an action, he does not make any set of such interests his own. "His reaction," Brandt declares, "would have been the same no matter what other individuals or groups were involved, as long as they had the same abstract properties."[22] Third, he is dispassionate and clearheaded.

However, it is not enough to put yourself in the prescribed frame of mind and to acquire the relevant information. It is necessary to bring your duly prepared mind to bear on an ordered series of proposed moral principles, each a correction of the one preceding it, until a principle is reached that is judged acceptable. You begin with a principle about which you are in doubt. You proceed to consider it in terms of an adequately varied range of specific cases, which you imagine vividly and with a tranquil mind, taking care that your judgement of the principle with respect to them is neither partial nor uninformed, nor unintelligible in the light of some consistent set of other comprehensible precepts.[23] If, as a result, you judge the principle acceptable, you need do no more. If you judge it unacceptable, the cases in terms of which you do so should suggest to you an amendment or a substitute. A different set of cases, although one overlapping in part the previous set, will be pertinent to the new principle, which must be considered in terms of them in the same way as the original principle was considered in terms of the original set of cases. The same procedure is then repeated until an acceptable principle is found.

Plausible though the method proposed by Brandt is, a simpleminded objection directs attention to its ambiguity and limitations. If it were asked, "Is 563 the sum of 179 and 384?" nobody would offer, as a step towards an answer, "It is, if it is the sum that an ideal calculator would reach by considering the question as an ideal calculator would," followed by a minute description of what ideal calculators are, and what faults they avoid in adding, but not of what they do in adding two numbers. Why then, when asked, "Is the principle that human beings are to be respected as rational creatures a true moral principle?" should anybody offer, as a step towards an answer, "It is, if an ideal observer would judge it to be so," followed by a minute description of what ideal observers are, and what faults they avoid in making such judgements, but not of what they do in arriving at a judgement on questions such as this? No doubt it is in part because there is now no difficulty in describing what adding is, whereas describing moral thinking seems, as Wittgenstein has said, "to run against the boundaries of language."[24] Yet, if there were a similar difficulty in describing how to add two numbers, would an answer in terms of an ideal calculator be less odd, or at all helpful?

The most direct reply to this objection appeals to the tradition from which the ideal observer theory grew. "Methods of addition which refer to ideal calculators are indeed superfluous," it may be answered, "because adding is an intellectual process, which can be described without referring to any calculator, ideal or other; by contrast, deciding whether or not a moral principle is true is a matter of employing one's moral sense, and that process cannot be described without referring to the possessors of such a sense. Furthermore, the process of employing one's moral sense effectively is well described in the method laid down in the theory, which is designed to ensure that the moral sense will be directed undistractedly and unobstructedly on all the relevant objects."

About the multiform theory that there is a moral sense I shall say nothing except that, if it is true, then the traditional lines of investigation followed in this study are radically in error. Kant's brief criticism of it in his *Grundlegung* seems to me decisive.[25] And if the theory of a moral sense be untenable, then the preliminary objection to the ideal observer theory which I described as simpleminded becomes strong. For if ideal observers arrive at their conclusions by rational processes, and not by employing a moral sense, why not describe those processes?

This task becomes urgent when attempts are made in terms of the ideal observer theory to decide between two established and consistent moral systems, the advocates of which are convinced of their systems' truth and eager to uphold it in argument: for example, between utilitarianism in one of its sophisticated forms and traditional common morality. There is nothing positive in the qualified attitude method advocated by Brandt to which either utilitarians or traditional moralists would object. They would agree that a moralist may be led into error by lack of information, by defects in imaginative insight; by partiality, passion, and foggy-mindedness; and by failure systematically to investigate all the pertinent varieties of case in relation to all the significant varieties of moral theory. Presumably they would acknowledge that they themselves are wanting to some degree in all these respects. But, confident that their individual shortcomings are corrected by others in the same tradition, they would deny that their conclusions are vitiated by them.

It does not follow from this that ideal observers may disagree about what the principles of morality are. An adherent of the ideal observer theory may properly protest that the advocates of neither of the competing moral systems under consideration have been shown to qualify as ideal observers. The difficulty is that the qualifications of ideal observerhood are such that no human being can be shown ever to possess them. It follows that nobody can establish that he has reached the conclusions an ideal observer would reach except by demonstrating them directly. If a conclusion in morality is demonstrated directly, it will have been established indirectly that an ideal observer would reach it. But no conclusion in morality can be established indirectly by directly demonstrating that it is one an ideal observer would reach.

In his comparison of the three hypothetical choice theories, Hare rightly placed the ideal observer theory together with universal prescriptivism in one subclass and Rawls's rational contractor theory in another. For both the ideal observer theory and universal prescriptivism attempt to determine the principles of morality by ascertaining what moral principles would be accepted by thinkers who satisfy certain conditions and follow a prescribed procedure. The objection that is fatal to both is that, provided that the conditions which must be satisfied by those who are to follow the procedure prescribed are not persuasively and so question-beggingly defined, either there are no principles that they will be obliged to accept by following the procedure prescribed or there is no way of assuring themselves that they have succeeded in following it.

No such objections against Rawls's theory can be sustained. It really does generate a definite moral system—a nonutilitarian one. And it does much more than that. It is a comprehensive theory of just social institutions, of which morality is only one. But in working it out, Rawls himself devotes comparatively little space to elaborating his moral system, which he divides into a system of natural duties and a system of obligations.[26] It is true that help in exploring the ramifications of the Rawlsian moral system may be had from David A. J. Richards's *Theory of Reasons for Action*; but it cannot be assumed that Rawls would endorse all of Richards's results.

Rawls's theory is accounted by Hare a hypothetical choice theory because it identifies just institutions (including a just moral system) with those that would be agreed upon by those who participate in them, provided that they were to reach their agreement in a sequence of four stages: beginning with an agreement as to fundamental principles arrived at in what Rawls calls "the original position," and then proceeding, in order, to a constitutional convention, to a functioning representative legislature, and to the general acceptance of the rules promulgated in the earlier stages, and their execution by judicial and administrative bodies.[27] Plainly, the last two stages cannot be hypothetical: a just society cannot do without a real legislature, judiciary, and administration, or without a real acceptance by its citizens of its institutions. But the second stage may be hypothetical: there could be a just society the political institutions of which developed gradually, without any constitutional convention. And the first must be: it is impossible that the members of any society should ever be in the original position. In this respect Rawls's theory diverges from the classical contractarianism of Hobbes and Locke. While it is improbable to the last degree that any set of social institutions has ever originated in a free agreement between persons in a state of nature, it is not historically impossible; but Rawls's original position confessedly is.

Nonetheless, Rawls maintains that the principles of morality are those principles of obligation and natural duty that would be agreed upon by all members of a society, if they were to make their agreement in that purely hypothetical original position, the nature of which is as follows. Each contractor, who is assumed to be rational, is for the purpose of the contract to consider only his own self-interest, which in view of subsequent characteristics of the position, is taken to consist in acquiring a sufficiency of primary human goods: namely of fundamental liberties, rights and opportu-

nities, of income and wealth, and of the social bases of self-esteem. [28]
In addition, each contractor is to be furnished with knowledge
which few in fact have: of the general truths of human psychology,
sociology, economics, and the theory of human institutions; and of
the fact that moderate scarcity obtains, given the resources and
capital of which his society disposes, and the talents and skills
possessed by its members. [29] On the other hand, all the contractors
are to be under a "veil of ignorance" as to their individual race, sex,
social position, wealth, talents, opinions, aspirations, and tastes.
They are thereby prevented, in making their self-interested decision
whether or not to accept a proposed moral precept, from favoring
either their own race, sex, or social or economic class, or persons of
similar talents and attitudes. [30] The effect is equivalent to that of
granting the worst-off representative person in the society a veto
over proposed precepts in its moral system; for when each contractor
considers his interests, he must take into account what they would
be if such a person were to turn out to represent him.

Rawls has, in my opinion, succeeded in showing that rational
contractors in the original position would necessarily accept not only
what he calls the "difference principle"—roughly, that the position
of the better-off is to be improved only if it is necessary for improv-
ing the position of the worst-off—but also a nonutilitarian moral
system having much in common with traditional morality. Yet how
is that supposed to provide a foundation for either that principle or
that moral system? Why should anybody accept a moral system
merely because a rational contractor in the original position (which
he is not) would accept it (which he has not)? *Prima facie*, Rawls's
hypothetical choice theory improves on universal prescriptivism and
the ideal observer theory in generating a definite moral system,
while falling ludicrously short of them in not even appearing to
justify that system.

Of course, this is only an appearance. For Rawls did not offer
his conception of the original position as a substitute for universal
prescriptivism or the ideal observer theory: it is not a hypothetical
procedure the sole purpose of which is to constrain the contractors
to deliberate in accordance with the laws of logic, and with the
morally neutral conditions which an analysis of moral concepts has
shown must be satisfied by any candidate for the status of moral
principle. Rather, as Rawls has explicitly stated, he designed the
original position "to nullify the effects of specific contingencies
which put men at odds and tempt them to exploit social and natural

circumstances to their own advantage."[31] He does not advance it as itself the foundation of morality but as a contrivance by which his "deeper" theory of morality (as Ronald Dworkin has called it) can be applied.[32] He has recently acknowleged this in an explanatory discussion:

> It might be thought that the original position is meant to be morally neutral. Rather, it is intended to be fair between individuals conceived as moral persons with a right to equal respect and consideration in the design of their common institutions.[33]

In other words, as Dworkin has divined, "the original position is an intermediate conclusion, a halfway point in a deeper theory that provides philosophical arguments for its conclusions."[34] And that deeper theory has been presented by Rawls as Kantian:

> The principles [an autonomous agent] acts upon are not adopted because of his social position or natural endowments, in view of the particular kind of society in which he lives or the specific things that he happens to want. To act on such principles is to act heteronomously. Now the veil of ignorance deprives persons in the original position of the knowledge that would enable them to choose heteronomous principles.[35]

The foundation of Rawls's moral system is therefore a theory of human rights, the inspiration of which is Kantian.[36] The contractarian hypothetical choice it employs is no more than an expository device, and as such it is both memorable and economical. But if that is so, Rawls's theory of morality is not a hypothetical choice theory at all. It does not attempt to establish the fundamental principles of morality indirectly, but rather accepts the task of justifying them directly. Not least, it confirms the historical judgement that in seeking how this may be done, it is well to turn to Kant.

7.3   The Limits of Purpose

We have seen, from the imperatives of skill derivable from the principle of the hypothetical imperative, that reason can be practical in its own right. And Foot's arguments that all imperatives of practical reason are hypothetical have brought home the fundamental nature of Kant's question whether practical reason can prescribe anything nonhypothetical.

Let us begin with the question whether all the imperatives of practical reason are imperatives of skill. Such imperatives, as we have seen (7.1), arise from the contemplation of ends that can be achieved by action; and for any such end they impose a choice—either abandon it or adopt the necessary effective means of achieving it. Evidently, if there is an end attainable by action which practical reason imposes, there will be all kinds of actions which it prescribes unconditionally: namely, those that are necessary effective means to attaining that end. Is there such an end?

According to the classical Western philosophical tradition there is: the end called *eudaimonia* in Greek, *felicitas* or *beatitudo* in Latin, and "happiness" in English. It is not to be identified with pleasure, although pleasure is an element in it. Aristotle's description of it has not been bettered: activity in accordance with human excellence (*arete*), in a complete life (*Eth. Nic.* 1098a 16-20). That happiness in this sense presupposes the enjoyment of primary human goods, such as health, a certain amount of wealth, and a respected place in a free society, has been brought out by Rawls.[37] There is no doubt at all that normal human beings naturally seek happiness. But they do not all in fact seek it; and when they do not, it may be presumed that they have reasons for not doing so which they consider of overriding importance. That is why Kant consistently held happiness to be the natural end of man but not an unconditional rational end. Action in pursuit of happiness is always intelligible in rational terms, but it is not imposed by reason.

Not only is the pursuit of our own happiness not imposed on us by reason, but, setting aside the duty to preserve one's life and health, even when happiness is one's end, reason seldom requires any specific action as a means to it. "[I]t is impossible," Kant maintains, "even for a most clear-sighted and most capable but finite being to form here a definite concept of that which he really wills."[38] A man can deduce from the Aristotelian analysis that he ought to form a rational plan of life, and act on it; but in almost all cases he will be able to think of a number of alternative rational plans, between which his idea of happiness will not determine his choice.

Practical reason, in short, can and does largely leave the pursuit of happiness to look after itself. It counsels prudence—the choice of *some* rational plan of life—and condemns imprudence; and it supplies imperatives of skill for the conduct of the various enterprises on which a man may embark in carrying out his plan. For the rest, it leaves him to his own devices and inclinations.

Does reason offer any prescriptions for the practical conduct of life other than these? Undoubtedly, many people are strongly inclined to believe that it does. Consider the following case, which is suggested by a passage from a paper by J. L. Stocks, from which I have stolen much besides the title of this section.[39] A manufacturer, with the innocent purpose of making a fortune, calculates that by bringing out a new product, which will drive out of the market one produced by another firm, he can make a great deal of money, much more than by adopting any of the other promising plans he is considering. It is true that the product he will drive out is the principal one made by a firm with which he started his career, and the major owner and chief executive of which was his guide, friend, and early financial backer. However, his former patron is well provided for, and not even loss of the market for its chief product would be likely to put his firm out of operation. Besides, as associates do not allow him to forget, business is business. Even so, he recoils from their advice. Stocks's remarks on this are worth quoting:

> This recoil or repulsion is not the opposite or contradictory of the former attraction. Nothing envisaged in the merely purposive attitude . . . is now disowned. All that is admitted and remains in view. But something new plainly has been seen which accounts for the change of mind. What is it? To the merely practical or purposive man, say a partner, who has followed [him] through his calculations, and understands the projected coup in all its bearings, [his] rejection will seem madness, something wholly irrational, a blind subservience perhaps to ancient superstition or old-fashioned business convention, or a lazy good-tempered acquiescence in wholly arbitrary and artificial limitations upon enterprise.[40]

It may, of course, be objected that the reluctant manufacturer has a purpose in conflict with that of making a fortune: namely, to take care that his old patron does not suffer. But that would be a mistake. It is supposed that if a third manufacturer were to do what he recoils from doing, he would not consider himself called upon to take any action at all. It should be remembered that his old patron is well-off.

Deliberately, the case has been so described as to leave its moral status ambiguous—cases of gratitude are at the frontiers of morality. My object is to elicit the rational considerations that lie at the heart of morality, but without presupposing any particular moral position. In the imaginary situation that has been presented, the manufacturer, in refraining from action that will further his purpose of making a fortune, has no other purpose to achieve. The suffering he would cause his old patron by invading his market does not, in itself, disturb him at all; nor is it his purpose to prevent it. And he would not scruple in the least to cause suffering of the same kind to anybody else, or think himself wronged if anybody caused it to him. What he cannot stomach is that he, or anybody in a like position, should cause suffering of that kind to a former patron.

How can refraining from action on such a ground possibly be thought to be demanded by reason? Let us begin by inquiring into the structure of purposive reasoning itself. Our imaginary manufacturer had an end, in view of which he made his business plans: namely, to make a fortune. It was not his only major end, but it was one of them. And that end was itself adopted in view of a further end. Making a fortune was an important element in his plan of life, the carrying out of which he hoped would constitute living happily. But although his end in making a fortune was to live happily, making a fortune was not a process, in itself neutral, that would ultimately lead to happiness. It was not a means in the instrumental sense, but rather in the sense in which getting a part is a means to getting the whole. Yet, even allowing for this distinction, both making a fortune and living a happy life are *producible* ends—ends brought into existence by the actions that are means to them—of which the latter is comprehensive, the former not. What we are trying to understand is how anybody can think it reasonable to act contrary to his own comprehensive end.

The case imagined points to an answer. Our manufacturer might himself have explained his reason for not doing the thing for which his own comprehensive purpose called by saying, "You can't do that to the old man who gave you your start!" He perceives the relation of a purposive action to a certain person as a reason for not doing the action—and one which overrides all purposive considerations. That suggests that he perceives his purposes—even the comprehensive one of living happily—as subordinate to some end yet more ultimate.

What is the point of seeking happiness? The question is not absurd: it does not call in doubt that it is natural for us to seek happiness. Rather, it brings a reminder that, however natural it may be to seek happiness, since we do not necessarily or always seek it, we would do well to reflect on our natural inclination to do so, and inquire whether there are grounds for following the inclination. Can a choice either to do what we think will make for our happiness, or to refrain, be anything but that—a sheer ungrounded decision? Or can it be made according to some judgement of its reasonableness? Suppose that our choice is to do what we think will make for our happiness: on what possible ground could it be made? I can think of only one: that we are beings of such a nature that our natural inclinations are worth following. If our happiness is a rational end, it will not be because of the multiform nature of happiness, but because we are beings of the kind we are.

Our imaginary manufacturer's recoil from entering into competition with his old patron can now be seen to have a ground which is not merely intelligible but also, in his mind, rational. His pursuit of his own happiness is neither instinctive, like the purposive activity of brute animals, nor a matter of arbitrary choice; it springs from his judgement that a being such as himself is one whose natural inclinations are worth satisfying. But besides affirming that he is of such a nature that his natural inclinations are worth satisfying, he also judges that his former patron is of such a nature that the fact that he is a benefactor and friend, and that a purposed action would cause him suffering, is a ground for refraining from that action. He does not make his old patron's purposes his own. But, for the patron's sake, he sets a limit on what he will do for his own sake.

Our investigation has therefore disclosed a twofold teleology in human action. The first is the teleology of purpose, which is in turn twofold: consisting, in the foreground, of a technical teleology of means to specific ends; and, in the background, of a teleology of part to whole, in which various specific ends are related, through a rational plan of life, to the comprehensive end of a happy human life. The second, which underlies the teleology of purpose, is the teleology of ultimate *ends for the sake of which*, or ends in themselves. These ends are not producible by the actions that are done for their sake, as ends in the teleology of purpose are producible by the actions that are means to them. (Human beings, although they are producible by procreative acts, are not, as individuals, ends for the sake of which the acts that produce them are performed: their parents' end is purposive, to have *a* child, or a child of certain characteristics; but it cannot be to have this child rather than that one.)

The analyses I have, with Kant in mind, derived from Stocks's work, show that some human beings at least think of their actions as done for the sake of beings—themselves or others—who are ends in themselves, and who are therefore considered to be beings for whose sake not only are purposive actions rationally performed but also limits on purposive actions are rationally set. And it is virtually certain that here is the source of the doctrine that practical reason issues nonhypothetical as well as hypothetical prescriptions. It remains to determine whether a nonpurposive teleology of ends in themselves is rationally justifiable, and, if it is, what practical principles can rationally be derived from it.

7.4 The Theory of the End-in-Itself

The ground of the fundamental principle of morality (*oberstes praktisches Prinzip*), according to Kant, is that rational nature exists as an end in itself (*die vernünftige Natur existiert als Zweck an sich selbst*).[41] From this ground it obviously follows that no rational being should ever be used merely as a means; always, even when he is being used as a means, he must at the same time be treated as an end. And that may also be expressed as: every rational creature is to be respected as such; which, in turn, in its application to human beings, yields the fundamental principle of common morality— every human being is to be respected as being a rational creature.

The argument from ground to principle is plain. The problem is whether the ground can be established. Has Kant an answer to Philippa Foot's denial that it is either inconsistent or irrational to reject it?

She is obviously right in denying not only that such a rejection is inconsistent but also that it is necessarily irrational in the sense of doing what is calculated to frustrate one's own purposes. A man may not care about rational nature—his own or anybody else's. We must therefore inquire whether irrationality in action is confined to the frustration of one's own purposes.

What Kant himself wrote directly on the question is meagre. It may be quoted in full:

> . . . rational nature exists as an end in itself. Man necessarily
> thinks of his own existence [*Dasein*] in this way; thus far it is a
> subjective principle of human actions. Also every other rational
> being thinks of his existence by means of the same rational
> ground which holds also for myself; thus it is at the same time,
> an objective principle.[42]

Kant appears to have thought these assertions to be so obviously true that nobody would wish to deny them; but they are not. Indeed, on one natural reading they are false: it is quite possible for human beings not to conceive their existence as an end in itself, but instead to consider it as utterly pointless.

Since Kant's moral theory becomes utterly unintelligible if he is interpreted as denying this, his assertion that human beings necessarily conceive their own existence as an end in itself must be understood as meaning that it is contrary to reason for them to conceive it in any other way. Yet not only is it possible for them so to conceive it, but disastrous. For their state of mind would then be like that expressed by Shakespeare's Macbeth, when he is reduced to utter despair:

> Life's but a walking Shadow, a poore Player,
> That struts and frets his houre upon the Stage,
> And then is heard no more. It is a Tale
> Told by an Ideot, full of sound and fury,
> Signifying nothing.

In maintaining that such a view of human existence is contrary to reason, Kant is obviously not suggesting that Macbeth is frustrating his own purposes; but what *is* he suggesting?

The answer to be found in the *Grundlegung* is along the following lines.

Analysis of imperatives of skill has shown that reason cannot be, in practice, the mere instrument or slave of wants and desires. For the hypothetical imperative, which must be valid if reason is to have a practical function in the service of desire, itself imposes choices, which are often undesired, between adopting means and relinquishing ends. In short, nobody whose action really is determined by himself as the result of deliberation, even if he embarks on deliberation with nothing else in mind than to gratify desire, can be subject to those desires; for his deliberation can lead him not to gratify them. If deliberating with a view to action is what human beings who conceive themselves as rational agents take it to be, then anybody who acts deliberately is free either to gratify his instincts and desires or not to gratify them. And this is part of the traditional conception of what it is to be human.[43]

The behavior of the higher brute animals is reasonably understood (and was implicitly understood by Kant)[44] to be a function of the strength of their various desires and drives, and of their perception of their situation, which comprises both perceptions of what is there and perceptions of what they can bring about in view of what is there. The function of perception in the behavior of a brute animal is therefore not to motivate but to present possible actions with foreseen outcomes (the foresight possibly erring) from among which its actual behavior will be determined by its strongest drives. These perceptions of possible actions and outcomes need not be interpreted as deliberative, and should not. Köhler's famous example of the ape who "deliberated" about how to put two sticks together as an instrument for drawing food into its cage is more economically interpreted as analogous to an animal's hesitating between several complex routes to a destination, and then, after a short pause, "seeing" the one that answers its purposes best and taking it confidently and rapidly. In such cases the "reflective" process, while not blind trial and error, at no time involves rational deliberation, which calls in question what the end shall be.

What distinguishes human beings from brute animals, then, is a twofold capacity: for rational deliberation, which enables them to call in question not only whether a necessary means to a contemplated end shall be chosen but also whether the contemplated end shall be pursued; and for making the choices rational deliberation presents. Paradoxically, the liberty of choice implicit in rational agency threatens to eradicate from human action the rationality found even in animal behavior: the rationality of being an efficient means to an end that the animal has by virtue of being the animal it is. Hence the very freedom of human action from determination by natural instinct and desire seems to deprive human beings of any ends proper to them as human. And if they have no ends as human, how can their actions be rational?

Of course it remains possible for them simply to act according to their inclinations. But not only is there nothing rational about following such a course, very few human beings in fact do follow it. Except in the degenerate sense of inclination in which one may be said to have been "inclined" to do or seek whatever one in fact chose to do or seek, most human ends are not chosen from inclination: as we have seen (4.1), they are usually motivated by chosen enterprises, or chosen plans of life, which more often than not are arrived at by reflections in which inclination is not a major consideration. And even though everybody wants to be happy, not only is it usually impossible, as Kant saw, to choose one rational plan of life as against another on the basis of any rationally grounded calculation as to which is more likely to result in happiness, but it may not be contrary to reason to choose a plan of life which is less likely to result in happiness for oneself than some other. Some plans of life, as self-defeating, may certainly be condemned as irrational; but often a plan must be chosen from among several, none of which can be condemned on that ground. Yet it would be superficial to conclude that therefore reason provides human beings with no end that is theirs as human; for such a conclusion would only follow if it were presupposed that all rational ends are ends producible by action. Kant's position was that, by the very fact that it supersedes all the producible ends set up by instinct and desire, reason provides man with an end of quite another sort. For by the very fact that there is no producible end, not even his own happiness, which a man cannot rationally choose to relinquish, it follows that he stands to all producible ends, even to those which are natural to him, in the position of what St. Augustine called a "judge." Having this power to judge his producible ends, which as such, is a higher kind of power than brute animals possess (there is nothing at all more excellent [*sublimius*] in nature, according to St. Augustine[45]—but the tradition can be traced to Anaxagoras, and beyond), human beings, as rational, are of a higher kind than any others they have yet encountered in nature. Nor can there be any creature higher in kind, although there may be some higher in degree. For reason will not acknowledge anything other than itself as its judge, although one rational being may well concede that another has greater rational powers than himself. In short, human beings may reasonably judge that any being of the same nature as theirs, any rational being, is an end for rational action. And since rational nature is not to be produced (*bewirkender*) but is self-existent (*selbständiger*), as an end it must be thought of "negatively," as something "which must never be acted against, and which consequently must be valued never merely as a means, but in every act of will [*Wollen*] always at the same time as an end."[46]

The foregoing considerations underlie Kant's statement, in *Grundlegung* sec. 3, that from the concept of the negative freedom of the human will, that is, the concept of each human agent as having the power to determine his actions independently of any cause external to reason itself, "there springs . . . a *positive* concept, which, as positive, is richer and more fruitful,"[47] namely, the concept of each human agent as autonomous—a law to himself. Since Kant certainly did not think that a richer concept can be extracted by logical analysis from a poorer one, he must have

thought of the connection between negative freedom and positive as
synthetic. And I submit that what in his moral theory connects the
two is the concept of an end in itself. Since they are negatively free,
the actions of a rational being have a causality higher than those of a
brute animal; and it is because of that higher kind of causality that
rational beings are ends in themselves—ends which are not producible but which exist independently of the actions done for their
sake. It is as ends in themselves that rational beings find in their
own natures a ground for the law they lay down to themselves.

In Hill's admirable summary, "moral conduct [in Kant's view] is
the practical exercise of the noble capacity to be rational and self-
governing, a capacity which sets us apart from the lower animals
and gives us dignity."[48] We are self-governing, at bottom, because
our rational agency entails that we are negatively free—that our
actions are not causally determined by anything, such as instinct or
desire, which is external to reason. Our negative freedom grounds
our status as ends in ourselves. And that status furnishes the content
of the fundamental principle of morality.

The objections that may be made to this position are not difficult
to anticipate. First of all, there is the metaphysical objection, which
Kant himself, in view of his own conclusions in *The Critique of Pure
Reason*, found intractable: that, since human beings belong to the
realm of nature, in which every occurrence, so far as it is explicable
at all, accords with laws which, if not deterministic, are at any rate
purely physical,[49] it is flatly impossible that human beings should be
agent-causes, as the conception of them as ends in themselves
presupposes. To meet such objections, as was observed in 2.1, is
beyond the scope of a study of moral theory, in which what is
presupposed about the nature of human action in traditional
Western civilization is provisionally assumed to be true. Of course,
if the moral system here developed is ultimately to be upheld, all its
presuppositions must be vindicated in appropriate independent
inquiries.

Even so, two remarks are in order. First, neither the determinist
nor the purely physicalist interpretations of human action are results
of modern science: rather, they are anticipations of what its results
will be, which are disputed within the relevant sciences.[50] Only
metaphysicians, such as Spinoza and Kant, seriously offer to prove
that all natural events are explicable in terms of deterministic or
physicalistic laws; and their proofs are disputed in metaphysics.
Despite Kant and the present vogue for materialism, the conception

of human action as agent-caused is neither scientifically nor philosophically indefensible. And secondly, if human beings are to be
regarded as human, then it is necessary to conceive of them not
merely as beings whose behavior can be explained in terms of
reasons (as, for example, an electronic computer's can), but as
beings who choose between the possibilities about which they
deliberate.[51]

The second objection to Kant's theory of the end in itself, and the
more familiar one, has to do with the concept of rationality. It may
take various forms. One of them we have already encountered, in
Foot's argument that the only rational imperatives are hypothetical, because practical rationality is a matter of consistency, and of
not acting in such a way as to frustrate the attainment of one's own
ends. Unquestionably, if the analysis of rationality presupposed in
this argument stands, then it cannot be true that a rational being,
inasmuch as it is rational, must prescribe that no rational being is to
be used merely as a means. And that analysis has at least internal
unity to recommend it; for the practical concept of not willing to act
in such a way as to frustrate the attainment of one's own ends is
derivable from the theoretical concept of consistency. Should Foot's
objection be met by a counterdefinition of rationality, supported by
persuasive considerations, it may be transformed into an objection
to settling the fundamental principle of morality by persuasive
definition. For, as has been argued in connection with Hare's resort
to a persuasive definition of fanaticism in deriving his moral
principles, no dispute that ultimately turns solely on persuasive
definitions can be rationally decided. In sum, if Foot's analysis of
rationality is correct, then the fundamental principle of morality is
false; but if it is one persuasive definition among others, and so
neither correct nor incorrect, then the fundamental principle,
whether it follows on one definition or not on another, is merely
trivial.

To meet this twofold objection, it is necessary to return to the
semantic interpretation of moral precepts advanced in 2.3, in which
they were taken to be true if and only if practical reason, functioning without error, would make certain prescriptions, and false
otherwise. The errors in functioning referred to would not be false
assertions; for, unlike precepts, which are propositions about them,
prescriptions themselves are neither true nor false. What is assumed
is that the power to reason practically may, in any rational creature,
function well or ill. An error in practical reasoning is prescribing

something as a result of a rational process in which there has been some malfunction. Some malfunctions are familiar. Everybody is aware that practical deliberation can be impaired by prejudice or passion, and that practical decisions can be aborted by precipitation or inattention. Nor have the varieties of such possible malfunctions ever been completely listed. For our purposes, it is enough that practical reason, like theoretical reason, may be used by its possessors well or ill. When they reason well, their rational processes accord with the nature of reason; when ill, they do not.

All this presupposes that the word "reason," as it is used here, has a reference that is fixed for all possible worlds.[52] But it seems reasonable to suppose that it has. It stands for a power, possessed by normal human adults, by which they do such things as propound propositions, assent to them or dissent from them, recognize that if a certain one is true then a certain other must also be true, and the like. What particular description is given does not matter, provided that it describes a power correctly to perform acts having contents belonging to the domain of logic; for in any possible world, one and the same power is referred to by all such descriptions. Hence the reference of "reason" is fixed, and it is possible to proceed to investigate its nature more deeply, and to discover new things about what is involved in possessing it.

The implication of this, that reason, considered as a thing (a certain power) found in the world, has a certain nature or essence, would not long ago have been dismissed by many logicians as unintelligible. Propositions purporting to assert necessity *de re*—that certain things, by virtue of their natures or essences, necessarily have certain properties—were held to be either confused or reducible to others purporting to assert no more than necessity *de dicto*—that certain propositions are logically true, that is, that their contradictories violate some law of logic. This familiar dogma is now discredited.[53] As Saul A. Kripke has observed, "The type of property identity used in science seems to be associated with *necessity*, not with a prioricity, or analyticity,"[54] and so once one finds out, say, what the atomic structure of gold is (and so necessarily is, for what does not have that structure cannot be gold), one can go on to determine all sorts of other properties necessarily possessed by gold, which can by no means be deduced from the descriptions by which the reference of the term was originally fixed.

Yet in seeking to establish what reason necessarily prescribes, when it functions without error, it would be preposterous to employ the a posteriori methods appropriate in determining laws of physical necessity. To begin with, the distinction between event causation and agent causation drawn in 2.2 entails that, even if reason does necessarily prescribe something, it is in the power of any rational agent to deny that it does, and to act contrary to what is prescribed. And furthermore, as we have seen, since the possibility of genuine error, whether culpable or not, cannot be excluded, it is possible in any given case that a rational agent may simply fail to grasp what reason prescribes. Questions about the fundamental prescriptions of practical reason can no more be answered by empirically investigating how rational agents behave, or what they will assent to, than can questions about the foundations of logic or arithmetic.

How then can questions about what practical reason prescribes be settled? What Kripke has said of the word "pain" is also true of the word "reason"; its "reference is determined by an essential property of the referent."[55] For, although the reference of "reason" may be fixed by many different descriptions, they must all mention acts the contents of which belong to the domain of logic, and which are stipulated to accord with its laws. Hence it is not merely necessary that reason, by its very nature, does not accord with assenting to self-contradictions, but this essential property of reason, being presupposed in any description of it by which the reference of "reason" is fixed, is also demonstrable a priori. And, as we have seen, it is likewise demonstrable a priori that reason, by its very nature, does not accord with dissenting from the general formula of hypothetical imperatives.

Since the reference of "reason" is fixed by stipulations relating to logic, it is possible to demonstrate a priori that reason necessarily forbids the denial of any truth that is analytic in Frege's sense: that is, of any truth the contradictory of which can be reduced, by purely formal operations, to the contradictory of a law of logic. And, as we shall see, some philosophers nurse hopes of demonstrating a priori more than that. But it is of the first importance that it be acknowledged that not all truths about necessities *de re* are established either by such a priori demonstrations, or by the a posteriori methods appropriate to establishing laws of nature. For example, the important proposition that temporal priority is transitive, from which it follows that for no observer can time run backwards, can be established in neither way.[56] It is neither experimentally testable (save by "thought experiments"), nor can it be shown that reason must affirm it, given the descriptions by which the reference of the word "reason" is fixed. Most of us are convinced that it is necessarily so, because we seem to ourselves to have sufficient insight into the nature of time for anything else to be unthinkable. Yet few would deny the abstract possibility that coherent observations and experiments of a bizarre kind could undermine our confidence.

What Kant had to say in justification of the fundamental principle of morality is in some ways like this, although what might undermine the confidence of those who agree with him would not be some totally unexpected observation or experiment but the elaboration of some hitherto unthought of but practicable possibility for human living. For, whatever he may have occasionally implied, Kant did not demonstrate a priori that reason must by its very nature prescribe for free and rational beings what the fundamental principle of morality says it must. Rather, he drew attention to certain characteristics implicit in being a rational creature, with regard to which he claimed to have sufficient insight into the nature of practical reason confidently to affirm that it must prescribe that rational creatures be unconditionally respected. They are: first, that rational creatures are negatively free because they exhibit a kind of causality by virtue of which their actions are not determined to any end by their physical or biological nature; and second, that because of that causality, they are creatures of a higher kind than any others in nature. These characteristics, according to Kant, provide rational creatures with an end which their own reason must acknowledge: their own rational nature. That end is not a producible one, like those of instinct and desire; but, as an end to be respected, by virtue of which things are to be done, it can generate action.

To me, these considerations seem as rationally compelling as they did to Kant. True, their force is not intuitively self-evident; for, in the abstract, it might be weakened by others not hitherto thought of. At present, however, in view of what has been pointed out by Kant, I have no doubt that practical reason must by its very nature prescribe what he said it must. And it may be that, on this matter, nothing further can or need be said. Certainly, if there is more to be said, save for disposing of objections and misunderstandings, traditional moralists did not say it.

Yet the temptation to try to demonstrate a priori that reason must prescribe at least part of what the fundamental principle of morality says it must is very hard to resist; for such demonstrations have certainly not been shown to be impossible. The most persuasive recent attempts at them have been made by Alan Gewirth and Thomas Nagel. Gewirth has endeavored to show that, in acting purposively, every rational agent "regards himself as justified in performing his actions, and in having the freedom and basic well-being which generically figure in all his actions, and implicitly makes a corresponding right-claim."[57] And he has argued that the right-claim which every rational agent as such necessarily makes cannot consistently be rejected by any rational agent.[58] Nagel has ingeniously contended that for any rational agent to disavow the objectivity of reasons for acting—to decry the existence of a reason for some given individual to do something as a motive for oneself and for everybody else to promote his doing it (although of course one may also have other motives for not promoting it)—is to reject the full reality of others, and so to be committed to a sort of practical solipsism.[59] And the rejection of solipsism, although not logically necessary, is not implausibly thought to be implicit in the essential properties that determine the reference of the word "reason."

Anybody who accepts the fundamental principle of morality after reflecting on the considerations articulated by Kant, but who acknowledges that they do not amount to an a priori demonstration, must hope that rejecting it may one day be shown to be incompatible with some essential property that determines the reference of the word "reason." Certainly, there seems to be no valid objection in principle to the possibility that attempts such as Gewirth's and Nagel's may prove to be sound. It should surprise nobody that rejecting what practical reason by its very nature prescribes may turn out to involve some hidden contradiction (as Gewirth holds) or some practical absurdity (as Nagel holds).

However, it must be repeated that, however desirable, a priori demonstrations such as those attempted by Gewirth and Nagel are not necessary to establishing the truth of the traditional system of morality. The traditional considerations upon which Kant accepted the fundamental principle, which are implicit in the earliest writings in the tradition, both Hebrew and Stoic, have seldom failed to move the minds of those who have been willing to reflect upon them. They are effective without a priori demonstrations of the fundamental principle; and they will remain effective even if such demonstrations should turn out to be impossible.

A different but complementary reflection is prompted by another line of thought that has recently been taken. Cannot a considerable part of traditional morality be justified simply as a system of rules which it would be irrational for human beings living in a society not to adopt, for the sake of protection from the evils which they can bring upon one another? In *The Moral Rules*, Bernard Gert has developed this line of thought thoroughly and persuasively. His main inspiration has been Hobbes, although he acknowledges debts to Kurt Baier, Marcus Singer, and John Rawls. But in following Hobbes, as he himself confesses, while he defends "traditional morality, or as much of it as can be defended," he neither can nor does defend traditional defences of it.[60] For his powerful defence of much of what I have called the traditional "first-order" code, every traditional moralist must be grateful. Yet they cannot regard such defences as other than secondary. For the spirit in which those who accept the traditional defences try to abide by the first-order code which they largely share with Hobbists, is not the same as that in which Hobbists try to abide by it. It is not clear to me whether Hobbists accept or reject the traditional doctrine that one must not do even the right thing for the wrong reason. But this is not the place to return to earlier results to argue either that the Hobbists' reasons for doing the right thing, however valid, are not the fundamental ones, or that they should act on the fundamental ones.

7.5   Respect for Rational Nature as a Condition of Self-Respect

It is widely agreed that self-respect is a primary human good, and want of it an evil. But the nature of self-respect is not always understood.

In his influential examination of the primary human goods, John Rawls has distinguished two elements of self-respect, which he identifies with self-esteem: first, "a person's sense of his own value, his secure conviction that his conception of his good, his plan of life, is worth carrying out"; and second, "a confidence in one's ability, so far as it is in one's power, to fulfill one's intentions."[61] As an analysis of self-esteem, this may do; for esteem is proportional to success. True, Rawls has taken pains to dissociate self-esteem from absolute success: the accomplishments that are to count are to be relative to one's plan of life, and within one's power. But even so, it seems to have been placed beyond the reach of the unrighteous and imprudent—say, of the Sir John Falstaffs of this world. And that is hard to accept.

Why? A clue may be found in one of the finest scenes in which Falstaff appears, and in which his creator compels us to see the limits of any conception of value as success. Falstaff has been conscripting troops for the Welsh wars, and lining his pockets with bribes for releasing the fit. "A mad fellow met me on the way," he remarks, "and told me, I had unloaded all the Gibbets, and prest the dead bodyes." But when the Prince complains, "I did never see such pittifull Rascals," he retorts, "Tut, tut, good enough to tosse; foode for Powder, foode for Powder: they'le fill a Pit, as well as better: tush man, mortall men, mortall men."[62] That the Prince never makes such a remark shows how different his mode of consciousness is from Falstaff's. He is a man of self-esteem: securely convinced that his plan of life is worth carrying out, and confident that he can carry it out; and he accurately registers that Falstaff's scarecrows have no plans and no confidence. Falstaff, while he esteems them no more than the Prince, is yet aware of them as "mortall men," for whose sake, although he does not say it, the state itself exists. True, he does not let his awareness trouble him much.

Yet, for all his misdeeds, Falstaff respects other human beings as he respects himself, irrespective of esteem. Respect, in this sense, has no degrees: you either respect somebody or you do not; and you respect him for what he is, not for what he does. The distinction here implied between respect and esteem shows itself in syntax. It makes sense to say of somebody what Falstaff constantly implies about Prince Hal: that he esteems himself too much. But it makes no sense to say of anybody that he respects himself too much.

The theory of traditional morality is inevitably moralistic; and that distracts attention from the fact that its foundation is not moralistic at all. Awareness of that foundation may be found in rascals like Falstaff, but never in precisians who observe the first-order precepts that follow from it, but merely for some secondary reason. Falstaff warned the Prince, who did not heed it, "Banish plumpe *Jacke*, and banish all the World." As D. A. Traversi has pointed out, the dramatic significance of this is: "Banish Falstaff . . . and banish everything that cannot be reduced to an instrument of policy in the quest for empty success."[63] In other words, banish Falstaff, and banish everything as a ground of morality that is not a matter of esteem.

Nietzsche's concept of the noble soul is a good philosophical

illustration of the implications of banishing the Falstaffian respect
for mortal men on which Hebrew-Christian morality rests.
A Nietzschean noble soul of course esteems itself. And it never
forgets that esteem is a matter of degree. It has no doubt at all that
its way of life is the one to be lived, and no diffidence about living it.
It has, as Nietzsche described it, "an unshakable faith that to a
being such as 'we are' other beings must be subordinate by nature
and have to sacrifice themselves."[64] "[T]he noble type of man," he
wrote in another place,

> experiences *itself* as determining values; it does not need
> approval; it judges, "whatever is harmful to me is harmful
> in itself"; it knows itself to be that which first accords honour
> to things; it is *value-creating*. Everything it knows as part of
> itself it honours; such a morality is self-glorification.[65]

It did not occur to him that a soul possessed of a faith that others
must sacrifice themselves to it must need what they sacrifice. Nor
did it occur to him that if according honor to things creates value,
then in themselves the things honored have no value. The noble
souls for whom morality consists in honoring whatever they know as
part of themselves (did Nietzsche perhaps suspect that they have
missed something fundamental?) are true *milites gloriosi*: all their
decorations are self-awarded.

In a society Nietzsche would consider healthy, what passes for
value is created by the masters, as Louis XIV multiplied distinctions
of rank at the court of Versailles. Yet the masters *find* value no-
where. Although, in extorting services from their slaves, they show
that they need them, they themselves recognize no rational purpose
in their extortions. The honors they confer, being grounded on
nothing but arbitrary will, can be upheld only by force. And,
inevitably, as their slaves divine the nullity that lies behind their self-
esteem, detestation will give way to contempt and anger.

That "slaves" and their spokesmen, the Hebrew-Christian moralists, reject master-morality because it is fraudulent, was unbearable
to Nietzsche's resentful mind. Since he would respect only that
whose value he had created, he resented the rationality in himself
which bore witness that respect cannot be accorded on such a
ground. Nor could he acknowledge that he resented it. And so, like
most thinkers whose consciousness is corrupt, he projected on the

hated thing that in himself which caused his hatred. It is not reason, he told himself, which demands that respect be given only to that which is valuable in itself, but rather resentment at the noble souls who can confer value upon things. Nothing is valuable in itself. All value is created.

Yet though self-respect is a primary human good, and though a condition of self-respect is the respect for rational nature as such that is the foundation of morality, it does not follow that self-respect justifies morality or that it is possible to accept the foundation of morality in order to gain self-respect. All respect rests on the recognition of something as intrinsically worthy of it. If one does not *find* rational nature intrinsically worthy of respect, to confer value on it in order to be able to respect oneself is impossible.

The grounds of morality must be sound in themselves. They cannot be made sound by the fact that things would be bad if they were not.

7.6   The Limits of Practical Reason

It is a prevalent delusion that, if acceptance of a system of prescriptions is in truth required by practical reason, a demonstration of it must ensure that those who accept the demonstration also accept those prescriptions.

According to the theory of action presupposed by traditional morality, knowledge is emphatically not virtue. It is perfectly possible for a rational creature to judge that a certain course of action is unconditionally required by reason, and yet to choose not to follow it. However, when a rational creature elects to flout his own judgement as to what is rational, he will necessarily do so for some reason or other, which *ex hypothesi* he recognizes as inadequate.

These reasons may be of two distinct kinds. Those of the first kind are often discussed in connection with the phenomenon of weakness of will. They are reasons which, in themselves, it would be perfectly rational to act upon, but not in a situation in which countervailing reasons are stronger. Thus, to avoid pain, or trouble, or even exertion is a perfectly good reason in itself for doing something; but not when there is adequate reason for putting up with it.

Those of the second kind are recognized in both the Jewish and the Christian religious traditions, but outside them are often ignored or denied. They arise out of refusal to accept the human condition itself, as traditional morality understands it: the condition of being finite rational creatures, limited in their physical and intellectual powers, inhabiting a world in which their race has never yet contrived to enjoy peace or plenty, but whose reason sets before them their own nature as something to be unconditionally respected. Refusal to accept the human condition may take the violent form of rebellion, of repudiating what reason presents as an end to be respected, and embarking on a life "beyond good and evil." Or it may take the abject form of treating the task of respecting every rational creature as such as an impossible one, which it is unfair of our nature to have imposed upon us. The result is a life of pettiness and resentment. In these ways, paradoxically, the recognition of the grounds of traditional morality (perhaps corruptly kept from full consciousness) gives rise to the worst offences against it.

These possibilities, however, have been implicit throughout what has been said about human action. Traditional moralists should be the last persons on earth to imagine themselves exempted from Kafka's admonition: *One must not cheat anybody, not even the world of its triumph.* [66]

Notes

Information about books and
articles cited by short titles, as
most are, may be found in the
Select Bibliography.

Chapter 1

1. Cf. Nietzsche, *The Will to Power*, tr. Kaufmann and Hollingdale, pp. 148-49, 151.

2. Diogenes Laertius, *Vitae Philosophorum* VII, 88, tr. Long (1970), p. 104.

3. Anscombe (1958), esp. pp. 5-9, 13-15.

4. Ibid., p. 15.

5. The point is not new. Aquinas, for example, held that *qua* virtuous, all virtuous acts belong to the moral law: "Si igitur loquamur de actibus virtutum inquantum sunt virtuosi, sic omnes actus virtuosi pertinent ad legem naturae" (*Summa Theologiae* I-II, 94, 3).

6. Aristotle, *Politics*, III, chap. 4; and cf. III, 1278a40, 1288a39; IV, 1293b5; VII, 1333a11. My view of the limitations of Aristotle and his predecessors as moral theorists owes much to Adkins, *Merit and Responsibility*, esp. pp. 341-54. For a criticism of Adkins which I cannot accept, see Hardie, *Aristotle's Ethical Theory*, pp. 124-28.

7. Maimonides, *Mishneh Torah*, XIV, 5, 9, 1 (Y.J.S., III, pp. 230-31).

8. Cf. Schwarzschild (1961), pp. 297-308, esp. 306-7; and (1962), pp. 30-65, esp. 40-50.

9. Romans, 2:14-15 (tr. Knox); cf. 1:24-32.

10. Aquinas, *Summa Theologiae*, I-II, 91, 2; cf. I-II, 100, 1.

11. "Porro haec ipsa quae ex *duabus tabulis* discenda sunt, quodam modo nobis dictat lex illa interior, quam omnium cordibus inscriptam et quasi impressam superius dictum est ... Proinde (quod tum hebetudini tum contumaciae nostrae necessarium erat) Dominus legem scriptam nobis posuit: quae et certius testificaretur quod in lege naturali nimis obscurum erat, et mentem memoriamque nostram, excusso torpore, vividius feriret" (John Calvin, *Institutio Christianae Religionis*, ed. postrema, 1559, II, viii, 1, in Baum, Cunitz, and Reuss, eds., *Joannis Calvini Opera quae supersunt Omnia*, vol. 2, being *Corpus Reformatorum*, vol. 30 (Brunswick: Schwetschke, 1864), p. 267.

12. Cf. Beck, *Early German Philosophy*, pp. 272–75; and Macmurray, Introduction to Kant, *Lectures on Ethics*, p. xvii.

13. Cf. Beck, *Early German Philosophy*, 489–90; and *Studies in the Philosophy of Kant*, pp. 221–24.

14. Cf. Beck and Macmurray, in Kant, *Lectures on Ethics*, pp. xi, xvii. Macmurray concludes that our text "represents substantially the lectures Kant was in the habit of giving between the years 1775 and 1781," during which he lectured on ethics five times (p. xvii).

15. Kant, *Grundlegung*, pp. 20–24 (pp. 403–5).

16. Hegel, *Phil. des Rechts*, §153 (p. 90). Hegel's theory of *Sittlichkeit*, and his attack upon Kant, are usefully examined in Walsh, *Hegelian Ethics*, esp. chaps. 4–7, and Charles Taylor, *Hegel*, pp. 164–70, 368–88, esp. p. 375 n. 3. While noting that, even though he recognized Socrates and Jesus as heroes, Hegel denied that they made real the spiritual truths they discovered, Taylor does not remark upon its paradoxicality (pp. 377–78).

17. Hegel, *Phil. des Rechts*, §150 (p. 107).

18. Ibid., §138 (p. 92).

19. Ibid.

20. Ibid., §138A (p. 255).

21. Ibid.

22. Oakeshott, *Rationalism in Politics*, p. 61. The structure of this section owes so much to Oakeshott's essay, "The Tower of Babel," from which this phrase is taken, that it is prudent to warn the reader of two disagreements: (1) that much of what Oakeshott says against morality as the reflective application of a moral criterion in my opinion applies only to one of his two forms of it, namely, to the self-conscious pursuit of moral ideals; and (2) that although Hebrew-Christian morality is one of reflective observance of moral rules, it is in my opinion *not* one of the self-conscious pursuit of moral ideals. Jewish and Christian religious ideals are for the most part *not* moral.

23. Ibid., pp. 64–65.

24. MacIntyre, *Secularization and Moral Change*, p. 24.

25. Ibid., p. 34.

26. Hegel, *Phil. des Rechts*, §135 (p. 90).

27. Kant, *Grundlegung*, p. 52 (p. 421), tr. Beck.

28. Cf. Beck, *Commentary on Kant's Critique of Practical Reason*, pp. 95–96; Paton, *Categorical Imperative*, pp. 61–62.

29. Kant, *Grundlegung*, pp. 66–67 (p. 429), tr. Beck.

30. For the argument of this paragraph I owe much to the succinct treatment in Beck, *Early German Philosophy*, p. 491. Rawls has taken a similar position: see *A Theory of Justice*, pp. 251–55.

31. Hegel, *Phil. des Rechts*, §138 (p. 92).

32. Dawes Hicks, *Stoic and Epicurean*, p. 144.

33. Oakeshott, *Rationalism in Politics*, p. 65.

34. See, e.g., Hörmann, *Moral Theology*, pp. 252–56.

35. Zahn, *In Solitary Witness*, p. 223.

36. Ibid., p. 233.

37. Ibid., pp. 165–66.

38. Ibid., p. 215.

39. Descartes, *Regulae ad Directionem Ingenii*..., in Adam and Tannery, eds.,

Oeuvres de Descartes, vol. 10, p. 368. The Latin text is: "Per *intuitum* intelligo . . . mentis purae et attentae non dubium conceptum, qui a sola rationis luce nascitur, et ipsamet deductione certior est, quia simplicior. . ."

40. Locke, *Essay concerning Human Understanding*, IV, 3, 20 (p. 552).

41. Butler, *Fifteen Sermons*, III, 4 (p. 63).

42. For expositions of Whewell's system, see Schneewind (1968), and Donagan (1974).

43. Sidgwick, *Methods of Ethics*, Preface to 2d ed. (1877), p.xx.

44. E.g., ibid., pp. 96-103.

45. Ibid., pp. 101-2.

46. Ibid., pp. 338-42.

47. The argument is summed up in ibid., pp. 342-43; it is elaborated in Book III, chaps. 2-10.

48. Ibid., p. 306.

49. Whewell, *Elements of Morality*, §281 (p. 155).

50. Cronin, *Science of Ethics*, vol. 2, pp. 301-2.

51. Broad, *Five Types of Ethical Theory*, pp. 222-23.

52. Ross, *Foundations of Ethics*, p. 187.

53. Ibid., p. 189.

54. Geach (1956), p. 41.

55. Oakeshott, *Rationalism in Politics*, p. 78.

56. Rawls, *A Theory of Justice*, p. 52.

57. Nietzsche, *Untimely Meditations*, III, sec. 6, quoted by J. R. Hollingdale in *Nietzsche: The Man and His Philosophy*, p. 127. I owe the reference to Rawls, *A Theory of Justice*, p. 325 n.

58. MacIntyre and Ricoeur, *The Religious Significance of Atheism*, p. 41. I have found both MacIntyre's argument that theism depends on a certain view of morality rather than the converse, and his view of Kant as "a coherent and consistent recorder and analyst of an incoherent . . . set of moral concepts . . . embodied in an incoherent . . . moral practice" valuable and suggestive, although I cannot wholly accept either.

59. Rather than "Judaeo-Christian," in order to signify its antiquity: the "Hebrew" conception of common morality may be found in the Mosaic Pentateuch, the compilation of which antedates rabbinic Judaism (which can be traced to about 200 b.c.).

60. Aquinas, *Summa Theologiae*, I-II, 94, 4.

Chapter 2

1. The example is from Nielsen (1972), p. 227.

2. Danto, *Mysticism and Morality*, p. 34. My information about Hinduism is largely derived from this book.

3. Ibid., p. 40.

4. Ibid., pp. 26-28. For the similar Buddhist view, see Tachibana, *Ethics of Buddhism*, pp. 90-92.

5. Fyodor Dostoevsky, *The Brothers Karamazov*, tr. David Magarshack (Harmondsworth: Penguin, 1958), vol. 1, pp. 287-88.

6. Cf. Geach, *Logic Matters*, p. 166.

7. In using "predicable," here and in the sequel, for an expression that gives us a

proposition about something if we attach it to another expression which stands for what we are forming the proposition about, I follow Geach, *Reference and Generality*, p. 25.

8. Geach, *Logic Matters*, p. 313.
9. Cf. Davidson (1967), pp. 393–94.
10. Russell, *Mysticism and Logic*, p. 180.
11. The term is Richard Taylor's; C. D. Broad prefers "occurrent causation" and R. M. Chisholm "transeunt-causation."
12. Cf. Popper, *The Logic of Scientific Discovery*, pp. 59–62.
13. Davidson (1967), pp. 699–702.
14. Mill, *A System of Logic*, III, 5, 3.
15. For a different view, see Goldman, *A Theory of Human Action*, chaps. 1–2. However, I cannot make out what Goldman takes the ontological status of his "act-tokens" to be.
16. This idea is Goldman's: cf. ibid., chap. 2.
17. Cf. Davidson (1971), pp. 21–23.
18. This idea is from Hart and Honoré, *Causation in the Law*, 67–69, a book to which in the remainder of this section I owe much.
19. Ibid., p. 67.
20. Ibid., p. 69.
21. Ibid., p. 153 n; cf. pp. 31–34, 68–69, 151–57.
22. Ibid., p. 129; cf. also pp. 127, 292–96, 348, 357–61.
23. The term is Richard Taylor's; C. D. Broad prefers "non-occurrent causation," and R. M. Chisholm "immanent causation."
24. Aristotle, *Physics*, VIII, 256a6–8, tr. Hardie and Gaye, but substituting "mover" for their neologism "movent."
25. Cf. Chisholm (1966), pp. 20–22; Taylor, *Action and Purpose*, pp. 9–56.
26. Hart and Honoré, *Causation in the Law*, p. 123.
27. I do not know whether my conception of unwitting agency has legal support; it is advanced as philosophically sound.
28. Feinberg, *Doing and Deserving*, pp. 169–73.
29. Ibid., p. 155.
30. Ibid., p. 169.
31. Ibid., p. 166.
32. Bennett (1966), p. 87.
33. Cf. Donnellan (1964), esp. pp. 49–50.
34. Cf. Anscombe (1958), pp. 11–12; Foot (1967), pp. 10–14.
35. The analysis of "consequence," in the wider sense discussed in the last four paragraphs of this section, is an attempt to adapt to a conception of consequences as events an analysis of them as states of affairs offered by Sobel (1970) and adopted by Gibbard (1973). Most technical discussions of the concepts of consequence and of alternative are now extraordinarily complex: cf. Brock (1973), pp. 249–53, where much use is made of Lars Bergstrom, *The Alternatives and Consequences of Action* (Stockholm, 1966). The most persuasive rejection of the distinction between consequentialist and nonconsequentialist moral theories on the ground of what I take to be the mistaken premise that sequences of events initiated by agents are only conventionally separated into "actions" and "consequences," is in Oldenquist (1966), esp. pp. 180–86. Brock's defence of the distinction, based on Bergstrom's analyses (Brock [1973], pp. 252–53) sufficiently coincides with mine in its results to encourage the

hope that my simpler treatment may not be vitiated by incorrigible technical defects.
36. Lottin, *Morale Fondamentale*, pp. 63–64, 231–32. "L'acte humain en effet se compose de deux éléments essentiels, la matière et la forme. La matière, ou objet matériel, est ce sur quoi se porte l'acte externe: dans un acte d'aumône, par exemple, l'objet matériel est la prestation d'une chose, considérée non dans son être physique, mais dans son être moral, en tant que de sa nature elle soulage la misère d'autrui. La forme, ou l'objet formel, est l'intention de la volonté. Cette intention peut s'identifier avec la finalité interne de l'acte; on peut vouloir l'aumône dans la seule intention de soulager son prochain, et dans ce cas le *finis operantis* est le *finis operis* lui-même; mais l'intention peut être différente, soit qu'on exclue la finalité interne d'aumône, soit qu'on la subordonne à une autre fin, la volonté de convertir le pauvre, par exemple" (p. 232).
37. Chisholm (1963), esp. pp. 1–3, 9–14.
38. Kant, *Grundlegung*, p. 79 (p. 436).
39. *Babylonian Talmud*, Shabbat, p. 31a.
40. Matt. 7:12.
41. Cf. Kant, *Grundlegung*, p. 68 n. (p. 430).
42. Sidgwick, *Methods of Ethics*, pp. 379–80.
43. Singer (1967), p. 365b.
44. Sidgwick, *Methods of Ethics*, p. 380.
45. Kant, *Grundlegung*, p. 52 (p. 421), tr. Beck.
46. Hare, *Freedom and Reason*, pp. 86–111, 157–85; cf. Hare (1975).
47. Maimonides, *Mishneh Torah*, List of Precepts, 206, 207 (Hyamson, p. 55a). But cf. Nelson, *Idea of Usury*, pp. xix–xxiii, esp. xix n. 1; pp. 135–38. Unfortunately, Nelson does not discuss Deut. 10:19.
48. Aquinas, *Summa Theologiae*, I–II, 100, 3 *ad* 1; and 11 *ad* 1.
49. Ibid., I–II, 100, 3.
50. Ibid., I–II, 94, 6.
51. Ibid., I–II, 94, 2.
52. Grisez (1965), pp. 184–90. Cf. Grisez (1970), pp. 65–66, and *Abortion: the Myths, the Realities, and the Arguments*, pp. 315–21; and Finnis (1973), pp. 125–29.
53. Aquinas, *Summa Theologiae*, I–II, 63, 1.
54. Ibid., I–II, 100, 10 *ad* 3.
55. Frankena, *Ethics*, p. 44; cf. Frankena (1964), esp. pp. 221–25. St. Augustine's enunciation, *Dilige, et quod vis fac*, is cited by Gilson from *In Epistolam Joannis ad Parthos*, 7, 4, 8; in Migne, *Patrologia Latina*, vol. 35, p. 2033.
56. Ramsey, *Deeds and Rules in Christian Ethics*, pp. 7–8, 111–13, 224–25. Cf. Gilson, *Christian Philosophy of St. Augustine*, pp. 140–41.
57. Frankena, *Ethics*, pp. 44–45; cf. p. 37.
58. For a dissection of some representative horrors, see Ramsey, *Deeds and Rules in Christian Ethics*, chap. 7.
59. Kant, *Grundlegung*, pp. 66–67 (p. 429), tr. Beck.
60. Sidgwick, *Methods of Ethics*, p. 390.
61. Ross, *Kant's Ethical Theory*, p. 51.
62. "Finis ultimus cuiuslibet facientis, inquantum est faciens, est ipsemet: utimur enim factis a nobis propter nos; et si aliquid aliquando propter aliud homo faciat, hoc refertur in bonum suum vel utile vel delectabile vel honestum" (Aquinas, *Summa contra Gentiles*, III, 17, [8]).
63. Aquinas, *Summa contra Gentiles*, III, 18, [4], tr. Bourke.

64. Levi, *Introduction to Legal Reasoning*, pp. 8–9.
65. (1932), *Appeal Cases*, p. 580.
66. Hare (1975), pp. 204–5. Hare's note here is: "Cf. Aristotle, *Nicomachean Ethics*, 5, 1137b20. I owe the roller-skate example to H. L. A. Hart."
67. Cf. Nozick (1968), pp. 4–7.
68. Ibid., p. 5.
69. Ibid., p. 5.

Chapter 3

1. Daube (1972), pp. 398, 414–15 (esp. n. 166).
2. Genesis, 9:5.
3. *Babylonian Talmud*, Avodah Zarah, p. 18a. Cf. Rosner (1970), p. 30.
4. St. Augustine, *De Civitate Dei*, I, 20; cf. Aquinas, *Summa Theologiae*, II–II, 64, 5.
5. Kant, *Met. der Sitten*, pt. 2, 73 (p. 423).
6. 2 Maccabees, 14:41–42. For the commandment forbidding compliance, see Maimonides, *Mishneh Torah*, I, 1, 5, 2 (Hyamson, p. 40a) and I, 1, 5, 7 (Hyamson, p. 40b).
7. *Babylonian Talmud*, Gittim, p. 57b.
8. Cicero, *De Officiis*, III, 23.
9. It can be held not to be so by appealing to the theory of the double effect, for which see 5.3.
10. Kant, *Met. der Sitten*, pt. 2, 74 (pp. 423–24).
11. I heard R. M. Hare discuss cases of this kind in a lecture at the University of Notre Dame in summer 1973.
12. Kant, *Met. der Sitten*, pt. 2, 73 (p. 423).
13. Aquinas, *Summa Theologiae*, II–II, 150, 1.
14. Paton, *Categorical Imperative*, pp. 155, 173.
15. Searle, *Speech Acts*, pp. 51–52.
16. Rawls, *Theory of Justice*, p. 55.
17. Cf. Noonan, *Morality of Abortion*, pp. 51–59.
18. Whewell, *Elements of Morality*, §§ 426–27 (pp. 231–32).
19. Boswell, *Life of Johnson*, vol. 3, pp. 202–4.
20. *Shorter Oxford English Dictionary*, "Violence" sb. (1). For a more comprehensive usage, in which "violence" is equivalent to "force," see Fraser, *Violence in the Arts*, pp. 140–43.
21. Maimonides, *Mishneh Torah* XI, 5, 1, 14 (Y.J.S., IX, p. 198).
22. Maimonides, *Mishneh Torah* XI, 5, 1, 13 (Y.J.S., IX, pp. 197–98).
23. Maimonides, *Mishneh Torah* XI, 5, 1, 9 (Y.J.S., IX, pp. 196–97). For a recent Roman Catholic view on similar lines, see Grisez (1970), p. 94.
24. "The Hebrew word in the Decalogue, *raṣaḥ*, is stronger than *occidere* [in the Vulgate]: it signifies "to murder" . . . and it is never used of a person dying by his own hand" (Daube [1972], p. 414 n. 166). The translation of the commandment given in the *Book of Common Prayer*, namely, "Thou shalt do no murder," is therefore preferable to that given in the King James Version, namely, "Thou shalt not kill."
25. This definition of a lie (*mendacium*) as a free utterance, which distinguishes lying from falsehood (*falsiloquium*) in general, is one of several traditional definitions. My immediate source is Kant, *Lectures on Ethics*, pp. 226–27. In his *Metaphy-*

sik der Sitten, pt. 2, 83–88 (pp. 429–31), Kant abandoned the distinction, in my opinion wrongly.
26. Kant, *Lectures on Ethics*, p. 228.
27. Whewell, *Elements of Morality*, §162 (p. 95).
28. Boswell, *Life of Johnson*, vol. 4, p. 306.
29. Kant, *Lectures on Ethics*, p. 227.
30. Boswell, *Life of Johnson*, vol. 3, pp. 376–77.
31. Ibid., vol. 4, 305–6.
32. Cf. Prichard, *Moral Obligation*, pp. 168–69; and Prior, *Logic and the Basis of Ethics*, chap. 5.
33. McNeilly (1972); and cf. Richards, *Theory of Reasons for Action*, pp. 164–69.
34. Ross, *The Right and the Good*, p. 18.
35. Ross, *The Foundations of Ethics*, pp. 94–99.
36. Cicero, *De Officiis*, III, 29.
37. Thomas Hobbes, *Leviathan*, ed. Michael Oakeshott (Oxford: Blackwell, n.d.) I, 14 (pp. 90–91).
38. Whewell, *Elements of Morality*, §293 (p. 169).
39. The most valuable study of the duty of preservation known to me is Passmore, *Man's Responsibility for Nature*. Passmore, however, blames man's past ecological arrogance on false theological doctrines of man's "tenure in the biosphere," which he connects with the metaphysical doctrine of the uniqueness of man, that is, of rational creatures, in nature (cf. pp. 183–84). In my view, Passmore's denial of man's uniqueness jeopardizes his doctrine of man's ecological responsibility.
40. Pope Leo XIII, *Rerum Novarum*, in M. Oakeshott, ed. *Social and Political Doctrines of Contemporary Europe* (Cambridge 1939), p. 67. Cf. John Locke, *Second Treatise of Civil Government*, secs. 25–51, esp, 27, "[W]hatsoever, then he removes out of the state that nature had provided and left it in, he hath mixed his labour with it, and joined to it something that is his own, and thereby makes it his property." On the view as a whole, see Cronin, *Science of Ethics*, vol. 2, pp. 115–47; and cf. Nozick, *Anarchy, State, and Utopia*, pp. 174–82.
41. Aquinas, *Summa Theologiae*, II-II, 66, 2 ad 1.
42. Nozick attributes such an argument to Fourier (in *Anarchy, State and Utopia*, pp. 178–79 n.). The following, by Pope Leo XIII, is on the same lines, and denounces forced labor: "It is a dictate of natural justice more imperious and ancient than any bargain between man and man . . . that wages ought not to be insufficient to support a frugal and well-behaved wage-earner. If through necessity or fear of a worse evil the workman will accept harder conditions because an employer or contractor will afford him no better, he is made the victim of force and injustice" (from *Rerum Novarum*, in Oakeshott, *Social and Political Doctrines of Contemporary Europe* [Cambridge, 1939], p. 67).
43. Nozick argues that "This compensation would be due those persons, if any, for whom the process of civilization was a *net loss*, for whom the benefits of civilization did not counterbalance being deprived of these particular liberties"—i.e. "liberties to gather, pasture, engage in the chase" (*Anarchy, State, and Utopia*, pp. 178–79 n.).
44. Collingwood, *New Leviathan*, 19.5–19.58, 19.8–19.94.
45. For the traditional Christian doctrine of the family, Catholic sources are the best. Aquinas's treatments of it are authoritative: see *Summa contra Gentiles*, III, 122–26, and *Summa Theologiae*, III, Supp. 41–68, esp. 41, 44–48, 51, 54, 65, 67. For a good summary account, see Vernon J. Bourke, *Ethics* (New York: Macmillan,

1951), pp. 419-23; and for a fuller account, Cronin, *Science of Ethics*, vol. 2, pp. 415-42. For the traditional Protestant view, Kant, *Metaphysik der Sitten*, pt. 2, 75-79 (pp. 424-26), is enlightening, although too ascetic to be representative; for a corrective, cf. Whewell, *Elements of Morality*, §§524-29, 720-49 (pp. 279-82, 373-86). For the Jewish view, besides the standard encyclopaedias, I have found Feldman, *Birth Control in Jewish Law* (which, despite its title, is comprehensive) very useful. For the relations of the Christian view to the Jewish, see Daube, *The New Testament and Rabbinic Judaism*, pp. 71-86; for later Christian influence on Judaism, see Falk, *Jewish Matrimonial Law in the Middle Ages*.

46. Aquinas, *Summa contra Gentiles*, III, 124 (1-3).

47. Ibid., III, 124 (4).

48. Cf. Aquinas, *Summa contra Gentiles*, III, 124 (8).

49. Kant, *Metaphysik der Sitten*, pt. 2, 77 (p. 425).

50. Ibid., 78 (p. 425).

51. Aquinas, *Summa Theologiae*, II-II, 154—*de luxuriae partibus*. Cf. esp. art. 11 *ad* 3: "luxuriosus non intendit generationem humanam, sed delectationem veneream, quam potest aliquis experiri sine actibus ex quibus sequitur humana generatio. Et hoc est quod quaeritur in vitio contra naturam."

52. Atkinson, *Sexual Morality*, p. 103.

53. Ibid., pp. 145-51, esp. 146-47.

54. "...me non libebat id quod furabar, sed quia furabar; quod me solum facere prorsus non liberet, nec facerem" (Augustine, *Confessiones*, II, 9).

55. Hegel, *Phil. des Rechts*, §§183, 260 (pp. 123, 160-61).

56. For the Christian view of Hegel's theory of *der Staat* see Foster, *Political Philosophies of Plato and Hegel*, chap. 5. Foster used the word "State" for those forms of civil society in which the citizens participate in legislation, and reserved "civil society" for systems of free nonpolitical social relations out of which the idea of legislative participation arises.

57. Hörmann, *Introduction to Moral Theology*, pp. 255-56.

58. Baxter, *Christian Directory*, IV, 7, dir. 2 (*P.W.* VI, p. 120).

Chapter 4

1. D'Arcy, *Human Acts*, pp. 6-8.

2. Cf. Sellars, *Science, Perception and Reality*, 11-12.

3. Aquinas, *Summa Theologiae*, I-II, 6-17.

4. "[V]oluntarium dicitur esse, secundum definitionem Aristotelis, et Gregorii Nysseni et Damasceni, non solum *cuius principium est intra*, sed cum additione *scientiae*" (Aquinas, *Summa Theologiae*, I-II, 6, 1). Cf. Aristotle, *Nicomachean Ethics*, 1111a 22-25.

5. Aquinas, *Summa Theologiae*, I-II, 6, 3 *ad* 1.

6. See Ryle, *Concept of Mind*, pp. 69-72; Austin, *Philosophical Papers*, pp. 139-40; and Searle, *Speech Acts*, pp. 142-43, 150. For contemporary restatements of the traditional position, see Anscombe, *Intention*, pp. 89-90, and D'Arcy, *Human Acts*, pp. 100-101.

7. Aquinas, *Summa Theologiae*, I-II, 6, 6; cf. Aristotle, *Nicomachean Ethics*, 1110a 4-19.

8. Goldman, *Theory of Human Action*, pp. 72-76, 130-37.

9. Cf. Anscombe, *Intention*, pp. 19–20, and Lawrence, *Motive and Intention*, pp. 83–88.

10. Nagel, *The Possibility of Altruism*, pp. 29–32.

11. Lawrence, *Motive and Intention*, p. 4.

12. Anscombe, *Intention*, pp. 20–23; D'Arcy, *Human Acts*, pp. 143–46.

13. Kneale and Kneale, *Development of Logic*, p. 609 (for the application of the word "function" to predicables, see pp. 499–502). For my use of "predicable," see ch. 2 n. 7.

14. Kneale and Kneale, *Development of Logic*, p. 609.

15. Anscombe, *Intention*, pp. 41–43. Cf. also Davidson (in Rescher), pp. 94–95 and Davidson (1971), pp. 6–8.

16. Aristotle, *Nicomachean Ethics*, 1110b 25; Aquinas, *Summa Theologiae*, I–II, 6, 8.

17. Davidson (1971), p. 8: Davidson, however, makes the point in connection with "is intentional" rather than with "is voluntary."

18. Austin (1966), pp. 439–40.

19. Sidgwick, *Methods of Ethics*, p. 202; for a justly severe criticism, see Anscombe (1958), pp. 11–12.

20. Austin (1966), p. 437.

21. Aquinas, *Summa Theologiae*, I–II, 12, 4.

22. Austin (1966), p. 432.

23. Ibid., p. 439. Cf. Lawrence, "We can start with these approximations: . . . an intention (for the future) is an action in prospect; . . . a purpose is a desired condition seen as achievable" (*Motive and Intention*, p. 4).

24. Anscombe, *Intention*, p. 46.

25. Cf. Thomas Gilby's note in the Blackfriars edition of *Summa Theologiae*, vol. 17, p. 15.

26. Abelard, *Ethics*, pp. 28–29 (Luscombe's translation slightly modified).

27. Aquinas, *Summa Theologiae*, I–II, 76, 3.

28. Ibid., I–II, 76, 1; Hall, *General Principles of Criminal Law*, pp. 375–94.

29. D'Arcy, *Human Acts*, p. 107.

30. Aquinas, *Summa Theologiae*, I–II, 6, 8.

31. Aristotle, *Nicomachean Ethics*, 1110b 20–27.

32. Aquinas, *Summa Theologiae*, I–II, 76, 1.

33. Cf. D'Arcy, *Human Acts*, p. 119.

34. Whewell, *Elements of Morality*, §§239, 343–46 (pp. 136, 180–91).

35. Hart, *Punishment and Responsibility*, pp. 152–56.

36. Mark Twain, *The Adventures of Tom Sawyer* and *The Adventures of Huckleberry Finn* (New York: The Modern Library, n.d.), p. 356.

37. Virtually everything that follows about the history of the concept of conscience is owed to D'Arcy, *Conscience and Its Right to Freedom*, parts I–II, of which the portion having to do with the medieval scholastics is in turn indebted to O. Lottin, *Psychologie et morale aux 12e et 13e siècles* (Gembloux: Duculot, 1948), vol. 2, pp. 103–50.

38. Aquinas, *Summa Theologiae*, I, 79, 13.

39. Ryle, *Collected Papers*, vol. 2, p. 185.

40. Butler, *Fifteen Sermons*, p. 54.

41. Newman, *Difficulties Felt by Anglicans*, vol. 2, p. 248.

42. For the use of the familiar contemporary term "disposition" in rendering *habitus* and *hexis*, see Anthony Kenny's editorial remarks in the Blackfriars edition of Aquinas's *Summa Theologiae*, vol. 22 (I–II, 49–54), esp. pp. xix–xxxiv and 113–16.
43. Aquinas, *Summa Theologiae*, I, 79, 12.
44. Ibid., I–II, 50, 4.
45. Ibid., I–II, 52, 1; cf. Kenny, in the Blackfriars edn., vol. 22, pp. xxvi–xxviii.
46. Whewell, *Elements of Morality*, Preface to 2d ed. (p. 3).
47. Ibid., (p. 2).
48. Taylor, *Ductor Dubitantium*, I, 3, Rule 3 (*W. W.*, vol. 9, p. 138).
49. Baxter, *Christian Directory*, I, 3, Direct. 17, Q. 5 (*P. W.*, vol. 2, p. 339).
50. Prichard, *Moral Obligation*, pp. 18–39, esp. p. 25; Ross, *Foundations of Ethics*, pp. 148–56.
51. Baier, *Moral Point of View*, pp. 146–47.
52. T. S. Eliot, *Murder in the Cathedral*, Part I (*Complete Poems and Plays* [New York: Harcourt Brace, 1952], p. 196).
53. Cf. D'Arcy, *Conscience and Its Right to Freedom*, pp. 258–72.
54. Mark Twain, *The Adventures of Tom Sawyer* and *The Adventures of Huckleberry Finn* (New York: Modern Library, n.d.), p. 360.
55. Collingwood, *Principles of Art*, p. 219; pp. 282–84.
56. Mark Twain, *The Adventures of Tom Sawyer* and *The Adventures of Huckleberry Finn* (New York: Modern Library, n.d.), pp. 509, 354. These passages are discussed by Lionel Trilling, *The Liberal Imagination* (London: Secker and Warburg, 1951), pp. 111–12.
57. Collingwood, *Principles of Art*, pp. 284–85.
58. Ibid.
59. Newman, *Difficulties Felt by Anglicans*, vol. 2, p. 261.

Chapter 5

1. "Sed horum testiculorum nervi perplexi sunt, quia suggestionum illius argumenta implicatis inventionibus illigantur, ut plerosque ita peccare faciant, quatenus si fortasse peccatum fugere appetant, hoc sine alio peccati laqueo non evadant; et culpam faciant dum vitant, ac nequaquam se ab una valeant solvere nisi in alia consentiant ligari" (St. Gregory the Great, *Moralium Libri sive Expositio in Librum B. Job* xxxii, 20, in J.-P. Migne, *Patrologia Latina*, vol. 76 [Paris: Garnier, 1878], p. 657). I owe the reference to Kirk, *Conscience and Its Problems*, p. 322.
2. St. Gregory the Great, *Moralium Libri*, xxxii, 20, 36–38 (Migne, *Patrologia Latina*, vol. 76, p. 658).
3. I owe this point to Geach, as reported by von Wright, *Essay in Deontic Logic*, p. 81 n. 1. Cf. Kirk, *Conscience and Its Problems*, p. 322 n. 1. The pertinent passages in Aquinas are *Summa Theologiae*, I–II, 19, 6 *ad* 3; II–II, 62, 2 *obj.* 2; III, 64, 6 *ad* 3; and *de Veritate*, 17, 4 *ad* 8.
4. Aquinas, *De Veritate*, 17, 4 *ad* 8. Cf. *Summa Theologiae*, I–II, 19, 6 *ad* 3: "Sicut in syllogisticis, uno inconvenienti dato, necesse est alia sequi, ita in moralibus, uno inconvenienti posito, ex necessitate alia sequuntur..."
5. Kant, *Met. der Sitten*, pt. 1, 24 (p. 224).
6. Chisholm (1963b), p. 33.
7. Ibid., p. 36.

8. Ibid., p. 35. Systematic investigations of the whole field have shown that there are sources of logical difficulty other than that noticed by Chisholm. For such investigations, see von Wright, *Essay on Deontic Logic*, and *Norm and Action*; and Castañeda (1973) and Castañeda, *The Structure of Morality*.

9. Kirk, *Conscience and Its Problems*, p. 331.

10. As Fletcher has noted with satisfaction: see Fletcher, *Situation Ethics*, pp. 36–37; but cf. Ramsey, *Deeds and Rules in Christian Ethics*, pp. 221–25.

11. Geach, *God and the Soul*, p. 124; cf. pp. 123–26.

12. Ibid., p. 128.

13. Rawls, *Theory of Justice*, p. 43; cf. Richards, *Theory of Reasons for Action*, pp. 30–31, 47–48.

14. Cicero, *De Officiis*, iii, 28 (102).

15. Blaise Pascal, *Pensées* and *The Provincial Letters* (New York: Modern Library, 1941), p. 390.

16. Kant, *Grundlegung*, p. 53 n. (p. 421 n.).

17. Paton, *The Moral Law*, p. 31.

18. Chisholm, (1963a), p. 4.

19. Bennett (1966), p. 102; cf. pp. 84–86.

20. Ibid., p. 102.

21. Concerning the nature and history of the theory of the double effect, I have relied chiefly on Mangan (1949).

22. J.-P. Gury, S.J., *Compendium Theologiae Moralis*, 5th ed. (Ratisbon, 1874), vol. 1, tr. *de actibus humanis*, c. 2, n. 9: quoted and tr. Mangan (1949), p. 60. Cf. Grisez (1970), p. 78.

23. For those who have held this interpretation, see Mangan (1949), pp. 43–50. See also Grisez (1970), pp. 66–73.

24. Grisez (1970), p. 88. For essentially the same point, differently formulated, see Foot (1967), pp. 6–7.

25. Grisez (1970), p. 90. Grisez conceives the unity of an action as that of an indivisible whole containing its effects; in 2.2 I have analysed it as that of a single event, the bringing about of something (a bodily movement, a mental event) by an agent, which is also the causing of those effects. This difference in analysis, however, seems not to affect what either of us has to say on the present topic.

26. Ibid., p. 88.

27. Ibid., p. 89.

28. The formulation is mine, but it is based on Grisez (1970), pp. 89–90, taking into account what he says about proportionately grave reasons on pp. 78–79.

29. Ibid., p. 94.

30. Maimonides, *Mishneh Torah*, XI, 5, 1, 9 (Y.J.S., IX, pp. 196–97).

31. Aquinas, *Summa Theologiae*, II-II, 64, 2 *ad* 3.

32. Grisez (1970), p. 69.

33. For a parallel conclusion, see Foot (1967), esp. pp. 13–14.

34. Aquinas, *Summa Theologiae*, II-II, 64, 7.

35. Quoted by Q. D. Leavis, "Lives and Works of Richard Jefferies," in F. R. Leavis, ed., *A Selection from Scrutiny* (Cambridge: University Press, 1968), vol. 2, p. 204.

36. A. J. P. Taylor, *English History: 1914-1945* (Oxford: Clarendon, 1965), p. 165.

37. Ibid.

38. Anscombe (1972b), 49; cf. Anscombe (1972a), p. 23.
39. Anscombe (1972a), pp. 21–22.
40. Wertheimer (1971), p. 81. Cf. Paul Ramsey, in Noonan, *The Morality of Abortion*, pp. 64–79. For a serious argument for a later (but still prenatal) beginning, see Becker (1975).
41. Thomson (1971), p. 65.
42. Warren (1973), p. 50.
43. Ibid., p. 56. Cf. Wertheimer (1970), pp. 87–89; and Tooley (1972), pp. 43–50.
44. Warren (1973), p. 56.
45. Tooley (1972), p. 40.
46. Ibid., p. 44.
47. Warren (1973), p. 56.
48. Contrary to Tooley's repeated assertion (Tooley [1972], pp. 51, 55). With regret, I have forborne examining Tooley's celebrated argument for it, which I think mistaken.
49. I have expressed no opinion upon whether abortion, when morally impermissible, should be a criminal offence. However, I incline to think that there may be circumstances in which the wrongful taking of life ought not to be prohibited by criminal law. The institution of duelling is evil, and leads to the wrongful taking of life; but there have been states of popular mores in which it would have done more harm than good legally to prohibit duelling. The present state of our mores with respect to abortion may be of such a kind.

Chapter 6

1. Maimonides, *Mishneh Torah*, I, 1, 5, 1 (Hyamson, p. 40a).
2. Ibid., I, 1, 5, 2–3 (Hyamson, p. 40a).
3. Anscombe (1958), p. 12; cf. pp. 9–13.
4. Cicero, *De Officiis*, III, 23 (84–90). There is a valuable historical discussion in Kirk, *Conscience and Its Problems*, pp. 138–49, esp. pp. 146–47.
5. Whewell, *Elements of Morality*, §314 (p. 173).
6. *Reports of Cases in Criminal Law*, vol. 15, 1882–84 (London: Horace Cox, 1886), pp. 624–38.
7. Ibid., p. 624.
8. Ibid., p. 632.
9. Ibid., p. 636.
10. Ibid., p. 636.
11. Ibid., p. 637.
12. Ibid., p. 638, n. (*b*).
13. Two versions of it are given in Foot (1967), p. 7, as "well-known to philosophers," although my own acquaintance with it began with this paper. Nielsen gives another version in Nielsen (1972), p. 228. Both Foot's and Nielsen's versions contain the comic irrelevancy of making the man fat, and the sole obstruction his body.
14. Nielsen (1972), pp. 228–29.
15. Ibid., p. 229.
16. Brock (1973), p. 251 n. 13. By chance Brock's paper was to hand when I sought an example of the position criticized. Other examples of it are too many to

count. Brock's proposed escape clause is further examined in 6.5.

17. John, 18:4.

18. Foot (1967), p. 10.

19. Daube, *Collaboration with Tyranny in Rabbinic Law*, p. 19. My account of rabbinic teaching is derived from this work.

20. Cf. ibid., pp. 7, 25–26.

21. Ibid., pp. 18–19.

22. Ibid., pp. 40–43.

23. Ibid., p. 83.

24. Ibid., pp. 76–79.

25. Ibid., p. 39.

26. John Plamenatz, *Man and Society*, vol. 1, p. 29.

27. Quoted in Walzer (1973), p. 161, from J.-P. Sartre, *Dirty Hands*, in *"No Exit" and Three Other Plays*, tr. Lionel Abel (New York, n.d.), p. 224.

28. Walzer cites Max Weber, "Politics as a Vocation," in Hans Gerth and C. Wright Mills, eds., *From Max Weber: Essays in Sociology* (New York, 1946), pp. 77–128, esp. 125–26. (See Walzer [1973], pp. 163–64, 176–78.)

29. Cf. Brandt (1972), and Hare (1972b).

30. Hegel, *The Philosophy of History*, tr. Sibree, pp. 22, 25.

31. Walzer (1973), p. 165.

32. Baxter, *Christian Directory*, IV, 19, dir. 9 (*P.W.*, pp. vi, 295).

33. Carl Sandburg, *Abraham Lincoln* (abridged ed., New York: Dell, 1959), vol. 3, p. 739.

34. Walzer (1973), pp. 167–68; cf. p. 174.

35. Anscombe (1958).

36. Ibid., p. 12; cf. pp. 10–13. Cf. Foot (1967), p. 10.

37. Sidgwick, *Methods of Ethics*, p. x.

38. Both historical information and terminology are owed to Rawls, *Theory of Justice*, pp. 22–27, 161–66, esp. p. 162 n. 1.

39. The formulations of both (1) and (2) owe much to Urmson (1953), p. 35, but depart from his in ways he may disapprove. Cf. Mabbott (1956), pp. 115–16; Anscombe (1958), pp. 3, 9.

40. Mandelbaum (1968), p. 220. Cf. Smart, *Outline*, pp. 42–43.

41. Mandelbaum (1968), p. 218, esp. n. 17. For a similar point, see Mabbott (1956), p. 116.

42. Mabbott (1956), p. 114.

43. Mill, *Utilitarianism*, p. 23.

44. Mandelbaum (1968), p. 218 n. 17.

45. Smart, *Outline*, pp. 9–12, 30–42.

46. Ibid., p. 10.

47. Quoted by Mill from Adam Sedgwick, "Discourse on the Studies of the University of Cambridge," *London Review*, April 1835, p. 64, in Mill, *Dissertations and Discussions*, vol. 1, p. 142.

48. Cf. Mill, *Dissertations and Discussions*, vol. 1, pp. 142–47; Smart, *Outline*, pp. 40–42. For criticism see 6.5.

49. Lyons, *Forms and Limits of Utilitarianism*, pp. 128–32.

50. The distinction was obscurely grasped by Mill in his attack upon Whewell, but he did not understand its implications; see Mill, *Dissertations and Discussions*, vol.

2, pp. 475–78. In recent philosophy, the fundamental paper is probably Brandt (1963), on which Lyons draws heavily in *Forms and Limits of Utilitarianism*, pp. 140–42, to which are owed the terms "conformance utility" and "acceptance utility." On Lyons's criticism of rule utilitarianism, see Ezorsky (1968). Hare has made use of the distinction in much of his work: see his *Applications of Moral Philosophy*, pp. 16–23 (a paper read in 1957), and the definitive Hare (1972a). A survey of recent work may be found in Brock (1973), pp. 255–57.

51. This double point is well made by Williams, *Critique*, pp. 119, 121–22.

52. I have defined "maximum" acceptance utility, which can be possessed by at most one code, and not "maximal," which can be possessed by more than one, because the possibility that two nonequivalent codes should have the same acceptance utility seems remote.

53. For the line of thought that follows I owe numerous debts: above all, to Diggs (1964), esp. pp. 4, 6–7; Gibbard, *Utilitarianisms and Coordination* (especially for his discussion of reformist rule utilitarianism); and Williams, *Critique*, pp. 120–21, 130, 134–35.

54. Smart, *Outline*, pp. 50–51.

55. Sedgwick, quoted by Mill, *Dissertations and Discussions*, vol. 1, p. 142.

56. Smart, *Outline*, p. 38; cf. pp. 32–33, 37–39.

57. Ibid., p. 41.

58. Mill, *Dissertations and Discussions*, vol. 1, p. 142; cf. pp. 145–47.

59. Isaac Asimov, *The End of Eternity* (New York: Signet, 1955), p. 12.

60. Smart, *Outline*, p. 54.

61. Whewell, *Elements of Morality*, Supp., chap. 2, §2.2 (p. 582). Whewell's emphases.

62. Whewell, *Lectures on the History of Moral Philosophy* (1852), p. 211, quoted by Mill, *Dissertations and Discussions*, vol. 2, p. 475.

63. Mill, *Dissertations and Discussions*, vol. 2, p. 477.

64. Ibid., p. 478.

65. Brandt (1972), pp. 152–61.

66. Smart, *Outline*, pp. 69–71.

67. Mill, *Dissertations and Discussions*, vol. 2, p. 478. For an admirable restatement of the point, see Hare (1972a), pp. 5–7.

68. Nielsen (1972), p. 227; in criticism of Donagan (1968), pp. 193–95.

69. Sidgwick, *Methods of Ethics*, p. 355.

70. Ibid., p. 443.

71. Whewell, *Elements of Morality*, §293 (p. 161).

72. Moore, *Principia Ethica*, p. 149; cf. Urmson (1970), pp. 344, 347–49.

73. Williams, *Critique*, pp. 134–35; Hare (1972a), p. 14.

74. Cf. Hare (1972b), pp. 177–78; Brock (1973), p. 252; Williams, *Critique*, p. 90.

75. Williams, *Critique*, pp. 98–99.

76. Kirk, *Conscience and Its Problems*, p. 340. In a note, Kirk acknowledged that the officer's assertion was not a lie, but added that a lie was "virtually . . . implied" by it. In my opinion, one cannot lie by virtual implication: cf. 3.4.

77. Williams, *Critique*, p. 116.

78. The argument of the concluding paragraphs of this chapter owes much to criticism by Gertrude Ezorsky, in conversation, of an unpublished paper of mine.

Chapter 7

1. I have in mind *Ethica Nicomachea*, III, chaps. 2-5, VI (the whole); *de Anima*, III, chaps. 9-11; and *de Motu Animalium*, chaps. 6-11. All are conveniently translated in J. L. Ackrill, ed., *Aristotle's Ethics* (London: Faber, 1973).

2. Hardie, *Aristotle's Ethical Theory*, p. 232.

3. Ibid., p. 229.

4. Anscombe, *Intention*, pp. 57-67; cf. also Anscombe (1965), pp. 151-55.

5. Anscombe (1965), p. 153.

6. Kant, *Grundlegung*, p. 41 (p. 415).

7. This, while not a translation of anything Kant wrote, preserves the gist of such remarks as: "Wer den Zweck will, will (so fern die Vernunft auf seine Handlungen entscheidenden Einfluss hat) auch das dazu unentbehrlich notwendige Mittel, das in seiner Gewalt ist"; and ". . . wer den Zweck will, will auch (der Vernunft gemäss notwendig) die einzigen Mittel, die dazu in seiner Gewalt sind" (*Grundlegung*, pp. 44-45 [p. 417], p. 46 [p. 417]).

8. Ibid., pp. 40-41 (pp. 414-15). My analysis is largely derived from Diggs (1960), esp. pp. 302-8, and from Hill (1973), esp. pp. 429-32, although with too many embroideries for me to venture to claim the sanction of either.

9. Hill (1973), p. 432.

10. Anscombe, *Intention*, p. 66; cf. p. 63.

11. Foot (1972), p. 310.

12. What is disadvantageous either coincides with what frustrates one's ends or it is hard to see how it can be shown that doing what is calculated to be disadvantageous is irrational. If for some serious purpose a man does what he calculates will be disadvantageous to him in some narrow sense (e.g., risks probable death to save his child's life), he does not act irrationally. Cf. Gert, *The Moral Rules*, pp. 42-43.

13. Hare (1973), p. 87.

14. The exposition which follows is largely based on *Freedom and Reason*, but *Applications of Moral Philosophy*, pp. 71-89, and Hare (1972a) have also been drawn upon.

15. Hare, *Freedom and Reason*, p. 176.

16. Hare, *Applications of Moral Philosophy*, pp. 81-82.

17. Stevenson, *Ethics and Language*, chaps. 9-10.

18. Ibid.

19. See Firth (1952) and (1955); Brandt (1955) and *Ethical Theory*, esp. pp. 175-76.

20. Adam Smith, *Theory of the Moral Sentiments*, 1st ed. 1759, 6th ed. 1790, in Selby-Bigge, *British Moralists*, vol. 1.

21. Selby-Bigge, *British Moralists*, vol. 1, p. 279.

22. Brandt, *Ethical Theory*, p. 174.

23. Ibid., pp. 244-52, 264-65.

24. Wittgenstein (1965), p. 12.

25. Kant, *Grundlegung*, pp. iii-viii (pp. 388-90), pp. 30-34 (pp. 409-11), pp. 90-91 (pp. 442-43).

26. Rawls, *Theory of Justice*, pp. 108-17.

27. Ibid., pp. 196-201.

28. Ibid., pp. 13-14, 144-45.

29. Ibid., pp. 137–38.
30. Ibid., pp. 18–19, 136–37.
31. Ibid., p. 136.
32. Dworkin (1973), pp. 25–26; cf. Rawls, *Theory of Justice*, pp. 21, 587.
33. Rawls (1975), p. 539.
34. Dworkin (1973), p. 26.
35. Rawls, *Theory of Justice*, p. 252.
36. Despite my debt to Dworkin (1973), I dissent from his opinion that Kant's theory of morality is "duty-based" as opposed to "right-based" (p. 41). So, I think, would Rawls; cf. *Theory of Justice*, pp. 256–57. Cf. also Hill (1973), p. 449 n.
37. Rawls, *Theory of Justice*, pp. 410–11, 424–29.
38. Kant, *Grundlegung*, p. 46 (p. 418), tr. Beck.
39. J. L. Stocks, "The Limits of Purpose," in *Morality and Purpose*, pp. 15–32, esp. p. 28.
40. Ibid.
41. Kant, *Grundlegung*, pp. 66–67 (pp. 428–29).
42. Ibid., tr. Beck. The German text reads: "... So stellt sich notwendig der Mensch sein eignes Dasein vor; so fern ist es also ein *subjektives* Prinzip menschlicher Handlungen. So stellt sich aber auch jedes andere vernünftige Wesen sein Dasein, zufolge eben desselben Vernunftgrundes, der auch für mich gilt, vor; also ist es zugleich ein *objektives* Prinzip ..."
43. Hill (1973), p. 449.
44. Cf. Kant, *Grundlegung*, pp. 4–5 (pp. 394–95), pp. 82–86 (pp. 437–39).
45. St. Augustine, *De Libero Arbitrio*, II, 6, 13.
46. Kant, *Grundlegung*, p. 82 (p. 437), tr. Beck, slightly revised.
47. Ibid., p. 98 (p. 446), tr. Paton.
48. Hill (1973), p. 449.
49. Cf. Dennett (1973), pp. 159–60.
50. Cf., e.g., J. C. Eccles, *The Neurophysiological Basis of Mind* (Oxford: Clarendon, 1953), pp. 271–79.
51. Cf. Dennett (1971), pp. 90–93; (1973), pp. 180–83. I agree with Dennett that there is no incompatibility between what he calls "Intentionality" and mechanism (a computer can be understood in Intentional terms); I differ from him in holding that what is essential to being human is not that an "Intentional stance" can be profitably taken towards one, but that one can take an Intentional stance. Intentionality without Intentional agency is not enough.
52. Thought and diction here are owed to Kripke (1972), esp. pp. 254, 258–59, 269–70, 275–76.
53. Although I learned slowly, I was taught this, as a graduate student, by William Kneale (see Kneale [1962], and, with M. Kneale, *The Development of Logic*, pp. 628–51, esp. pp. 637–38). Afterwards, in private exchanges over more than fifteen years, Henry B. Veatch also did what he could to teach it to me (see Veatch, *Two Logics*, chaps. 3–4). In his *For an Ontology of Morals*, and Veatch (1975), Veatch has shown how his logical and metaphysical doctrines apply to ethics; but the moral theory he has developed is rather a cousin than a sibling of mine. A recent defense of "good, old-fashioned Aristotelian essentialism," in the logical style of today, may be found in Brody (1973). Gratitude is owed to many that now, among philosophical analysts, even formalizers are unlikely to refuse a hearing to a moral theory simply because it is essentialist; but perhaps chiefly to the late Richard Montague (see his

Formal Philosophy, papers 1, 5; and to Saul A. Kripke (see Kripke [1972], esp. pp. 260–69, 327–34).

54. Kripke [1972], 330. Cf. Kneale and Kneale, *The Development of Logic*, 650–51.

55. Kripke (1972), p. 340.

56. Both the example, and my use of it, are owed to Kneale and Kneale, *The Development of Logic*, pp. 637 ff.

57. Gewirth (1974), p. 52; cf. Gewirth (1967).

58. Gewirth (1974), pp. 53–57.

59. Nagel, *The Possibility of Altruism*.

60. Gert, *The Moral Rules*, p. ix.

61. Rawls, *Theory of Justice*, p. 440.

62. Shakespeare, *Henry the Fourth, Part I*, act IV, scene 2.

63. D. A. Traversi, "Henry the Fourth, Part I," *Scrutiny* 15 (1947–48), p. 29.

64. Nietzsche, *Jenseits von Gut und Böse*, §265. Friedrich Nietzsche, *Beyond Good and Evil*, tr. Kaufmann (New York: Random House, 1966), p. 215.

65. Nietzsche, *Jenseits von Gut und Böse*, §260. *Beyond Good and Evil*, p. 205.

66. Kafka, "Reflections on Sin, Pain, Hope, and the True Way," no. 51. In Franz Kafka, *The Great Wall of China and Other Pieces*, 2d ed. rev., tr. Willa and Edwin Muir (London: Secker and Warburg, 1946), p. 149.

Select Bibliography

Books

Abelard, Peter. *Peter Abelard's Ethics*. Edited and translated by D. E. Luscombe. Oxford: Clarendon Press, 1971.

Adkins, Arthur W. H. *Merit and Responsibility: A Study in Greek Values*. Oxford: Clarendon Press, 1960.

Anscombe, G. E. M. *Intention*. 2d ed. Oxford: Blackwell, 1963.

Atkinson, Ronald. *Sexual Morality*. London: Hutchinson, 1965.

Austin, J.L. *Philosophical Papers*. Oxford: Clarendon Press, 1961.

Babylonian Talmud, The. Translated into English . . . under the editorship of Rabbi Dr. I. Epstein. London: The Soncino Press, 1948-52.

Baier, Kurt. *The Moral Point of View: A Rational Basis of Ethics*. Ithaca: Cornell University Press, 1958.

Baxter, Richard. *A Christian Directory, or a Sum of Practical Theology and Cases of Conscience. The Practical Works of Richard Baxter*. Edited by W. Orme. 23 vols. London: Duncan, 1830. References are to part, chapter, and (where appropriate) direction and question, to which a reference to the volume and page of the *Practical Works (P.W.)* is added.

Beck, Lewis White. *A Commentary on Kant's Critique of Practical Reason*. Chicago: University of Chicago Press, 1960.

———. *Early German Philosophy*. Cambridge, Mass.: Belknap Press-Harvard University Press, 1969.

———. *Studies in the Philosophy of Kant*. Indianapolis: Bobbs Merrill, 1965.

Binkley, Robert; Bronaugh, Richard; and Marras, Ausonio, eds. *Agent, Action, and Reason*. Oxford: Blackwell, 1971.

Boswell, James. *Life of Johnson. Boswell's Life of Johnson*. Edited by G. Birkbeck Hill and revised by L. F. Powell. Vols. 1–4, 1934, vols. 5–6, 2d. ed., 1964. Oxford: Clarendon Press.

Brandt, Richard B. *Ethical Theory: The Problems of Normative and Critical Ethics*. Englewood Cliffs, N.J.: Prentice-Hall, 1959.

Broad, C. D. *Five Types of Ethical Theory*. London: Kegan Paul, 1930.

Butler, Joseph. *Fifteen Sermons . . . and a Dissertation upon the Nature of Virtue*. Edited by W. R. Matthews. London: Bell, 1949.

Castañeda, Hector-Neri. *The Structure of Morality*. Springfield, Ill.: Charles C. Thomas, 1974.

Collingwood, R. G. *The New Leviathan*. Oxford: Clarendon Press, 1942.

———. *The Principles of Art*. Oxford: Clarendon Press, 1938.

Cronin, Michael. *The Science of Ethics*. 2d ed. 2 vols. Dublin: Gill, 1920.

Daniels, Norman, ed. *Reading Rawls*. New York: Basic Books, 1975.

Danto, Arthur C. *Mysticism and Morality: Oriental Thought and Moral Philosophy*. New York: Basic Books, 1972.

D'Arcy, Eric. *Conscience and Its Right to Freedom*. New York: Sheed and Ward, 1961.

———. *Human Acts: An Essay in Their Moral Evaluation*. Oxford: Clarendon Press, 1963.

Daube, David. *Collaboration with Tyranny in Rabbinic Law*. London: Oxford University Press, 1965.

———. *The New Testament and Rabbinic Judaism*. London: Athlone Press, 1956.

Falk, Ze'ev W. *Jewish Matrimonial Law in the Middle Ages*. London: Oxford University Press, 1966.

Feinberg, Joel. *Doing and Deserving: Essays in the Theory of Responsibility*. Princeton, N.J.: Princeton University Press, 1970.

Feldman, David M. *Birth Control in Jewish Law: Marital Relations, Contraception, and Abortion as Set Forth in the Classic Texts of Jewish Law*. New York: New York University Press, 1968.

Fletcher, Joseph. *Situation Ethics*. Philadelphia: The Westminster Press, 1966.

Foster, Michael B. *The Political Philosophies of Plato and Hegel*. Oxford: Clarendon Press, 1935.

Frankena, W. K. *Ethics.* Englewood Cliffs, N.J.: Prentice-Hall, 1963.

Fraser, John. *Violence in the Arts.* Cambridge: Cambridge University Press, 1974.

Geach, Peter. *God and the Soul.* London: Routledge and Kegan Paul, 1969.

———. *Logic Matters.* Oxford: Blackwell, 1972.

———. *Reference and Generality.* Ithaca, N.Y.: Cornell University Press, 1962.

Gert, Bernard. *The Moral Rules: A New Rational Foundation for Morality.* New York: Harper and Row, 1970.

Gibbard, Allan F. "Utilitarianisms and Coordination." Ph.D. dissertation, Harvard University, 1971.

Gilson, Etienne. *The Christian Philosophy of Saint Augustine.* Translated by L. E. M. Lynch. New York: Random House, 1960.

Goldman, Alvin I. *A Theory of Human Action.* Englewood Cliffs, N.J.: Prentice-Hall, 1970.

St. Gregory the Great. *Moralium Libri, Sive Expositio in Librum B. Job.* In *Patrologia Latina,* vol. 76. Edited by J.-P. Migne. Paris: Garnier, 1878.

Grisez, Germain. *Abortion: the Myths, the Realities, and the Arguments.* New York: Corpus Books, 1970.

Hall, Jerome. *General Principles of Criminal Law.* 2d ed. Indianapolis: Bobbs-Merrill, 1960.

Hardie, W. F. R. *Aristotle's Ethical Theory.* Oxford: Clarendon Press, 1968.

Hare, R. M. *Applications of Moral Philosophy.* Berkeley and Los Angeles: University of California Press, 1973.

———. *Freedom and Reason.* Oxford: Clarendon Press, 1963.

Hart, H. L. A. *Punishment and Responsibility: Essays in the Philosophy of Law.* Oxford: Oxford University Press, 1968.

Hart, H. L. A., and Honoré, A. M. *Causation in the Law.* Oxford: Clarendon Press, 1959.

Hegel, G. W. F. *Werke.* Vol. 8, *Grundlinien der Philosophie des Rechts.* Edited by E. Gans. References are by section, with the *Zusätze* printed by Gans at the end of some sections indicated by *A.* I have used (occasionally parting from) T. M. Knox's translation: *Hegel's Philosophy of Right* (Oxford: Clarendon Press, 1942), where the *Zusätze* are separated from Hegel's own text and printed as an appendix. In a parenthesis, I have added page references to Knox.

Hicks, R. D. *Stoic and Epicurean*. New York: Scribner's, 1910.

Hollingdale, R. J. *Nietzsche: The Man and His Philosophy*. Baton Rouge: Lousiana State University Press, 1965.

Hörmann, Karl. *An Introduction to Moral Theology*. Translated by Edward Quinn. London: Burns and Oates, 1961.

Kant, Immanuel. *Grundlegung zur Metaphysik der Sitten*. Riga: 1st ed., 1785; 2d ed., 1786. Page references are to the second edition, given in some German texts; and, in parentheses, to vol. 4 of the Prussian Academy's edition of Kant's *Gesammelte Schriften* (Berlin: G. Reimer, 1902–42). I have used the translations of L. W. Beck and H. J. Paton.

————. *Kritik der praktischen Vernunft*. Riga: 1788.

————. *Lectures on Ethics*. Translated by Louis Infeld. New York: Harper and Row, 1963. Except for the Foreword by L. W. Beck, this is a reprint of the edition published by Methuen & Co., London, 1931.

————. *Die Metaphysik der Sitten*. Königsberg: 1st ed., 1797; 2d ed., 1798. Page references are, for the first part (*Rechtslehre*) to the second edition; and, for the second part (*Tugendlehre*) to the first edition, as in some German texts; and also, in parentheses, to vol. 6 of the Prussian Academy's edition of Kant's *Gesammelte Schriften*, pp. 202–483. I have used the translations of John Ladd (*Rechtslehre*), Mary J. Gregor (*Tugendlehre*), and James Ellington (*Tugendlehre*).

Kirk, Kenneth E. *Conscience and Its Problems*. London: Longmans, 1927.

Kneale, William, and Kneale, Martha. *The Development of Logic*. Oxford: Clarendon Press, 1962.

Lawrence, Roy. *Motive and Intention: An Essay in the Appreciation of Action*. Evanston: Northwestern University Press, 1972.

Lehrer, Keith, ed. *Freedom and Determinism*. New York: Random House, 1966.

Levi, Edward H. *An Introduction to Legal Reasoning*. Chicago: University of Chicago Press, 1949.

Locke, John. *An Essay concerning Human Understanding*. Edited by Peter H. Nidditch. Oxford: Clarendon Press, 1975.

Lottin, Odon, O.S.B. *Morale Fondamentale*. Tournai: Desclee, 1954.

Lyons, David. *Forms and Limits of Utilitarianism*. Oxford: Clarendon Press, 1965.

MacIntyre, Alasdair. *Secularization and Moral Change*. London: Oxford University Press, 1967.

———, and Ricoeur, Paul. *The Religious Significance of Atheism.* New York and London: Columbia University Press, 1969.

Maimonides, Moses. *Mishneh Torah*. This work is cited by book, treatise, chapter, and paragraph, except for the list of 613 precepts prefixed to the code, which are cited by number. Two translations have been used:

Mishneh Torah: Book of Knowledge and Book of Adoration, vol. 1. Edited and translated by M. Hyamson.

The Code of Maimonides, edited and translated by various authors. In Yale Judaica Series, vols. 2–5, 8–9, 11–12, 14–16, 19. New Haven: Yale University Press, 1949–. (Y.J.S.)

Mill, John Stuart. *Utilitarianism, Liberty, and Representative Government*. New York: Dutton, Everyman's Library, 1951.

Montague, Richard. *Formal Philosophy*. Edited by Richmond H. Thomason. New Haven: Yale University Press, 1974.

Moore, G. E. *Principia Ethica*. 2d ed. Cambridge: Cambridge University Press, 1922.

Nagel, Thomas. *The Possibility of Altruism*. Oxford: Clarendon Press, 1970.

Nelson, Benjamin. *The Idea of Usury: from Tribal Brotherhood to Universal Otherhood*. 2d ed. Chicago and London: University of Chicago Press, 1969.

Newman, John Henry, Cardinal. *Certain Difficulties Felt by Anglicans*. 2 vols. London: Longmans, 1891.

Nietzsche, Friedrich. *Jenseits von Gut und Böse*. Leipzig: Naumann, 1886. Translated by Walter Kaufmann, *Beyond Good and Evil*. New York: Random House Vintage Books, 1966.

———. *The Will to Power*. Edited, with commentary, by Walter Kaufmann. Translated by Walter Kaufmann and R. J. Hollingdale. New York: Random House Vintage Books, 1968.

Noonan, John T., Jr., ed. *The Morality of Abortion*. Cambridge, Mass.: Harvard University Press, 1970.

Nozick, Robert. *Anarchy, State, and Utopia*. New York: Basic Books, 1974.

Oakeshott, Michael. *Rationalism in Politics and other Essays*. London: Methuen, 1962.

Passmore, John. *Man's Responsibility for Nature: Ecological Problems and Western Traditions*. London: Duckworth, 1973.

Paton, H. J. *The Categorical Imperative*. London: Hutchinson, n.d.
──────. *The Moral Law, or Kant's Groundwork of the Metaphysics of Morals; a New Translation with Analysis and Notes*. London: Hutchinson, n.d.
Popper, Karl R. *The Logic of Scientific Discovery*. London: Hutchinson, 1959.
Prichard, H. A. *Moral Obligation*. Oxford: Clarendon Press, 1949.
Prior, Arthur N. *Logic and the Basis of Ethics*. Oxford: Clarendon Press, 1949.
Quinton, Anthony. *Utilitarian Ethics*. London: Macmillan, 1973.
Ramsey, Paul. *Deeds and Rules in Christian Ethics*. New York: Scribners, 1967.
Rawls, John. *A Theory of Justice*. Cambridge, Mass.: Harvard University Press, 1971.
Rhees, Rush. *Discussions of Wittgenstein*. London: Routledge and Kegan Paul, 1970.
Richards, David A. J. *A Theory of Reasons for Action*. Oxford: Clarendon Press, 1971.
Ross, W. D. *The Foundations of Ethics*. Oxford: Clarendon Press, 1939.
──────. *Kant's Ethical Theory: A Commentary on the Grundlegung zur Metaphysik der Sitten*. Oxford: Clarendon Press, 1954.
──────. *The Right and the Good*. Oxford: Clarendon Press, 1930.
Russell, Bertrand. *Mysticism and Logic*. London: Allen and Unwin, 1950 (1st ed. 1917).
Ryle, Gilbert. *The Concept of Mind*. London: Hutchinson, 1949.
──────. *Collected Papers*. 2 vols. London: Hutchinson, 1971.
Schneewind, J. B., ed. *Mill: A Collection of Critical Essays*. Garden City, N.Y.: Doubleday, 1968.
Searle, John R. *Speech Acts: An Essay in the Philosophy of Language*. Cambridge: University Press, 1969.
Sellars, Wilfrid. *Science, Perception and Reality*. London: Routledge, 1963.
Sidgwick, Henry. *The Methods of Ethics*. 7th ed. London: Macmillan, 1907.
Singer, Marcus George. *Generalization in Ethics*. New York: Knopf, 1961.
Smart, J. J. C. *An Outline of a System of Utilitarian Ethics*. 2d ed., rev. In *Utilitarianism: For and Against*, by J. J. C. Smart and Bernard Williams, pp. 1–74. Cambridge: Cambridge University Press, 1973.

Smart, J. J. C., and Williams, Bernard. *Utilitarianism: For and Against.* Cambridge: Cambridge University Press, 1973.

Stevenson, C. L. *Ethics and Language.* New Haven: Yale University Press, 1945.

Stocks, John Leofric. *Morality and Purpose.* Edited by D. Z. Phillips. London: Routledge and Kegan Paul, 1969.

Tachibana, Shundo. *The Ethics of Buddhism.* London: Oxford University Press, 1926.

Taylor, Jeremy. *Ductor Dubitantium, or the Rule of Conscience. The Whole Works of Jeremy Taylor.* Edited by R. Heber. Revised and corrected by C. P. Eden. 10 vols. London: Longmans and Others, 1855. References are to book, chapter, and rule, to which a reference to the volume and page of the *Whole Works (W. W.)* is added.

Veatch, Henry B. *For an Ontology of Morals: A Critique of Contemporary Ethical Theory.* Evanston: Northwestern University Press, 1971.

————. *Two Logics: The Conflict between Classical and Neo-Analytic Philosophy.* Evanston: Northwestern University Press, 1969.

von Wright, Georg Henrik. *An Essay on Deontic Logic and the General Theory of Action.* Amsterdam: North Holland Publishing Company, 1968.

————. *Norm and Action.* London: Routledge and Kegan Paul, 1963.

Walsh, W. H. *Hegelian Ethics.* New York: St. Martin's Press, 1969.

Wasserstrom, Richard, ed. *Today's Moral Problems.* New York: Macmillan, 1975.

Whewell, William. *The Elements of Morality, Including Polity.* 4th ed., with a supplement. Cambridge: Deighton Bell, 1864. Citations are by section, followed by a page number in parentheses.

Williams, Bernard. *A Critique of Utilitarianism.* In *Utilitarianism: For and Against,* by J. J. C. Smart and Bernard Williams, pp. 75–150. Cambridge: Cambridge University Press, 1973.

Zahn, Gordon C. *In Solitary Witness: The Life and Death of Franz Jägerstätter.* New York: Holt, Rinehart and Winston, 1964.

Articles

Anscombe, G. E. M. (1958). "Modern Moral Philosophy." *Philosophy* 33 (1958):1–19.

Anscombe, G. E. M. (1965). "Thought and Action in Aristotle." In
New Essays on Plato and Aristotle, edited by Renford Bambrough,
pp. 143–58. London: Routledge and Kegan Paul, 1965.
——— (1972a). "Contraception and Chastity." *The Human World*,
no. 7 (May 1972):9–30.
——— (1972b). "Comments." *The Human World*, no. 9 (November
1972):48–51.
Austin, J. L. (1966). "Three Ways of Spilling Ink." *Philosophical
Review* 75 (1966):427–440.
Becker, Lawrence C. (1975). "Human Being: The Boundaries of the
Concept." *Philosophy and Public Affairs* 4 (1974–75):334–59.
Bennett, Jonathan (1966). "Whatever the Consequences." *Analysis*
26 (1965–66):83–102.
Brandt, R. B. (1955). "The Definition of an 'Ideal Observer' Theory
in Ethics." *Philosophy and Phenomenological Research* 15 (1954–
55):407–13.
——— (1963). "Toward a Credible Form of Utilitarianism." In
Morality and the Language of Conduct, edited by Hector-Neri
Castañeda and George Nakhnikian, pp. 107–43. Detroit: Wayne
State University Press, 1963.
——— (1972). "Utilitarianism and the Rules of War." *Philosophy
and Public Affairs* 1 (1971–72):145–65.
Brock, Dan W. (1973). "Recent Work in Utilitarianism." *American
Philosophical Quarterly* 10 (1973):241–76.
Brody, Baruch M. (1973). "Why Settle for Anything Less than Good
Old-Fashioned Aristotelian Essentialism?" *Nous* 7 (1973):351–65.
Castañeda, Hector-Neri (1972). "On the Semantics of the Ought-to-
Do." In *The Semantics of Natural Language*, Synthese Library,
vol. 40, edited by Donald Davidson and Gilbert Harman. Dor-
drecht, Holland: Reidel, 1972.
Chisholm, R. M. (1963a). "Supererogation and Offence." *Ratio* 5
(1963):1–14.
——— (1963b). "Contrary-to-Duty Imperatives and Deontic Logic."
Analysis 24 (1963–64):33–36.
——— (1964). "The Ethics of Requirement." *American Philosophical Quarterly* 1 (1964):147–53.
——— (1966). "Freedom and Action." In *Freedom and Determinism*, edited by Lehrer, pp. 11–44.
Danto, Arthur C. (1965). "Basic Actions." *American Philosophical
Quarterly* 2 (1965):141–48.

Daube, David (1972). "The Linguistics of Suicide." *Philosophy and Public Affairs* 1 (1971-72):387-437.

Davidson, Donald (1967). "Causal Relations." *The Journal of Philosophy* 64 (1967):691-703.

———— (1971). "Agency." In *Agent, Action, and Reason,* edited by Robert Binkley, Richard Bronaugh, and Ausonio Marras, pp. 3-25. Oxford: Blackwell, 1971.

————. "The Logical Form of Action Sentences," and "Reply to Comments." In *The Logic of Decision and Action,* edited by Nicholas Rescher, pp. 81-95, 115-20. Pittsburgh: University of Pittsburgh Press, n.d.

Dennett, D. C. (1971). "International Systems." *Journal of Philosophy* 68 (1971): 87-106.

———— (1973). "Mechanism and Responsibility." In *Essays on Freedom of Action,* edited by Ted Honderich. London: Routledge and Kegan Paul, 1973.

Diggs, B. J. (1960). "A Technical Ought." *Mind* 69 (1960):301-17.

———— (1964). "Rules and Utilitarianism." *American Philosophical Quarterly* 1 (1964):32-44.

Donagan, Alan (1968). "Is There a Credible Form of Utilitarianism?" In *Contemporary Utilitarianism,* edited by Michael D. Bayles. New York: Doubleday, 1968.

———— (1974). "Whewell's *Elements of Morality.*" *Journal of Philosophy* 71 (1974):724-36.

Donnellan, Keith S. (1964). "Comments" (on Feinberg's "Causing Voluntary Actions"). In *Metaphysics and Explanation,* edited by D. D. Merrill, pp. 48-51. Pittsburgh: University of Pittsburgh, n.d.

Dworkin, Ronald (1973). "The Original Position." *University of Chicago Law Review* 40 (1973):500-533. Reprinted in *Reading Rawls,* edited by Norman Daniels, pp. 16-53. New York: Basic Books, 1975.

Ezorsky, Gertrude (1968). "A Defense of Rule Utilitarianism Against David Lyons Who Insists on Tying It to Act Utilitarianism, Plus a Brand New Way of Checking Out General Utilitarian Properties." *Journal of Philosophy* 65 (1968):533-44.

———— (1972). "How Many Lives Shall We Save?" *Metaphilosophy* 3 (1972).

Finnis, John (1973). "The Rights and Wrongs of Abortion." *Philosophy and Public Affairs* 2 (1973-74):117-45.

Firth, Roderick (1952). "Ethical Absolutism and the Ideal Observer." *Philosophy and Phenomenological Research* 12 (1951–52):317–45.

———— (1955). "Reply to Professor Brandt." *Philosophy and Phenomenological Research* 15 (1954–55):414–21.

Foot, Philippa (1967). "The Problem of Abortion and the Doctrine of the Double Effect." *Oxford Review*, no. 5 (1967):5–15.

———— (1972). "Morality as a System of Hypothetical Imperatives." *Philosophical Review* 81 (1972):305–16.

Frankena, William K. (1964). "Love and Principle in Christian Ethics." In *Faith and Philosophy*, edited by Alvin Plantinga, pp. 203–25. Grand Rapids, Mich.: Eerdmans, 1964.

Geach, P. T. (1956). "Good and Evil." *Analysis* 17 (1956–57):33–42.

Gewirth, Alan (1967). "Categorical Consistency in Ethics." *Philosophical Quarterly* 17 (1967):289–99.

———— (1970). "Some Comments on Categorical Consistency." *Philosophical Quarterly* 20 (1970):380–84.

———— (1974). "The "Is-Ought" Problem Resolved." *Proceedings and Addresses of the American Philosophical Association 1973–1974* 47 (1974):34–61.

Gibbard, Allan F. (1973). "Doing More Harm than Good." *Philosophical Studies* 24 (1973):158–73.

Grisez, Germain G. (1965). "The First Principle of Practical Reason: A Commentary on the *Summa Theologiae*, 1–2, Question 94, Article 2." *Natural Law Forum* (now *The American Journal of Jurisprudence*) 10 (1965):168–201. Of this article, most of pp. 168–96 is reprinted in Anthony Kenny, *Aquinas: A Collection of Critical Essays* (New York: Doubleday, 1969), pp. 340–82.

———— (1970). "Toward a Consistent Natural Law Ethics of Killing." *The American Journal of Jurisprudence* 15 (1970):64–96.

Hare, R. M. (1972a). "Principles." *Proceedings of the Aristotelian Society* 73 (1972–73):1–18.

———— (1972b). "Rules of War and Moral Reasoning." *Philosophy and Public Affairs* 1 (1971–72):166–81.

———— (1973). "Rawls' Theory of Justice." *Philosophical Quarterly* 23 (1973):144–55, 241–51. Reprinted in *Reading Rawls*, edited by Norman Daniels, pp. 81–107. New York: Basic Books, 1975. References given are to the version in Daniels.

———— (1975). "Abortion and the Golden Rule." *Philosophy and Public Affairs* 4 (1975):201–22.

Hill, Thomas E., Jr. (1973). "The Hypothetical Imperative." *Philosophical Review* 82 (1973):429–50.

Kenny, Anthony (1966). "Intention and Purpose." *Journal of Philosophy* 63 (1966):642–51.

Kneale, William (1962). "Modality, De Dicto and De Re." In *Logic, Methodology and Philosophy of Science: Proceedings of the 1960 International Congress*, edited by E. Nagel, P. Suppes, and A. Tarski, pp. 622–33. Stanford: Stanford University Press, 1962.

Kripke, Saul A. (1972). "Naming and Necessity." In *Semantics of Natural Language*, edited by Donald Davidson and Gilbert Harman, pp. 253–355. Dordrecht-Boston: Reidel, 1972.

Long, A. A. (1970). "The Logical Basis of Stoic Ethics." *Proceedings of the Aristotelian Society* 71 (1970–71):85–104.

Mabbott, J. D. (1956). "Interpretations of Mill's Utilitarianism." *Philosophical Quarterly* 61 (1956):115–20.

McNeilly, F. S. (1972). "Promises De-Moralized." *Philosophical Review* 81 (1972):63–81.

Mandelbaum, Maurice (1968). "Two Moot Issues in Mill's *Utilitarianism*." In *Mill: a Collection of Critical Essays*, edited by Schneewind, pp. 206–33. Originally published in *Philosophy* 43 (1968).

Mangan, Joseph T., S.J. (1949). "An Historical Analysis of the Principle of Double Effect." *Theological Studies* 10 (1949):41–61.

Murphy, Jeffrie G. (1973). "The Killing of the Innocent." *The Monist* 57 (1973):527–50.

Nielsen, Kai (1972). "Against Moral Conservativism." *Ethics* 82 (1972):219–31.

Nozick, Robert (1968). "Moral Complications and Moral Structures." *Natural Law Forum* 13 (1968):1–50.

Oldenquist, Andrew (1966). "Rules and Consequences." *Mind* 75 (1966):180–92.

Rawls, John (1975). "Fairness to Goodness." *Philosophical Review* 84 (1975):536–54.

Rosner, F. (1970). "Suicide in Biblical, Talmudic, and Rabbinic Writings." *Tradition* 11 (1970):25–40.

Schneewind, J. B. (1968). "Whewell's Ethics." *American Philosophical Quarterly*, Monograph Series, no. 1 (1968):108–41.

Schwarzschild, Steven S. (1962a). "Do Noachites Have to Believe in Revelation?" *Jewish Quarterly Review* 52 (1961–62):297–98.

Schwarzschild, Steven S. (1962b). "Do Noachites Have to Believe in Revelation? Cont." *Jewish Quarterly Review* 53 (1962-63):30-65.

Sellars, Wilfrid (1966). "Thought and Action" and "Fatalism and Determinism." In *Freedom and Determinism*, edited by Lehrer, pp. 105-39, 141-74. New York: Random House, 1966.

Singer, Marcus G. (1967). "The Golden Rule." In *The Encyclopedia of Philosophy*, edited by Paul Edwards, vol. 3, pp. 365b-367a. New York: Macmillan, 1967.

Sobel, J. Howard (1970). "Utilitarianisms: Simple and General." *Inquiry* 13 (1970):394-449.

Thomson, Judith Jarvis (1971). "A Defense of Abortion." *Philosophy and Public Affairs* 1 (1971-72):47-66.

Tooley, Michael (1972). "Abortion and Infanticide." *Philosophy and Public Affairs* 2 (1972-73):37-65.

Urmson, J. O. (1953). "The Interpretation of the Moral Philosophy of J. S. Mill." *Philosophical Quarterly* 3 (1953):33-39.

———— (1970). "Moore's Utilitarianism." In *G. E. Moore: Essays in Retrospect*, edited by Alice Ambrose and Morris Lazerowitz, pp. 343-49. London: Allen and Unwin, 1970.

Veatch, Henry B. (1975). "The Rational Justification of Moral Principles: Can There Be Such a Thing?" *Review of Metaphysics* 29 (1975-76):217-38.

Waismann, Friedrich (1965). "Notes on Talks with Wittgenstein." Translated by Max Black. *Philosophical Review* 74 (1965):12-16.

Walzer, Michael (1973). "Political Action: The Problem of Dirty Hands." *Philosophy and Public Affairs* 2 (1972-73):160-80.

Warren, Mary Anne (1973). "On the Moral and Legal Status of Abortion." *The Monist* 57 (1973):43-61.

———— (1975). "Postscript on Infanticide." In *Today's Moral Problems*, edited by Richard Waiserstrom, pp. 135-36. New York: Macmillan, 1975.

Wertheimer, Roger (1971). "Understanding the Abortion Argument." *Philosophy and Public Affairs* 1 (1971-72):67-95.

Wittgenstein, Ludwig (1965). "Lecture on Ethics." *Philosophical Review* 74 (1965):3-12.

Index

Abelard, Peter, 126–27
Abortion, 83, 87, 168–71
Act, human, 113–14. *See also* Action, human
Action, human, 41–47, 50, 112–14, 116–17, 125, 160–64, 228–29, 231–33, 237; circumstances of, 39–41, 50–51, 123–24; consequences of, causal, 41–42, 44–47, 115–17, 123, 161, 164; consequences of, in extended sense, 51–52, 124, 189, 200–201; deliberate, 120; ignorant, 127–35; intentional, 124–25; judicative, 55–56, 111, 121–22, 125–26, 164; objective or material, 52–53, 55–56; by secondary agents, 47–48; subjective or formal, 54–56, 136–37; voluntary, 114–18, 120–21, 124, 127–29, 164. *See also* Act, human; Human beings
Anscombe, G. E. M., 3, 117–18, 123–24, 167, 189–90, 211
Aquinas, Saint Thomas: on action, human, 114–15, 127–29, 164; on angels, 32; on conscience, 132–33; on double effect, theory of, 158–59, 163; on ends, 64; on family, the, 102, 105–6; on law, moral, 6, 8, 29, 60, 61, 64–65; on love and charity, 61–63; on perplexity, moral, 144–46; on property,

99; on reason, practical, 60–61; on sexuality, 105–6
Aristotle, 3, 4, 45, 115, 210–11
Asimov, Isaac, 201
Atkin, J. R. (Lord), 68–69
Augustine (of Hippo), Saint, 62, 107, 232
Austin, J. L. 115, 120, 122–23

Baier, Kurt, 137, 239
Baumgarten, A. G., 8
Baxter, Richard, 111, 136, 186–87
Beneficence, principle of, 85–86, 153–56
Bennett, Jonathan, 49–51, 156–57
Bentham, Jeremy, 19, 26, 192
Brandt, R. B., 184, 203, 215, 217–20
Bribery, 186–87
Broad, C. D., 22–23, 26
Brock, Dan, 180, 206–7
Butler, Joseph, 18, 19, 133

Calvin, John, 6
Casuistry, 8
Causation: agent, 45–47, 50, 111, 123, 231–33, 237; event, 38–39, 41–47; want-and-belief, 115–17. See also *Novus actus interveniens*